ALTERNATIVE DISPUTE RESOLUTION:

A DEVELOPING WORLD PERSPECTIVE

Routledge·Cavendish
Taylor & Francis Group

ALT

RE

A DEVELOPING WORLD PERSPECTIVE

Albert Fiadjoe, LLB (Hons) (Ghana)
LLM, PhD (London)
Professor of Public Law
formerly Dean, Faculty of Law
University of the West Indies
Barbados

Routledge·Cavendish
Taylor & Francis Group

First published in Great Britain 2004 by
RoutledgeCavendish Publishing Limited
2 Park Square, Milton Park, Abingdon, Oxon, OX14 4RN
Website: www.routledgecavendishpublishing.com

Published in the United States by RoutledgeCavendish Publishing
c/o International Specialized Book Services,
270 Madison Ave, New York NY 10016

Transferred to Digital Printing 2006

Published in Australia by RoutledgeCavendish Publishing (Australia) Pty Ltd
45 Beach Street, Coogee, NSW 2034, Australia
Website: www.routledgecavendishpublishing.com.au

© Fiadjoe, A   2004

British Library Cataloguing in Publication Data
Fiadjoe, Albert
Alternative dispute resolution: a developing world perspective
1 Dispute resolution (Law)
I Title
347'.09

Library of Congress Cataloguing in Publication Data
Data available

ISBN 1-85941-912-7
ISBN 978-1-85941-912-0

1 3 5 7 9 10 8 6 4 2

*This book is dedicated to my brothers and sisters
who taught me through practical living the
very important virtues of conciliation,
negotiation and mediation
and
my students, both past and present*

FOREWORD

In the last 25 years, throughout the common law world, traditional arrangements for the delivery of civil justice have come under scrutiny, challenge and change. The search for alternative processes to litigation in the resolution of disputes gained momentum and a great debate has ensued.

There is now a veritable mountain of literature and learning on ADR, the acronym for Alternative Dispute Resolution. More and more, universities and law schools have recognised the need to teach ADR as a separate and discrete course of study. This book will undoubtedly find a place of eminence in the libraries of law students at the Faculty of Law of the University of the West Indies.

With his customary scholarship, skill in handling legal materials and a felicitous writing style, Professor Fiadjoe has produced a work of exceptional merit. It is a timely and relevant publication, for it locates much of its learning and discussion in the realities of the contemporary Caribbean and the wider global environment.

Caribbean people, lawyers and non-lawyers alike, must become conversant with the dispute settlement Articles of the Revised Treaty of Chaguaramas which provides for the establishment of the CARICOM Single Market and Economy. Equally, they must understand the dispute settlement mechanisms of the World Trade Organization. On these matters this book is a storehouse of necessary information.

The timeliness and relevance of *Alternative Dispute Resolution: A Developing World Perspective* are well exemplified by the efforts of several States of the Commonwealth Caribbean to reform their rules of civil procedure to conform to a more judge-driven paradigm, at the heart of which will be ADR and its companion case management. In addition to treating of those techniques, Professor Fiadjoe examines attempts in the region to incorporate processes of mediation in the area of criminal law. This is a novel departure from traditional works on ADR.

In commending this book to the widest possible readership, I feel a sense of profound satisfaction that, once again, my expectations of the Faculty of Law of the UWI have been fulfilled. One dared to hope in 1970, on inauguration of the Faculty, that it would have been a catalyst for the publication of first class legal literature. That hope has been realised beyond measure in the last 30 years.

Professor Albert Fiadjoe has been an indefatigable author and a prolific contributor to legal learning in the Commonwealth Caribbean. His vast knowledge and intellectual agility have enabled him, apparently seamlessly, to make the transition from expert in Public Law to expert in an exciting, developing area of the law. I have every confidence that the same large measure of acclaim that attended his highly successful *Commonwealth Caribbean Public Law* will be accorded *Alternative Dispute Resolution: A Developing World Perspective*.

All lawyers in the Commonwealth Caribbean are advised to read this book and digest the contents of its pages. The monopoly of lawyers in the management and settlement of disputes is under threat from a new class of professional mediators and others offering services in ADR in the common law world. It is a counsel of prudence to be forewarned and forearmed. Professor Fiadjoe amply provides the intellectual armour to meet the competition.

David Simmons
Chief Justice
Supreme Court of Barbados

PREFACE

I pioneered the introduction of a course in Alternative Dispute Resolution (ADR) in the curriculum of the Faculty of Law of the University of the West Indies, Cave Hill Campus, in 1998. Little did I then realise that the level of student interest in the subject would be so overwhelming, and that this interest would, as in 1995 when my students' commitment led me to write *Commonwealth Caribbean Public Law*, result in the creation of this book.

When the Faculty of Law at the University of the West Indies decided to make ADR a part of its curriculum offering, I had the undeserved honour of being asked to teach the course. This text owes a great deal to those students who put their faith in me blindly, by enthusiastically enrolling for the course, far in excess of the cut-off numbers. That show of enthusiasm also revealed to me that our students were forward-looking in their vision and thinking as to where the jurisprudence in the Caribbean region ought to be heading. Despite limitations in student numbers, the Faculty has been forced to accommodate unusually large student numbers. This phenomenal growth in student interest also attests to the importance of ADR worldwide.

I dedicate this book to my brothers and sisters and also to all my students who have embraced this subject in the full knowledge that lawyering in this millennium has to take into account processes of dispute resolution other than litigation through the courts. The discerning client of today is asking a simple but very fundamental question: has my attorney delivered results for me which are quick, effective and creative to my needs?

Never in the history of litigation has there been more focus and purpose in the area of client services and results. The attorney without legal wisdom and business vision is out of step with the ethos of our times. The attorney of today has to focus on the client's short-term and long-term objectives and interests. That requires forward-thinking, uncompromising quality and exceptional client service. That is why all respectable law schools now carry a course in ADR.

This book has two equally important objectives. The first goal is to examine ADR techniques from a societal perspective. In spite of the impression that one gets from examining law schools' curricula, the vast majority of disputes are not filed in court. Even those few disputes that are filed as lawsuits are generally resolved before trial, primarily through settlement or some dispositive motion. Increasingly, disputes are being resolved by litigants using private agreements to bind themselves to such alternatives to litigation. In addition, sometimes the state itself requires parties to resolve their disputes using methods other than litigation. The underlying question which we need to address is whether this rushing tide toward ADR is a good thing. The second goal is to provide readers with some of the knowledge and skills required to function in a legal system that resolves many disputes through negotiation, mediation and arbitration, as well as through litigation.

Today's practice of the law does not provide a simple 'yes' or 'no' answer to dispute resolution. In both large and small jurisdictions, it is, indeed, a verifiable truism that the lawyer of today requires a marriage of both litigation and dispute resolution skills. There is now no option for the attorney to choose to work primarily in either a litigation context or, instead, in an ADR setting. In fact, virtually all attorneys will need to be well-versed in both styles of dispute resolution. For example, the attorney will need to know how to interview clients and witnesses and how to negotiate agreements, but even in that role, he will also need to know how to represent clients in mediations, arbitrations, mini-trials, etc, and how to advise them on which technique would be preferable.

In this book, I have included an ample discussion of arbitration. There is some disputation as to whether arbitration properly falls within ADR. This is because arbitration is a hybrid system which closely approximates to litigation. Brown and Marriott in *ADR Principles and Practice* justify some discussion of arbitration in their book on the grounds that the history of arbitration forms a 'part of ADR and because its practices and procedures have influenced some hybrid ADR processes. An understanding of its operation is essential to an application of dispute resolution generally'.[1] In the case of this book, the justification for discussing arbitration as a part of ADR is far easily explained.

It is a strategic part of the Faculty's mandate to promote regional development. International commercial arbitration has become a critical tool for the promotion of international trade. All the global treaties of modern times mandate the use of arbitration as one of the modes for the settlement of international disputes. Reference is easily made to the Caribbean Community and Common Market (CARICOM) Protocol 9 where arbitration may be invoked in addition to the original jurisdiction of the Caribbean Court of Justice, the WTO and, soon to come, the Free Trade Area of the Americas (FTAA). In the Law of the Sea Convention, arbitration is the default system for contentious proceedings. All these impact directly on the Commonwealth Caribbean region and influence the legal system in a significant way. In the WTO, arbitration is a subsidiary appendage to the institutionalised processes of dispute resolution.

I have sought to discuss in some detail the dispute resolution processes within the WTO and CARICOM, principally because of the impact of those treaties on Caribbean trade, commerce and economies.

The rapid adoption of case management techniques in the Commonwealth Caribbean has also given added impetus to ADR. As the region moves to modernise its civil court procedures to simplify and expedite the resolution of disputes, thus providing greater access to justice, questions remain as to whether case management should be practised in conjunction with mandatory ADR systems, which many would regard as essential to an effective civil justice system. The developing need for the resolution of conflicts and disputes not hitherto taken seriously drives the motivation to include some discussion, albeit briefly, on the Ombudsman and the Small Claims Court.

In sum, I have tried to address the 'why', 'what' and 'how' of ADR, while also dealing also with some policy issues and considerations.

In putting together this text, I have tried to provide the required Caribbean, and sometimes developing world, perspective and flavour, thus making the book refreshingly current, topical and relevant to the needs of developing countries.

I have also provided opportunities for role plays and de-brief exercises, because a skills training course will not be complete without some opportunity to practice some skills.

---

1   *ADR Principles and Practices*, 1999, Sweet & Maxwell, p 12.

All the role play materials used in the book have been graciously supplied by Donna Parchment of the Dispute Resolution Foundation in Jamaica. Her contribution is gratefully acknowledged as well as that of the Jamaica/Capital Project 1991.

My thanks also go to Sir David Simmons, KA, BCH, QC, Chief Justice of Barbados for readily agreeing to write the Foreword to this book. I wish to thank him also for his constant encouragement to me over the years. My grateful thanks also go to my colleagues, Professor AR Carnegie, Executive Director of the Caribbean Law Institute Centre, and Mr Endell Thomas, both of whom read the manuscript and made several constructive suggestions and comments.

Miss Pat Worrell continues to exhibit extraordinary skills in deciphering my awful calligraphy. I am indeed eternally grateful to her for secretarial assistance.

I thank my family for their patience and forbearance during the preparation of this book. Cavendish Publishing continues to support my efforts. I thank them for the confidence.

I have tried to illustrate the breadth and depth of conflict resolution as an academic field as well as the many levels of experience and analysis that practitioners of the subject and theorists bring to the dialogue.

I hope that this book will help to stimulate greater interest, awareness and discussion of issues related to the prevention and resolution of conflict peacefully. May our societies continue to drink deep from the wells of conflict resolution and management.

Albert Fiadjoe
Law Faculty
University of the West Indies
Barbados
August 2004

CONTENTS

CHAPTER 1

ADR: ORIGINS, CONTEXTUAL BACKGROUND AND PURPOSE

INTRODUCTION

There is no question but that conflict resolution, through the processes of negotiation, mediation and arbitration, has become an acceptable and, indeed, inevitable part of creative lawyering in the 21st century. That explains why all self-respecting law schools now provide for skills training in the field of Alternative Dispute Resolution (ADR) as part of their core offerings. Today, ADR processes are being applied worldwide to a universality of situations hitherto governed by either litigation or, in extreme cases, by warfare between nations. Obvious examples of such situations are in the areas of international peace and world order, environmental and public policy, science and technology, sports, social development and community-related issues, crime control and prevention, schooling, restorative justice and the family. To this list may be added the more traditional areas such as commercial contracts, employment, labour relations and insurance.

Indeed, there is now increasing recognition of the fact that every type of dispute can be the subject of a dispute resolution process. From business controversies to labour management disputes, ADR is becoming the preferred choice for the resolution of conflict and disagreement, and the reasons are not hard to find. Litigation is a stressful undertaking. It is a costly, lengthy, public exhibition of differences, leading to a great deal of ill-will between litigants. In contrast, ADR processes are usually faster, less expensive, less time-consuming and more conclusive than litigation. Some of the perceived advantages of ADR can be summarised as follows:

(a) speed;

(b) choice and expertise of impartial neutrals;

(c) informality and flexibility;

(d) privacy;

(e) economy;

(f) finality;

(g) diversity and adaptability of ADR;

(h) recognition of the needs of the parties;

(i) win-win situation;

(j) involvement of the parties in creating imaginative solutions;

(k) savings in public expenditure;

(l) private savings in time and energy;

(m) retention of beneficial business and personal relationships;

(n) shortening of court dockets;

(o) more efficient legal systems;

(p) qualitative improvement in the delivery of justice; and

(q) increased participation and access to justice.

ORIGINS

What then is ADR? In its pristine form, ADR originally referred to a variety of techniques for resolving disputes without litigation. But, having regard to the evolution of modern techniques, such as caseload management and the ever-growing prevalence of ADR within the litigation context, it might be more accurate now to describe ADR not as an alternative to litigation but one technique which is appropriate in the context of dispute resolution generally. Following that way of thinking, litigation is considered as just one of a variety of methods of dispute resolution.

Reading through the vast literature on ADR, one is left with the impression that ADR is of recent vintage and that its genesis traces to the USA. Without in any way detracting from the enormous, innovative and creative contribution of American scholars to this discipline, the point has to be made that both these propositions are false. Until now, western writers have assumed or given the impression that the traffic in ADR travelled in one direction, across the Atlantic from west to east. That is a fallacy.

The origins of ADR trace to traditional societies. Traditional societies, without the trappings and paraphernalia of the modern state, had no coercive means of resolving disputes. So, consensus building was an inevitable and necessary part of the dispute resolution process. The court system only developed as a necessary by-product of the modern state. Societies in Africa, Asia and the Far East were practising non-litigious means of dispute resolution long before the advent of the nation state, for the building of long-term relationships was the bedrock on which those societies rested.

Kaplan, Spruce and Moser chronicle early examples of dispute settlements by means of arbitration.[1] They write:

> In respect of arbitration, its history may be linked to the genesis of human society itself, parents are normally arbiters in disputes between their children. Mythological references to arbitration have been chronicled thus:
>
>> There are mentions of disputes between two gods being submitted to a third for decision in the earliest myths. Stories from Ancient Egypt tell of disputes between Osiris and Seth, and Horus and Seth, being decided in that way ... The earliest Greek arbitration myth is of a mortal arbiter, Paris, deciding between immortal parties, Hera, Athene and Aphrodite ...

References to arbitration were made around 350 BC by Plato, in *The Laws*, stating, *inter alia*, as follows:

> Whenever someone makes a contract and fails to carry it out ... an action may be brought in the tribal courts if the parties have been unable to resolve it before arbitrators or neighbours.

Another renowned historian, Plutarch, wrote of an arbitration anecdote:

---

1 *Hong Kong and China Arbitration Cases and Materials*, 1994, Butterworths (Asia), p xxxiii, quoted in a speech by VP Pradhan entitled 'Mediation and Alternative Dispute Resolution: Developments in the Various Jurisdictions: Have the Lawyers Caught On?'.

Plutarch tells of two men appointing the King, Archidamus II, to resolve their dispute. He took them into a remote temple and made them swear they would abide by his award. He then gave it: 'Stay here till you have made up your quarrel.'

Similarly in Rome, it is said that:

... there was a well-established practice of arbitration separate from the procedures of litigation. Cicero, writing before 50 BC, knew arbitration as part of the highly developed legal system of which he was the master:

A court hearing is one thing, the award of an arbitrator quite another. The trial concerns a definite sum, an arbitrator's award an indefinite. When we go to court we know that we are going to win all or lose all. But we go to arbitration with different expectations – that we may not get all we want but we will not lose everything. The very words of the arbitration contract are proof of that. What is a trial like? Exact, clear cut, explicit. And arbitration? Mild, moderate.[2]

In respect of commercial arbitration, the following has been said:

Commercial arbitration must have existed since the dawn of commerce. All trade potentially involves disputes, and successful trade must have a means of dispute resolution other than force. From the start, it must have involved a neutral determination, and an agreement, tacit or otherwise, to abide by the result, backed by some kind of sanction. It must have taken many forms, with mediation no doubt merging into adjudication. The story is now lost forever. Even for historical times it is impossible to piece together the details, as will readily be understood by anyone who nowadays attempts to obtain reliable statistics on the current incidence and varieties of arbitrations. Private dispute resolution has always been resolutely private.[3]

In the Malaysian context, RH Hickling, in his book on Malaysian law,[4] points out that conciliation and mediation are the traditional dispute resolution processes of the different races in Malaysia, with the emphasis upon *adat* and Confucian values of yielding and compromise. Traditionally, mediation is the key to reconciliation, with the mediator taking a broader view of the issues involved than any common law judge, whose area of investigation is limited by narrow concepts of what is relevant or irrelevant.

Early advocates of ADR include Abraham Lincoln, to whom is attributed the following exhortation: 'Discourage litigation. Persuade your neighbours to compromise whenever you can. Point out to them how the nominal winner is often the loser in fees, expenses and cost of time.' While advocating compromise may not be the same as advocating ADR, it represents a path away from litigation which is in line with the traditional thrust of ADR. Mahatma Ghandhi is quoted as saying of his practice:

I realized that the true function of a lawyer was to unite parties ... A large part of my time during the 20 years of my practice as a lawyer was occupied in bringing about private compromises of hundreds of cases. I lost nothing thereby – not even money, certainly not my soul.

---

2   *Ibid* at p xl.
3   Mustill, 'Arbitration: History and Background' (1989) 6 Journal of International Arbitration, p 43.
4   *Malaysian Law*, 1987, Professional (Law) Books Publishers, pp 136–41.

By way of further example, Professor G Woodman reminds us that among the ethnic groups of the Aruba and Tanzania, modes of dispute resolution existed before the advent of colonial rule and the inception of the modern state.[5]

Much nearer home, Helen Alves of Trinidad & Tobago has this to say on the point with respect to mediation:

> Mediation has had a long and varied history, and has traditionally been used as a means of dispute resolution and as a means of ensuring in several cultures, that societal cohesion was maintained in the face of individual and communal conflicts.
>
> Mediation had its genesis in traditional decision making procedures used at some stage in the history of almost all cultures of the world. The Hindu villages of India which have traditionally engaged the *panchayat* justice system, (and which system, in traditional times, was also used in Trinidad and Tobago as a means of dispute resolution). In traditional African societies, respected notables were often called to mediate disputes between neighbours, and Islamic traditional pastoral societies in the Middle East also established mediation methodologies. In the Jewish culture, a form of mediation was, in Biblical Times, practised by both religious and political leaders. Mediation has also been widely practised in Japan and a number of other Asian societies. The Christian religion has as well, traditionally used mediation among its members.
>
> Whilst factors such as cultural values, belief, self concepts, the relationship between the parties will affect the process used, the introduction of an impartial third party to the resolution process appears to transcend these differing factors.
>
> Despite the established historical background of mediation, it has only been since the mid-1990s that the process has become formalized, and, only within the last twenty-five years that the process has gained ground as an institution and as a developing profession.[6]

This viewpoint is also echoed by P Britton of Guyana, who writes:

> We are all aware that in African rural Communities, eg Victoria Village on the East Coast of Demerara, there existed what was known as the Village Committee, and in the administration of the Village affairs it was a stipulated condition precedent that disputes – especially with respect to the ownership of land – had to be brought before the Committee before recourse was had to the Courts ...
>
> In like manner, it must not be overlooked that in the East Indian Communities there were the famous Panchayat which means, 'the settlement of dispute by the elders within the East Indian Community'. The Panchayats operated in the open preferably sitting under a tree, either by themselves or together with the disputants. Marriages have been saved, family honours have been restored and family property preserved through the intervention of these wise men.

---

5 'The Alternative Law of Alternative Dispute Resolution' (1991) 32 Les Cahiers de Droit 2. Attention is drawn to the copious citations of literature on the subject of alternative dispute resolution practised under the umbrella of the state as well as non-state adjudication.

6 Alves, H, 'Mediation: A Method of Alternative Dispute Resolution' (1999) Hugh Wooding Law School Journal, The Junior Counsel 36.

In our impatient endeavour to leap into the new millennium the roles which were and still are being played by Priests, the Parsons, the Moulvis and the Pandits have been overlooked, if not all together forgotten. It is worthy to note that the functioning of the Panchayat has been recognised by the High Court of Trinidad and Tobago, where a settlement which was formulated by the Panchayats and agreed to by the parties, was later enforced by an Order of Court.[7]

It is well-documented that mediation has a long and varied history in all the major cultures of the world. As stated by CW Moore in his book, *The Mediation Process*,[8] 'Jewish, Christian, Islamic, Hindu, Buddhist, Confucian and *many indigenous cultures* all have extensive and effective traditions of mediation practice'.

In the case of Ghana, for example, there is abundant evidence showing the historical existence of ADR processes. In the Privy Council case of *Kwasi et al v Larbi*,[9] there is the discussion in the judgment of the Board on the question whether there is a right to resile from an arbitration after the award has been made. Reference was made to Sarbah's *Fanti, Customary Laws (Gold Coast)* published in 1887 and the case of *Ekua Ayafie v Kwamina Banyea*,[10] reported in 1884.

Also, in the present day customary law regime of Ghana, there is still a recognition of non-litigious modes of dispute resolution whereby the parties to a dispute may refer their disagreement to conciliation, mediation or arbitration, outside of the formal court system, to a chief or some respected elder of the community.[11] In a general sense, this respect for a non-litigious process of dispute resolution was underpinned by a society that was then largely culturally homogenous. Respect for the lineage, the household and personal abhorrence of crime and the focus on community rather than personal interests, all served, in large measure, to preserve the equilibrium of the society. The introduction of the court system, as part of the modern state, was an indication of the loss of society's homogeneity through the growth of internal fecundity or external admixture. In that kind of a mix, old sanctions tended to become inadequate to the new needs of maintaining law and order.

The second fallacy (in addition to the supposed one-way flow of ADR from west to east) is that ADR is of recent vintage. According to the American Arbitration Association, a public-service, not-for-profit organisation that has been in existence since 1926, the movement toward ADR in the USA began after World War I and reached its first milestone with the passage of the first modern arbitration statute in New York in the mid-1920s. Since then, the movement has grown steadily, achieving explosive growth since 1980. A chronology of significant dates is then provided in the development of the ADR movement.

It is indeed a significant fact that today, ADR methods have achieved broad acceptance by America's business, labour-management and legal communities. The

---

7   'Alternative Dispute Resolution' (1999) 1(1) The Guyana Law Review 108–09.
8   2nd edn, Jossey-Bass, pp 20 *et seq*. Emphasis added.
9   [1953] AC 164.
10 (1884) Fanti LR 38. For those interested in pursuing the point, several cases on customary arbitration are discussed in the judgment. See also Agbosu, LK, 'Arbitration Under the Customary Law' (1983–86) XV Review of Ghana Law 204.
11 Numerous records can be found in the holdings of the Institute of African Affairs, University of Ghana, Legon. See also an incisive and well-researched article by Professor G Woodman entitled 'The Alternative Law of Alternative Dispute Resolution' (1999) 32 Cahiers de Droit 2, and also Brukum, *Conflict and Conflict Resolution among the Nehumuru*, Transactions of the Historical Society of Ghana, New Series, no 2, p 39.

annual ADR caseload processed by the American Arbitration Association alone has surpassed 60,000 cases – a figure equivalent to one-quarter of the cases now handled each year in the Federal Courts. In fact, the courts have recognised the value of ADR. Today, in many state and federal jurisdictions in the USA, there are mandatory and voluntary court-sponsored ADR programs to divert cases which might be settled without litigation.

What can truly be said, therefore, is that the USA deserves credit for putting a modern face to the process and bringing to it some coherence and internal logic. That is acknowledged by Brown and Marriott when they say that:

> ... the reforms in court procedures have provided an increasing interest in the use of ADR, regarded hitherto by English lawyers with very considerable scepticism and initially seen as an American device to cope with the severe and supposedly unique problems of the USA litigation system. But there is now, we believe, an awareness that the problems which face our civil justice system are not unique to this country; and, that there is much we can learn from what happens elsewhere, particularly in common law countries with which we share a legal tradition and heritage.[12]

As has been shown in the preceding paragraphs, ADR long pre-dated World War I. It is important to acknowledge the ancient and long-standing roots of ADR while clothing it with a modern facade.

The additional point must also be made that international law has long recognised mediation, conciliation and good offices as essential tools of conflict resolution, long before the new fad in municipal law to wholeheartedly embrace ADR. Indeed, in international law, it is litigation which is the latecomer. Mediation, conciliation and good offices were in use before the establishment of the Permanent Court of International Justice (PCIJ) after World War II, and the confusingly named Permanent Court of Arbitration is earlier than the World Court. In earlier times, international lawyers never talked about an 'alternative' to the package of modes of 'pacific settlement of disputes' which included mediation, conciliation and good offices.

CONTEXTUAL BACKGROUND

Contemporary global politics teaches that the world is essentially a village, firing on the cylinders of free and fair trade. It is a marvel to contemplate the threshold on which the world economy stood at the turn of the century. The end of the Cold War had led to the abolition of geopolitical and ideological divisions between the capitalist west and the communist east. Divisions of economic ideology and mutual hostility that had existed between north and south had been significantly reduced.

Furthermore, enormous developments in information and communications technologies had accelerated the integration of the world and, at least in theory, led to wealth creation on a global scale. In her brilliant book, *The Death of Distance*,[13] Frances Cairncross writes that the reality of our times is that geography, borders and time zones are all rapidly becoming irrelevant to the way we conduct our business and

---

12 *ADR Principles and Practices*, 1999, Sweet & Maxwell, p viii.
13 1999, Harvard Business School Press.

personal lives, courtesy of the communications revolution. She predicts that this death of distance will be the single most important economic force shaping all of society over the next half century.

That may well be so, but that will not prevent disputes among individuals and nations. It may well, indeed, accelerate disputes. Indeed, as 'the death of distance' opens up enormous possibilities for increased economic interface, so the need for fast and efficient dispute resolution mechanisms will grow more, not less. At the national and international levels, the Cold War era may be gone but terrorism has replaced that as the principal outcome and form of international conflict. These wars include wars of terrorism, guerilla wars, civil wars and inter-state conflicts,[14] and the reasons may not be too hard to fathom. Generally, global trade has led to greater wealth-creation among states, but Utopia has not arrived for many in the world. Indeed, from a developing world perspective, the pace of technological change has caused income gaps to widen both between countries and within them. Widespread poverty, disease, ignorance and perceived injustices remain critical issues that need to be vigorously addressed if conflict reduction is to be achieved in the world. These are big issues which will be with us for a long time to come. They underscore the need for societies to put in place mechanisms for a quick resolution of conflict as a critical tool in diffusing tension. But that is not all. Our common law system of jurisprudence is also suspect. It carries within it the seeds of continued conflict.

The common law is very much an adversarial system of jurisprudence. The notion of a plaintiff versus a defendant, appellant versus respondent, the legal principles established through judicial precedents, the rules of court, the rules of admissibility, hearsay, etc, are all manifestations of this adversarial approach to dispute resolution.

Two cases that illustrate the ills of present day litigation very well are the civil and criminal trials of OJ Simpson, accused of the murder of his wife. This is not to suggest that ADR can be used for the resolution of serious crimes, but merely to underscore the ills of litigation. In both cases, millions of dollars were expended in litigation costs and expenses. The world was treated to a protracted criminal trial, thousands of rulings by Judge Lance Ito, and the jury suffered an unduly harsh sequestration for several months. OJ Simpson was eventually acquitted, but that was not all. That trial was followed by a subsequent civil trial, involving basically the same parties, in which OJ Simpson was found liable.

If this is an exaggerated example of the problems of modern litigation, everyone can, on their own, at least, begin to enumerate the normal, every-day criticisms of the judicial process. Some of these are:

(a) the adversarial nature of the trial;

(b) delay;

(c) expense;

(d) court overcrowding;

(e) rising demands on scarce public resources;

(f) escalating legal and emotional costs;

(g) an increasingly long, arduous litigation process; and

(h) inefficiency and popular frustration with litigation.

---

14 The attack of 11 September 2001 on the USA is a prime example but several examples of conflict remain in the world – Bosnia, Kosovo, Macedonia, Chechnya, Azerbaijan, Tajiskitan Kashmir, the Philippines, Indonesia, the Middle East, Sudan, Nigeria, etc.

One of the main driving forces towards ADR is public dissatisfaction with litigation. It is not a secret that the search for alternatives to the adjudicative model through courtroom litigation has been fuelled by the growing client dissatisfaction with traditional legal methods. There are the usual complaints of spiraling costs, lengthy delays, increasing levels of litigation and court overload. Then there are also the unusual complaints – clients being left out of the decision making process once they have instructed a lawyer, complete loss of control when they turn their claim to the lawyer, client intimidation by the formality of the adjudicative processes. Also, there is the not uncommon feeling that the burning issue, which originally belonged to the disputants, becomes detached from them once it is placed in the hands of the legal system. In the process, the original, personal facts of the case are reconstructed to fit the relevant legal rules.

ADR seeks to address one fundamental question – what is the best way for people to deal with their differences? Before an attempt is made to answer this question, an examination, albeit brief, of the nature of conflict is needed.

THE NATURE OF CONFLICT

The imagery that conflict evokes is that of clashing passions, intense emotional upheaval, the turmoil of battle and the tension of struggle. To the ordinary mind, therefore, conflict represents a sharp disagreement, a negative collision of ideas, values and interests. There is some sympathy for this viewpoint. For as 'cultural programming' well illustrates, individuals have different experiences, and are influenced by personal biases on life. Surely, all individuals cannot see things in the same light. Conflict is, therefore, a fact of life. It illustrates the simple fact that individuals and nations are uniquely different.

The word 'conflict' is derived from two Latin words *con* (together) and *fligere* (to strike). To take a straight definition from *The Concise Oxford English Dictionary*,[15] conflict means a 'fight, struggle, collision'. Some of its synonyms are belligerency, hostilities, strife, war or clash, contention, difficulty, disdain, dissension, dissent, friction and strife. Additionally, conflict has been defined to include a clash of opposed principles, statements or arguments.

Several theories seem to explain the genesis of conflict. Morton Deutsch[16] explains conflict in terms of incompatible activities of man. Folberg and Taylor[17] explain away conflict in terms of the divergent aims, methods or behaviour of people. Interesting though these theories may be, conflict can simply be viewed as the result of the differences which make individuals unique and the different expectations which individuals bring to life.[18]

While conflict is inevitable, disputes need not be. Disputes occur when we are unable to manage conflict properly. The main traditional responses are to fight, coerce or force a solution, usually of the win-lose variety. In other circumstances, compromise

---

15   7th edn, p 197.
16   Deutsch, M and Coleman, P, *The Handbook of Conflict Resolution*, 2000, Jossey-Bass, pp 9–16.
17   *Mediation: A Comprehensive Guide to Resolving Conflicts Without Litigation*, 1984, Jossey-Bass, p 24.
18   For an indepth study of conflict, see Hocker & Wilmot, *Interpersonal Conflict*, 6th edn, 2000, McGraw-Hill.

may be struck, the difference split or the dispute referred to a counsellor or simply a chance taken with a solution.

According to Boulle and Kelly:

> ... conflict is often regarded as being symptomatic of a pathology which should be cured as quickly as possible, either through compromise or by getting someone else to fix it. If there is a problem in a contractual relationship, in a planning application, or in neighbourly relations, this is perceived as a negative phenomenon which requires a 'remedy', often involving the payment of money, to 'resolve' it.[19]

But conflict need not be so narrowly construed: it can have productive consequences too. If managed properly, conflict can be harnessed into constructive change. If mismanaged, it can lead to destructive consequences, threaten relationships, systems and institutions. It is therefore in the interest of societies that aspire to be well-managed to develop processes and institutions for the resolution of conflict. Such processes generally revolve around negotiation, mediation, arbitration and adjudication.[20]

A diagrammatic representation of the origins of and responses to conflict is reproduced below.

ORIGINS OF CONFLICT

Different values	Unmet basic needs	Limited resources
Convictions	Belonging	Time
Priorities	Power	Money
Principles	Freedom	Property
Beliefs	Fun	

RESPONSES TO CONFLICT

Principled	Soft	Hard
Understanding	Withdrawal	Threats
Respect	Ignoring	Aggression
Resolution	Denial	Anger

A few words about the changing nature of disputes is in order, by way of setting the scene. Dispute resolution hitherto has been based on the assumption that where there is a conflict between two or more individuals or organisations, the party with the strongest (or best argued) legal claim will emerge the winner. This is based on a culture of rights, a culture which has permeated western civilisation and thought for over 100 years. The UN, for example, has consistently used the language of rights in its considerations of human welfare. Caribbean constitutions, too, speak about fundamental rights. So, whether in international law or municipal law, the focus is on 'rights', 'rights' and more 'rights'. Of course, the Commonwealth Caribbean has inherited this culture of 'rights'.

---

19 *Mediation: Principles, Processes, Practice*, 1998, Butterworths, p 47.
20 The next chapter addresses the full range of ADR possibilities.

Even in the majority of cases where the resolution of a conflict is without recourse to either lawyers or the courtroom, dispute resolution strategies are characterised by the language of rights, whether moral, legal, political or economic, all of which assert some basis of 'right'.

True, a focus on rights has played a significant part in the transformation of western political culture from the 'harmony ideology' of feudal societies into 20th century participatory democracies. But there is increasing recognition of the fact that legal standards alone cannot in themselves ensure an end to systematic inequalities, or change attitudes.

As observed by Dr Julie Macfarlane,[21] legal standards do not guarantee access to realistic solutions that meet the needs of individuals whose lives are ruptured by legal disputes. As a consequence, some now propose a rethinking of the rights ideology, as both a method of dispute resolution and a definition of social relations, as well as the development of alternative processes for dealing with conflicts and claims traditionally characterised as being over 'rights'.[22]

The current interest in ADR is stimulated, in part, by the potential to facilitate early settlement of disputes. Early settlement can be both financially and emotionally advantageous to the disputant. It may also mean that an important relationship can be repaired and maintained, rather than finally ruptured by the trauma of litigation. True, lawyers do engage in negotiation and settlement, but a successful negotiation often depends on the strength of the legal rights-based arguments, which can only be fully developed following expensive and time-consuming processes such as disclosure. This legalistic approach often overlooks other avenues of settlement opportunity, which may better address underlying client interests and needs. Interests are the essence of a mediation alternative to the dispute resolution. A focus on interests reflects a complex set of values about the understanding of disputes and how best to resolve them. ADR is, thus, more than a new fad. It represents a paradigm shift in how disputants think about the resolution of their conflict, based on an understanding of their interests.

UNDERLYING ISSUES

There is said to be an iceberg factor in all disputes. Many causes lie below disputes but very few of those surface in a courtroom dispute. Take, for example, the common thief on the block who is stealing because he is hungry. The court will punish him, send him to jail and release him after he has served his time. The court does not address the underlying issue.

There are wider ramifications to a dispute than meet the eye. Some of the factors which may affect a party's attitude to a dispute are set out by Brown and Marriott as follows:

---

21 *Rethinking Disputes: The Mediation Alternative*, 1996, Cavendish Publishing Ltd, pp 1–21.
22 Fiadjoe, A, 'Of Conflicts and Dispute Resolution Processes' (2000) 10(1) Caribbean Law Review 58.

(a) financial and economic implications;

(b) issues of principle;

(c) perceptions of fairness and justice;

(d) cultural differences;

(e) claims and defences that may be made;

(f) liberty of the party or parties;

(g) desire to establish a precedent;

(h) publicity;

(i) emotions;

(j) personality factors of the parties, the lawyers, the judge, the jury; and

(k) practical considerations.

To conclude, Brown and Marriott say that: 'It is clear that there are disputes about different kinds of subject matters, and the kinds of issues that may arise can be very different from one case to another ... Submerged issues may have a profound effect on the way each party views the dispute.'[23]

NON-TRADITIONAL APPROACHES

In the preface, some mention was made of the developing need for the resolution of conflicts and disputes not hitherto attended to or taken seriously. Under this rubric, reference may be made to the ombudsman and the small claims court.

THE OMBUDSMAN

The basic law on the ombudsman is set out in a number of texts such as *Commonwealth Caribbean Public Law*[24] and *Commonwealth Law and Legal Systems*[25] and *The Ombudsman: Caribbean and International Perspectives*.[26] For present purposes, the topic of the ombudsman will be examined from the viewpoint of unclogging the bottlenecks in the present litigation culture and providing access to justice to the citizenry.[27]

Issues relating to access to justice have become a focal point for contention and polemics in constitutional human rights law. Whereas all the constitutions of the Commonwealth Caribbean jurisdictions confer fundamental freedoms on the citizen, none speaks directly to mechanisms to ensure that those rights are properly accessed. That is problematic.

Modern law reform efforts in the Commonwealth, as a whole, now focus on access to justice. While access to justice may take different forms, it is submitted that one of the cheapest and potentially most effective means to achieve that desirable goal is

---

23 *Op cit*, fn 12, p 6.

24 Fiadjoe, A, 2nd edn, 1999, Cavendish Publishing, Chapter 10.

25 Antoine, R, 1999, London, Cavendish Publishing, Chapter 17.

26 Emmanuel, P (ed), 1993, University of the West Indies.

27 The contents on this section have been adopted from a public lecture presented by the author in Belize titled 'Access to Justice – Where Does the Ombudsman Of Belize Fit In?'. The original lecture is reproduced on the web at www.uwichill.edu.bb/bnccde/belize/conference/papers/fiadjoe.html.

through revamping the institution of the ombudsman. But has the Commonwealth Caribbean done so, as a region? Sadly, the answer is no. Granted that there is no significant financial cost to revamping the institution of the ombudsman, it is a pity that, as a region, the Commonwealth Caribbean has not focused on putting in place a few simple steps designed to strengthen and fortify the institution as a bedrock of the protection worthy of the citizenry.

The Commonwealth Caribbean has neither fully appreciated the potential of the institution nor sought to adapt it to become an effective source of 'people power'. The dilemma, therefore, is how to anchor these aims in the constitutional ethos of the region. A number of practical suggestions, which, if implemented, could give true meaning to the legal empowerment of the citizenry will be addressed below.

At a time of significant clamour for more civil justice, the region has no option but to explore alternative dispute resolution solutions. Legal aid, for example, is one of the means by which society ensures access to justice through the courts. While it may be true that law offices and officers in the region are fully committed to an expanded legal aid regime, it is also true to say that, at present, no Commonwealth Caribbean jurisdiction has a credible or established legal aid regime which covers both criminal offences and civil wrongs. Reform efforts – whether of the 'civil justice improvement' variety or the legal aid species – reveal that they are not only time-consuming but very expensive too. Modern governments are not known to be generous in relation to law reform efforts.

In order to fill the vacuum, the ombudsman must take on a pivotal role. The reforms which are needed in order to turn it truly into a people's institution should not be that daunting or difficult to achieve. They are relatively inexpensive. In his recent book, *Winner Takes All*,[28] Professor Selwyn Ryan deals with some proposals for reforming Caribbean democracy. Among his reform proposals is the suggestion to 'provide the office of the Ombudsman ... with material and other resources needed to enable him to monitor administrative abuse and to intervene more efficiently to minimize it'. The problem with that formulation is that it is couched in very general terms and is therefore susceptible to various interpretations.

The point has already been made that the Commonwealth Caribbean has neither fully appreciated the potential of the institution nor sought to adapt it to become an effective source of 'people power'. How then can this situation be improved? Before addressing specific recommendations, it may be helpful to set such recommendations in their proper context.

CONSIDERATIONS WHICH UNDERPIN PROPOSED REFORM

A number of critical considerations underpin the submissions to follow. It is a verifiable truism that a modern government relies on a huge bureaucracy for the carrying out of its business. That bureaucracy is accountable only to the political masters, never to the populace, yet the enormous discretion which it exercises is unparalleled.

---

28 1991, UWI Multimedia Production Centre, p 254.

In far colder climes, Sir Cecil Carr was able to observe, as early as 1941,[29] that 'we nod approvingly when someone tells us that, whereas the State used to be merely policeman, judge and protector, it has now become schoolmaster, doctor, house builder, road-maker, town-planner, public utility supplier and all the rest of it'.

This statement acknowledges the enormous growth in the nature and ambit of state power. The state has assumed an ever-increasing range of responsibilities. Through nationalisation it controls most of the basic industries and the goods and services they supply. It runs a comprehensive system of social services providing benefits from just before the cradle (by way of pre-natal services) to the grave and, inbetween, it provides education, a health service, sickness benefits and old age pensions. Such enormous power must have profound implications for traditional understanding of what constitutes basic freedoms. The dilemma of the modern state is therefore how to control this executive power through acceptable constitutional arrangements.

This is a critical challenge, which faces all constitutional systems that aspire to a democracy. How are structures and measures devised and implemented whereby state bureaucracy may be made accountable for its actions?

The Commonwealth Caribbean operates a system where the Constitution guarantees fundamental rights to all, but provides no full system of legal aid to enable aggrieved citizens to vindicate their rights and seek recourse to justice. To litigate a case involving a breach of fundamental freedoms is tantamount to putting together a powerful armoury of wealth, legal expertise, power and process – all of which are very much beyond the reach of the ordinary citizen.

Also, not many territories in the region have a human rights body to which citizens may refer their complaints and to which they may look for any form of minimal recourse to justice – not even a citizen's advisory bureau.

Finally, few territories in the region have integrity legislation or integrity commissions. Integrity commissions have been found by the citizenry of, for example, Trinidad & Tobago to be a most important adjunct to the mechanisms for the protection of the public against abuse and intolerable conduct on the part of those in authority.

It is submitted that the institution of the ombudsman ought to be the critical focal point to enable the ordinary citizen to have some affinity to the Constitution and to enjoy the benefits of constitutional protection.

The recommendations which follow will seek to capitalise on these considerations. They have been expressed in no order of importance, but they are all critical to the issues at stake if the constitutional protection of the Commonwealth Caribbean citizen is to be taken seriously.

---

29 Quoted in Harlow, C and Rawlings, R, *Law and Administration*, 1984, Weidenfeld & Nicolson, p 1.

SPECIFIC RECOMMENDATIONS

Reformed legal framework

In this cluster of recommendations it is prudent to start with issues which revolve around a reformed legal framework, and which are designed to give greater efficiency to the operations of the ombudsman.

First on the list is the need to address the problem of inordinate delay in the settlement of disputes between the individual and the state. It is a problem which is common to all the offices of the ombudsman in the region. One way to address the problem is to give the ombudsman a fast track authority to encourage settlements of disputes between the individual and the state. Once the ombudsman invokes a fast track authority, then parties should be obliged to comply with the terms set out by the ombudsman.

In the 2002 Report to Parliament, the Ombudsman of Barbados highlights delay as one of the biggest problems faced by his institution during the year 2001–02. Berating government departments for the tardy responses to complaints from the general public and even from his office, the Ombudsman indicated that the average time for the first response from government agencies, after being advised of a complaint by his office, was 95 days. Highly critical of the more than three months' delay, the Ombudsman of Barbados added that he also wished that public service agencies would re-examine their practice of not acknowledging correspondence, even after two or three requests. 'While some agencies reply promptly as a matter of course, some are particularly bad, embarrassing this office, their agency and the public service as a whole, but most importantly, doing the public whom they serve, a great disservice', he charged, insisting that the public deserved better.

The Ombudsman also noted that while he did not believe public servants were deliberately committed to disappointing the public, 'the short-comings arise out of a certain thoughtlessness and lack of consideration for the troubles of their customers and clients'. These are very strong words.

Next, it would be helpful to have the ombudsman invested with the power to refer cases for mediation or other alternative dispute resolution process.

Also, there should be an enhancement of the jurisdiction of the ombudsman in two ways, bearing in mind the absence of other supportive processes for the enforcement of legal rights and obligations. One way would be to seek to clarify the grey areas of the ombudsman's authority. The other way, in the mould of Lord Woolf's recommendations, would be to grant enhanced jurisdiction whereby cases may be referred to the ombudsman's office by the courts as they see fit. This would help, also, to ease the caseload of the courts. But more importantly, references may be made for cases which are more suited to the inquisitorial style of the ombudsman, who can be more proactive and aggressive than a judge, rather than the investigative style of the trial process.

And when the job of the ombudsman is done, the law should put some weight behind the conclusions reached by the ombudsman. At present, there is no obligation on parliaments in the region even to debate the reports of the ombudsman. The constitutional requirement is that the reports should be tabled and no more. This is a self-defeating and, indeed, contradictory provision in the law.

The reports of the ombudsman should not only be tabled, but should be discussed in parliament. To that end, a joint standing committee of parliament should be established to consider the reports of the ombudsman. These discussions should be afforded the widest publicity.

One could go further. The ombudsman should be given express power to publicise cases of non-compliance with recommendations that have been made.

Finally, a strong case can be made for a separate fund to be set up by parliament, from which payments of claims, jointly agreed upon by the ombudsman and the relevant public body, may be made. One important consequence of these recommendations is a cost and efficiency factor.

The enhanced role being argued for the office of ombudsman may require that the office be staffed with in-house counsel to assist it in its work. Is that too much for any country to bear? The efficiency of output that will benefit the populace as a result should far outweigh the costs.

Also, the ombudsman can only truly be the common man's lawyer in a milieu where his office is bolstered and assisted by state supported systems, such as the existence of a code of conduct for public officers and the imposition of an obligation on the bureaucracy to conduct public affairs fairly and reasonably.

There is also a compelling need for a code of conduct to regulate the operation of the public services. Many countries in the wider Commonwealth, for example, New Zealand and South Africa, have found the wisdom to adopt such a code. Some have even gone further to establish an integrity commission. One need not go so far. A voluntary code of conduct, which would provide some objective yardstick, in broad general terms, as to what is acceptable conduct in a public officer, would be a beginning.

Finally, a last lesson could be drawn from the Constitution of South Africa, which imposes a constitutional obligation on the public services of South Africa to maintain a just administrative system. Section 33 of the Constitution of the Republic of South Africa speaks to a right conferred on the citizen to expect nothing short of administrative action that is lawful, reasonable and procedurally fair. Section 195 sets out basic values and principles governing public administration, two of which are that 'peoples' needs must be responded to' and also that 'public administration must be accountable'.

Legislation is sometimes a useful instrument in setting norms and standards of correctitude and good behaviour in public administration. This is the backdrop against which delay and apathy in the decision making process ought to be tackled.

A small claims court?

Despite the stupendous pressure placed on the magistracy in the Commonwealth Caribbean region, the simple device of a small claims court to ease the caseload is not being applied universally.

Small claims constitute the vast majority of cases which pass through the litigation system. What this means is that the small claims system remains a key component in the provision of access to justice. It assists those who cannot afford the costs normally associated with civil litigation and who are not eligible for legal aid either. As Lord Woolf puts it in his report, *Access To Justice*: 'In an increasingly consumer based society there is a need to provide an effective forum for the sensible resolution of such disputes.'

He explains the rationale for a small claims court in terms of proportionality, fairness and speed:

> My approach to litigation in general ... is that it should provide a means of resolving disputes which is proportionate to the amount or importance of the matter at issue, which is achieved within an appropriate timescale and which ensures fairness of procedure and reasonable equality between the parties involved.[30]

A small claims court should not be bound by any rules of procedure except those of fair play and common sense. Nor should it be manned by other than lay personnel. Its jurisdiction should cover debt collection, petty civil claims and consumer matters. Hearings should be informal and strict rules of evidence must not apply. The role of the magistrate in a small claims court should be clearly distinguished from that of a regular magistrate. To quote Lord Woolf on this point:

> The role of the judge in small claims is not only that of an adjudicator. It is a key safeguard of the rights of both parties. In most cases, the judge is effectively a substitute for a legal representative. His duty is to ascertain the main matters at issue, to elicit the evidence, to reach a view on the facts of the matter and to give a decision. In some cases he may encourage the parties to settle. In doing so, he should ensure that both parties have presented the evidence and called the witnesses germane to their case and that he has identified and considered any issue of law which is pertinent to the case in hand. He must also hold the ring and ensure that each party has a fair chance to present his own case and to challenge that of his opponent. And since there is only a very limited right of appeal, the judge's decision, very unusually, is effectively final.[31]

It is rather surprising that, in a region where there is very little consumer protection, there is no pressure on governments to plump for a small claims court which is accessible, quick, cheap and informal. Such consumer credit claims, as well as simple debt cases, do not usually involve complex legal issues. Litigants should therefore be able to represent themselves on a do-it-yourself basis without the need for an attorney.

There is a minuscule reference in the Jamaica Judicature (Resident Magistrates) Act and the Resident Magistrates Court (Amendment) Rules 1999 (1973 Rev) to a small claims action.[32] But that is a far cry from the establishment of a small claims court. The Jamaican legislation only deals with the commencement of small claims actions, service of small claims summons and transfer of small claims actions to regular sittings, but these are designed for the regular court proceedings.

Perhaps the time is ripe for a serious regional push towards the establishment of small claims courts by way of an alternative to the present system of dispute resolution through the regular courts. Until then, a credible case can be made that the gap created by the absence of small claims courts should be filled by the ombudsman.

---

30 1996, HMSO, Chapter 16, para 1.
31 *Ibid*, Chapter 16, para 26: for 'judge' in the quotation, substitute 'Lay Magistrate'.
32 Sections 3–6.

In the absence of a human rights commission, and in the absence of a system of legal aid for civil cases, someone ought to fill that vacuum in the meantime. The office of the ombudsman is the most logical one to double up as both a small claims court and a human rights commission. Cases of a limited jurisdiction may be assigned to the ombudsman on the understanding that the ombudsman's decision would be final. This would be akin to the lay magistracy system in Belize. The ombudsman would determine such cases using basic common sense and rules of fair play.

CONCLUSION

In conclusion, this chapter has sought to highlight a few critically important points about ADR. First, ADR is linked in most people's minds with alternatives to the traditional judicial process, with which it is usually favourably contrasted.[33] Whatever ADR is, the argument runs that it is quicker, cheaper and more user-friendly than the courts. It gives people an involvement in the process of resolving their disputes that is not possible in a public, formal and adversarial justice system perceived to be dominated by the abstruse procedures and recondite language of the law. It offers choice: choice of method, of procedure, of cost, of representation, of location. Because it is often quicker than judicial proceedings, it can ease burdens on the courts. Because it is cheaper, it can help to curb the upward spiral of legal costs and legal aid expenditure. There have been many attempts throughout history to do what the proponents of ADR wish to do, namely, to balance fairness in dispute resolution with speed, informality and flexibility and to contain costs.

Secondly, the lawyer today requires both litigation and dispute resolution skills. However, more and more, the balance is tilting in favour of dispute resolution.

Thirdly, even in the heart of litigation, ADR has forced a complete rethink, a *volte-face*, of the trial process by introducing the concept of case management. Case management now mandates a re-examination of issues, such as who controls the trial process, costs, time frames within which to dispose of a case and access to justice.

Fourthly, ADR is growing in importance as society and the legal profession grapple with the problems associated with traditional litigation. People's motivations for using of ADR are varied. Some people are in search of new processes that could resolve the issues in a way that makes sense for all involved. Some simply want a binding decision imposed, but quickly and in private, with a minimum of monetary and emotional expense. Others want a less intimidating process where the parties have control over the decision, and can explore an increased number and range of options and solutions, rather than being confined to 'win' or 'lose' options. In short, people want a process where they will have an opportunity to express their interests, without fear that their legal rights will be jeopardised, and where their relationships will not be unnecessarily impaired by the very process of resolving the dispute.

---

33 In the words of Lewis Carroll's *Alice in Wonderland*: 'It seems very pretty but it is rather hard to understand. Somehow it seems to fill my head with ideas – only I don't exactly know what they are!' Or, as someone said in Trinidad & Tobago: 'Mediation? I know what that is, that is something like *Judge Judy*.'

Fifthly, ADR demonstrates the tremendous possibilities of our legal systems but requires a massive change of focus. Ordinary trial procedures never contemplated the use of electronically generated evidence or the resolution of disputes on line or through cyberspace. ADR leads to an examination of the future direction of the law. Some of these themes are developed in subsequent chapters in this book.

CHAPTER 2

THE ADR SPECTRUM

INTRODUCTION

In the past, ADR was the term which described a group of processes through which disputes and conflicts were resolved outside of formal litigation procedures. At present it is, perhaps, more accurate to include in these processes some aspects of litigation, such as case management. In any case, primarily in the USA, ADR has developed as an adjunct to the legal systems, rather than in direct contrast to litigation.

ADR covers a variety of devices which are not static. Indeed, they continue to expand as society gains a better appreciation of the nature of disputes. So, from the traditional methods of dispute resolution,[1] society is reorganising more and more of those processes which attempt, first and foremost, to reconcile the interests of the parties. A rights determination and a power resolution are involved only as a fallback in case of a failure in reconciling interests.

Many processes or devices claim a place under the *chapeau* of ADR. There are three classifications: adjudicative, evaluative and mediative.

In the adjudicative process, the neutral third party makes a decision for the parties. In the evaluative process, some feedback is provided to the parties about the relative merits of their cases by way of a non-binding evaluation of the case. In the mediative process, the neutral third party does not render a decision or an evaluation. Underpinning all these processes are the basic principles of negotiation. However, there is also a recognition of the fact that not all negotiations succeed.[2]

Unfortunately, there is no scientific formula by which we can make a definitive determination as to which process or device is suitable for or appropriate to a conflict situation. At times, a combination of processes may be required where a single one may not yield the desired results. A great deal also depends on the role and assistance provided by the neutral third party.

The ADR spectrum or umbrella covers the following processes:

(a) dispute prevention;

(b) negotiation;

(c) mediation;

(d) a mix of mediation/arbitration or arbitration/mediation;

(e) the institution of the ombudsman;

(f) private mini-trial;

(g) judicial mini-trial;

(h) pre-trial conference;

(i) early neutral evaluation;

---

1   Among these are the use of force and coercion, avoidance, compromise and splitting the difference.

2   Mnookin R, 'Why Negotiations Fail: An Exploration of Barriers to the Resolution of Conflict' (1993) 8 Ohio St J on Dispute Resol 235.

(j) arbitration;

(k) administrative hearing;

(l) case management; and

(m) renting a judge.

Contrasted with all of the above is the judicial trial.

The question of whether ADR should be court annexed or not is not wholly free from difficulty. That question is addressed later in this chapter.

ADR encompasses a spectrum of several different processes – from negotiation, to non-binding third party intervention (such as mediation), to binding third party intervention (such as arbitration). As noted by WD Brazil, the debate over the introduction of ADR revolves around the notion that:

> One of organized society's most fundamental responsibilities is to provide means by which people can resolve disputes without violence. In other words, providing effective dispute-resolution processes is an essential public responsibility. It is because we recognize that fact, and because we are concerned that the formal adjudicatory process might not, in all the circumstances, deliver the best dispute resolution services, that we are interested in having public courts explore the wisdom of sponsoring the ADR programs.[3]

In response to these needs and desires, ADR processes have developed both independently and as part of the court process. Many ADR processes can be considered as either forms of arbitration, in which a neutral party provides a binding or non-binding decision about the likely outcome if the case was to go to trial, or as forms of mediation, a non-binding process where a neutral third party assists the disputants to negotiate a resolution of the dispute.

To the question, 'what is ADR an alternative *to*?', the traditional response is that ADR is an alternative to litigation. But even that has all changed. The language has developed very fast. So, there is ADR on its own, court annexed ADR, court facilitated ADR and multi door ADR. There is even some talk of a threshold point beyond which a case may not proceed to trial without, first, a reference to some form of ADR. Now there is talk of 'case flow management' in which the court adopts an interventionist role in matters before it.

A pictorial rendition of the ADR spectrum would look something like this:

Prevention	Mediation	Ombudsman	Judicial mini-trial	ENE	Administrative hearing	Trial (including case management)
Negotiation	Mediation/arb or Arbitration/med		Private mini-trial	Pre-trial conference	Arbitration	Rent-a-judge

THE SPECTRUM INTERPRETED

As the spectrum illustrates, ADR refers to several processes for resolving disputes, inclusive of some aspects of litigation. Dispute resolution processes, including

---

3   'Institutionalizing Court ADR Programs', in Sander, FEA (ed), *Emerging ADR Issues in State and Federal Courts*, 1991, Chicago: ABA (Litigation Section), pp 52–165 at 56.

litigation, can be arranged along a spectrum according to the level of control the disputants have over the process. At the beginning of the spectrum, the parties are in full control of the process. As we move from negotiation to mediation, we find that the process involves a neutral third party who does not have the power to impose a binding decision. By the time arbitration, administrative hearing or a trial is reached in the spectrum, a neutral third party makes a binding decision for the parties.

These processes in the spectrum are often arranged to correlate with increasing costs and third party involvement, decreasing control of the parties over the process and, usually, increasing likelihood of having the relationship between the disputants deteriorate during and after the resolution of the dispute.

A few generalised descriptions about each process in the spectrum follow. Detailed discussions about each process will be addressed later.

1 Dispute prevention

It is an obvious fact that preventing unnecessary disputes saves time and money. It also has the potential to prevent a relationship from being damaged. Of course, one very obvious, but unrealistic, way of 'solving' a dispute is by ignoring the conflict. This is usually possible when the parties have sufficient resources and the patience to remove themselves from the conflict causing situation. At the same time, it is acknowledged that ignoring conflict can lead to an exacerbation of the root causes of that conflict, thus creating far more serious consequences for the parties, and for society, further down the road.

This is particularly so where the parties have an ongoing relationship. In that context, the conflict does not fade away merely because the parties ignore it. While the conflict may superficially fade away, the underlying causes ferment, thus reappearing later or emerging in a different form.

Another method of dispute prevention is compromise, whereby the parties shift position incrementally until they reach a middle ground. The principal difficulty with this approach is that, once again, it fails to address the underlying interests of the parties and the power relationships between them.

Another form of avoiding responsibility for managing conflict is with the intervention of a third party, for example, the judge. The parties are hardly involved in the creation of solutions to their problem and are easily able to blame the system responsible for the final outcome.

A more realistic way of preventing disputes is by providing dispute resolution training, as training provides people with the skills to prevent unnecessary disputes. In the USA, one method of dispute resolution is referred to as 'partnering'. Partnering requires all of the disputants or participants involved in a project to meet to discuss how to resolve any conflicts which may arise. For example, in the construction industry, the contractor, the subcontractors and tradespeople may attend a meeting to agree a process or processes to be used in case of future conflict. While that in itself may not prevent a dispute, what it does is to prevent a second dispute over which resolution mechanism should be applied to resolve the primary dispute.

Another method used is a 'systems design', which is a similar concept to partnering. It involves determining, in advance, what processes will be used for handling conflicts which arise within an organisation or between an organisation and other organisations or individuals. What that does is to provide, in advance, mechanisms for resolving the disputes in an efficient and effective manner.

An equally valid example may be found in private contracts where the parties provide, in advance, for a mode of settling any future disputes, for example, a reference to arbitration in case of a dispute.

Also in this category are processes of dispute prevention where mediation takes place before a formal dispute has arisen, for example, where the state wishes to undertake a major development in an area to which the citizens object.

2   Negotiation

Negotiation is any form of communication between two or more people for the purpose of arriving at a mutually agreeable solution. In a negotiation, the disputants may represent themselves or may be represented by a negotiating agent or agents. The people involved in the negotiation, whether the disputants or their agents, maintain control over the negotiation process.

In the context of ADR, when speaking about negotiation, there are certain terms such as competitive bargaining, co-operative bargaining and principled negotiation. These modes of negotiation are said to arise from different styles of negotiating. In competitive bargaining, the negotiators are so concerned with substantive results that they may advocate extreme positions, create false issues, mislead the other negotiator or bluff in order to gain advantage, try to ascertain the other negotiator's bottom line and only make concessions rarely and grudgingly.

On the other hand, co-operative negotiators focus on building a relationship of trust and co-operation. They may, therefore, be prepared to make concessions on substantive issues, principally in order to preserve the relationship.

Principled negotiation, on the other hand, requires the negotiators to focus on the interests of each of the disputants, with the goal of creating satisfactory and elegant options for resolution which may be assessed by objective criteria.[4]

3   Mediation

Among the mediative processes, mediation is the most popular. The other processes under the umbrella are conciliation and consensus building.

Mediation is a non-binding process in which an impartial third party, called the mediator, facilitates the negotiation process between the disputants. As the mediator has no decision making power, the disputants maintain control over the substantive outcome of the mediation.

However, the mediator controls the process with the help of the disputants. With the consent of the disputants, the mediator sets and enforces the ground rules for the mediation process. Mediation can be 'interests-based' or 'rights-based'.

---

4   See Chapter 3 for a detailed discussion.

Interests-based mediation, broadly speaking, refers to a style of mediation in which the mediator facilitates communication between the disputants and encourages the disputants to focus on their interests. In an interests-based mediation, the parties are encouraged to focus on the underlying interests, goals and needs rather than on the perceived outcome of litigation.

In a *rights-based* mediation, however, the mediator provides an opinion on the disputants' legal rights and encourages resolution of the dispute in accordance with the law in the view of the mediator.

In either form of mediation, both parties are encouraged to consider what course of action they will pursue if no agreement is reached, and the resulting consequences. The disputants have the option whether to attend mediation or not. Mediation may be court-connected or private.[5]

One important feature of the mediation process is that it is flexible and easily adaptable to all types of cases, especially those in which the parties have an interest in maintaining a relationship of one kind or another. Sometimes, the mediator may meet with the parties separately in a 'caucus' to explore various options designed to lead the parties to a settlement. Such agreements may be enforced in the same way as other settlement agreements.

The flexible nature of the mediation process has enabled it to be used at the appellate level during trial, prior to filing a suit or prior to trial. Mediation may be ordered or allowed by the courts or entered into voluntarily by the parties.

A number of advantages may be gained through the use of mediation. Among these are the following:

(a) informality of the process;

(b) swiftness in resolving disputes;

(c) relatively inexpensive cost;

(d) focusing on the parties' interests and concerns, rather than their legal rights only;

(e) encouragement to the parties to fashion their own solutions;

(f) involvement of the parties in the process;

(g) confidentiality of the process; and

(h) high success rate for mediators.

However, against these advantages must be weighed the disadvantages. Among these are the following:

(a) the absence of procedural protections for the parties;

(b) the consensual nature of the process means that both parties can walk away from the table at any time;

(c) the ability of a strong and powerful party to bully or browbeat the other into a result which may not necessarily be fair or just; and

(d) the absence of opportunities to measure the objectiveness of the process.

Conciliation and consensus building have been described as follows:[6]

---

5   See Chapter 4 for a detailed discussion.

6   Kovach, K, *Mediation: Principles and Practice*, 1994, West Publishing, p 12.

While historically the terms mediation and conciliation have been used interchangeably, there are some differences worth noting. Usually, mediation, while quite an informal process, maintains more structure than pure conciliation. For instance, it may be possible to achieve conciliation over the telephone, whereas telephonic mediation is rarely used. Moreover, the term conciliation usually denotes that the disputing parties have been reconciled, and the relationship has been mended. In mediation, although maintenance of the relationship is an important factor, often resolution of a case will occur without an actual reconciliation between the disputants.

Consensus building is another process which is mediative in nature. Consensus building may be thought of as an extended mediation, with large groups, which involves a number of conflicts. Unlike traditional mediation which is, by design, usually a one time, one day intervention, the consensus building process takes place over a more extended period of time. Additionally, because there are a number of individuals within groups, it is unlikely that everyone attends the process. Each group will have representatives who then must obtain ratification of any decision reached at the consensus building session.

4 Ombudsman

An ombudsman is a person who investigates complaints against public authorities and comes up with a non-binding recommendation. A case has been made elsewhere for the development of a symbiotic relationship between the courts and the office of the ombudsman.[7] Lord Woolf has strong views on this subject. In his 1995 *Report on Civil Justice*, he called for an expanded role for the institution far beyond the present arrangement where the ombudsman does not interfere with matters which are justiciable before the courts. In his own words:

> There are improvements, however, which could be made in the relationship between the public ombudsman and the courts without interfering with their independence. The public ombudsmen are concerned with issues of mal-administration, which do not manifestly fall within the province of court proceedings and judicial review. While the courts' jurisdiction should not be curtailed in any way, there would advantages if the public ombudsmen had wider scope to take on issues, which could be resolved, by the courts.

> It would also be an advantage if the courts were able to refer issues to an ombudsman, with his and the parties' consent.

The following specific recommendations by Lord Woolf ought to be of interest to ADR enthusiasts. They touch on the expanded role of the ombudsman but, also, go beyond that:

(a) Developments abroad, particularly those in the USA, Australia and Canada, in relation to ADR should be monitored, the Judicial Studies Board giving as much assistance as is practicable in relation to this exercise.

(b) The retail sector should be encouraged to develop private ombudsman schemes, to cover consumer complaints, similar to those which now exist in relation to service industries. The government should facilitate this.

---

7   See Fiadjoe, A, *Commonwealth Caribbean Public Law*, 2nd edn, 1999, Cavendish Publishing, Chapter 10.

(c) The relationship between ombudsmen and the courts should be broadened, enabling issues to be referred by an ombudsman to the courts and by the courts to the ombudsman with the consent of those involved.

(d) The discretion of the public ombudsmen to investigate issues involving maladministration, which could be raised before the courts, should be extended.

5 Evaluative processes

Evaluative processes have one principal aim: to provide the disputants with feedback as to the merits of their cases. Such objective, non-binding, confidential evaluation by a neutral third party comes in handy in further settlement negotiations.

6 Private mini-trial

The private mini-trial is usually used in complex commercial disputes between companies. The format may vary and can be determined by agreement between the companies. The essence is that a mini-trial usually involves the summary presentation of each disputant's case before a panel consisting of decision makers from each of the companies and a neutral third party. The representatives of the companies often have not been personally involved in the dispute or attempts at settlement. The advantage is that they are then able to bring fresh perspectives on the dispute.

Following the case presentations, the decision makers from both sides attempt to negotiate a settlement with the assistance of the neutral third party, who may or may not provide an opinion.

The advantages of this process in the case of a major dispute between large business entities are fairly obvious. To the extent that this process requires high level business executives to focus on the dispute and hear the opponent's version of the dispute at first hand, it increases each party's appreciation of the issues before pursuing litigation. It also provides an opportunity for business executives to take control of the dispute and help directly to attempt a resolution. Obviously, a successful resolution may mean substantial savings in costs and time to the business enterprises. Apart from its confidential nature, the process can be particularly helpful in resolving highly technical disputes.

Its disadvantages may also be dramatic. The requirement of substantial preparation may mean the diversion of valuable time by the business executives from their managerial responsibilities. But what is more, in the case of a failure to resolve the matter, it could lead to a situation where one side obtains an unfair advantage by being able to preview the other side's arguments and witnesses. Additionally, this process may not be suitable to the type of dispute which depends, for example, on the credibility of witnesses.

7 Judicial mini-trial

In some jurisdictions, such as the USA, the judicial system allows disputants to participate voluntarily in a judicial mini-trial. In that process, disputants' lawyers present brief arguments to a judge, who will not be the judge if the case goes to trial. The judge hears the summaries and then meets with the disputants and their lawyers and they, together, attempt to resolve the dispute. In doing so, the judge points out the strengths and weaknesses of each party's case and helps the parties to resolve the dispute.[8]

8   Pre-trial conference

A pre-trial conference is similar to a judicial mini-trial, though less formal.

Typically, counsel for the disputants present an overview of their respective clients' cases and may refer to the evidence upon which they would rely at a trial. The pre-trial judge frequently provides a non-binding opinion as to how the case would likely be resolved at trial. The disputants themselves are encouraged to attend the pre-trial conference.

If the disputants cannot settle the case at the pre-trial conference, the pre-trial conference judge will attempt to narrow the issues for trial and obtain agreement from the disputants regarding evidence and the anticipated length of the trial. As a result, a pre-trial conference combines an attempt to resolve a dispute prior to trial and preparation for trial.

9   Early neutral evaluation

If disputants cannot agree as to which one of them would be successful at arbitration or trial, they may retain a respected neutral third party to provide them with an early neutral evaluation (ENE). The disputants and their counsel present their cases to the evaluator, who then provides an opinion about the likely outcome of the case were it to proceed to arbitration or trial. This opinion may be presented to the parties jointly or, instead, privately to each party. Unlike a pre-trial conference, ENE usually occurs early in the dispute, generally upon the filing of the response. This process also forces the disputants to confront their case, narrow down the issues for resolution, develop a speedy disclosure process and, where possible, effect a settlement.[9] Even where a settlement fails, it is said that ENE is useful because it helps the parties to establish time limits for the administration of the case.

Among the advantages of this process are that it is informal, relatively inexpensive and allows each party the opportunity to reach a mutually acceptable agreement, other than one which is available only through the courts. It may also assist parties, who may have unrealistic expectations about their case, to form a view as to the prospects in litigation. Furthermore, the proceedings are confidential.

---

8   For a description of court mini-trials, see Plapinger, ES, 'The Minitrial in the District of Massachusetts' in Fine, E and Plapinger, ES (eds), *ADR and the Courts*, 1987, CPR Legal Program, pp 99–118; and 'A Federal Judge's ADR Technique: Minitrials With Special Masters' (January 1987) Alternatives 9. For a case illustration, see 'Minitrial Resolves Major Federal Gas Case; Shows Value of "Private" Procedure in Court' (May 1990) Alternatives 75. See also the following CPR resources: *CPR Practice Guide: The Minitrial* (1988); *CPR Model Minitrial Procedure* (revised 1989); and *Out of Court: The Minitrial*, a videotape of a minitrial with expert commentaries.

9   Levine, D, 'Early Neutral Evaluation: The Second Phase' (1989) J Disp Res 15.

The disadvantages of this process are similar to those identified under mediation. Where ENE fails, it could add extra time and cost to the resolution of the dispute.[10]

10 Arbitration

Arbitration is a process in which a neutral third party, or an odd-numbered panel of neutral parties, renders a decision based on the merits of the case.

The parties to arbitration can maintain some control over the design of the arbitration process. In some situations, the scope of the rules for the arbitration process are set out by statute or by contract; in other circumstances, the parties work together to design an arbitration process which is appropriate to their dispute.

For example, in some instances the parties may choose the arbitrator, may limit the length of opening statements, or may decide that there will be no disclosure or no oral hearing. In this way, the process can be tailored to meet the needs of the parties. Once the parties have set the parameters for the arbitration, the arbitrator assumes full control of the process.

The decision of an arbitrator may be advisory, though it is usually binding. In the case of non-binding arbitration, the parties or their attorneys present their cases, with supporting legal arguments, to the arbitrator who makes a decision based on the merits. Although the proceedings are fairly formal, the rules of evidence are somewhat relaxed. Accordingly, a case may be presented through witnesses or documents or summaries. Where the decision of the arbitration, in this case, is non-binding, the parties are not required to accept it. They are at liberty to commence proceedings if they are not satisfied with the decision. The power to inflict costs may be deftly deployed to make it difficult for a party to resile from a non-binding decision. Non-binding arbitration is usually court-ordered even though, on occasion, the parties may choose that mode of dispute resolution.

Two principal advantages attend this process. Where the parties accept the result of the non-binding arbitration, they may save considerably in terms of time and money. Additionally, the proceedings may be more amicable than the trial process, thus helping to better preserve the relationship between the parties.

Among the disadvantages are the following:

(a) the proceedings may turn out to be costly in terms of time and money where the dispute is taken to trial *de novo*;

(b) the parties could use the proceedings to claim an unfair advantage by obtaining a preview of the opponent's case;

(c) the process and results are private and so cannot be measured against objective standards of fairness; and

(d) not all arbitrations are held to one standard in adjudication. While some may be legalistic, others may be more oriented to basic fairness.

---

10 For explanations of ENE, see Brazil, WD, 'A Close Look at Three Court-Sponsored ADR Programs' (1990) University of Chicago Legal Forum 46; Fine, E and Plapinger, ES (eds), *ADR and the Courts*, 1987, CPR Legal Program, pp 163–91; Federal Judicial Center, *Court-Based Dispute Resolution Programs* (1991), pp 35–42 and appendix. For an account of the effectiveness of ENE, see Levine, DI, 'Northern District of California Adopts Early Neutral Evaluation to Expedite Dispute Resolution' (December–January 1989) 72 Judicature 235.

A binding arbitration follows the same process as a non-binding arbitration except that, this time, the decision is binding upon the parties. It is extremely difficult to upset a binding arbitral award. A binding arbitration is usually agreed to voluntarily by the parties, prior to the occurrence of the dispute.

Some of the advantages claimed for this process are that, due to the relaxed rules of evidence and procedure, the parties make considerable savings in time and money, compared to a trial, and the limited possibility of vacating an arbitral award lowers costs and ensures finality of outcome. Another possible claim is that such proceedings may be more amicable than a trial, thus better preserving the relationship between the parties.

As with all these processes, there is also the downside. There is a lack of sufficient appellate opportunities. The privacy and confidentiality of the process may deny the public access to information and precludes the creation of precedents. Also, binding arbitration now approximates too closely to litigation, thus attracting the usual complaints which accompany litigation. Binding arbitration is still to resolve the issue of strict enforcement of legal rights versus the application of principles of fairness.

In the USA, court annexed arbitration is widely used for small to moderate-sized disputes, based on specific authorising statutes.[11]

11 Administrative hearing

As the name suggests, an administrative hearing takes place before an administrative tribunal. Such tribunals are established by statute and have the power to enforce certain statutes. Generally, procedural rules are more relaxed at a hearing, contrasted with civil or criminal trials, though they are often more formal than arbitration.

The big difference between an administrative hearing and an arbitration is that in the former the parties cannot select the members of the tribunal and cannot set the procedural rules.[12]

12 Summary jury trial

Summary jury trial process is an avenue, that of a trial, to satisfy the desires of those disputants who insist on their day in court. This process saves time and money for the parties.[13] It involves the presentation of an abbreviated version of the evidence to an advisory jury. That evidence is the summary of the case for each party. Attorneys may present closing arguments based on the abbreviated evidence.

---

11 Two good overviews of court annexed arbitration are Hensler, DR, 'Court-ordered Arbitration: An Alternative View' (1990) University of Chicago Legal Forum 399; and Meierhoefer, BS, *Court-Annexed Arbitration in Ten District Courts*, 1990, Federal Judicial Center. For a good description of the CAA program in the Eastern District of Pennsylvania by one of its senior judges, see Broderick, RJ, 'Court-annexed Compulsory Arbitration: It Works' 72 Judicature 217–25 (December–January 1989). Generally, see also Center for Public Resources, *CPR Practice Guide: ADR Use in Federal and State Courts*, 1990, pp A267–A291; and Federal Judicial Center, *Court-Based Dispute Resolution Programs*, pp 83–95 and appendices (1990) (including the text of Federal Court Arbitration Rules).

12 See an example in the Administrative Appeal Tribunal Act 1981 of Barbados (Cap 109A).

13 See Lambros, T, 'The Summary Jury Trial – An Alternative Method of Resolving Disputes' (1986) 69 Judicature 286. The origins of this procedure are credited to Judge Thomas Lambros of the District Court for the Northern District of Ohio who established that a trial of six to eight weeks could be compressed into one or two days, using the summary jury trial procedure.

Upon the completion of the process, the jury offers a non-binding, advisory verdict. This information can then be used as a basis for further settlement negotiations. The beauty of this process is that the parties could limit the reference to the jury to a specific issue of grave importance, such as liability in a negligence dispute or the quantum of damages.

It is not unusual, following delivery of a 'verdict' by the jury, for the parties or their attorneys to question the jurors about their reasoning, to further the negotiation process. It is said that this process is infrequently invoked as it is reserved for complex cases.

Its main advantages, however, are that it provides the parties with valuable insights as to how a jury might find in a contested case, thus aiding the facilitation of a settlement, and it is faster, quicker and cheaper than a protracted trial. Among its chief disadvantages are the fact that it may not accurately predict the results of a trial, and it may prove to be wasteful of time and money, where a settlement is not reached. Additionally, as the process is not usually invoked until the eve of a trial, it cannot eliminate substantial costs of case preparation.[14]

13 Judicial evaluation

Kimberlee Kovach, in her book, *Mediation: Principles and Practice*, describes the process of judicial evaluation succinctly. She says:

> In some instances, the knowledge, experience and temperament a retired judge can bring to a case can be quite helpful in assisting the parties reach a settlement.[15] In contrast to private judging where the judge actually decides the case, in a case evaluation process the judge will merely point out to the lawyers and litigants the strengths and weaknesses of the case. This assessment is based, in part, upon past judicial experience. As with other types of case evaluation, the parties may engage in dialogue to gain additional feedback. They are then free to accept or reject the evaluation. Judicial evaluation may also take place in a less formal setting, such as when the judge presides over a pre-trial conference during a pending case.

14 Specialist or expert evaluation

To the extent that there are conflicts of a technical nature, well beyond the comprehension of judges, attorneys and jury, the specialist or expert process is most useful. The know-how of an expert may be used to promote a quick resolution of a dispute. Examples of such situations may include matters of a scientific nature, computer related issues and the regulation of the financial markets. For example, the question as to why *The Titanic* sank may well be more of an engineering question, to be resolved by engineers, rather than a legal one to be resolved by a judge.

---

14 For explanations of summary jury trials and sample forms, see Fine, E and Plapinger, ES (eds), *ADR and the Courts*, pp 79–99 (CPR Legal Program) (1987); and Federal Judicial Center, *Court-Based Dispute Resolution Programs*, 1991, pp 103–06 and appendices. For case examples, see 'Many Millions Saved by SJT', *Alternatives*, May 1990, p 73; 'GE, Utilities End $1B Case With Summary Jury Trial', *Alternatives*, February 1988 p 21; and other case studies collected in *CPR Practice Guide: ADR Use in Federal and State Courts*, 1990, CPR Legal Program, pp C10–C20.

15 This was the theory behind the creation of Judicial Arbitration and Mediation Service (JAMS) which was founded by retired judge Hon Warren Knight in 1979 in Orange County, California.

15 Rent-a-judge

Under this process, the parties usually utilise the services of a retired or former judge who hears the case and renders a decision. The parties select and hire a private neutral party to try the case, just as it would be in a court of law. The rules of evidence are followed strictly, including the application of strategy and precedents. The decision of the private neutral party is treated as a judgment of the court. A fee is normally payable to the retired judge. While this has led to the legitimate criticism that this type of process is only available to the rich and wealthy,[16] it is acknowledged that considerable savings result from the use of this procedure, compared with the usual litigation process.

Other advantages claimed for this process are that the parties have the opportunity to pick their own judge, who may have special expertise in the area of the dispute and who can devote their full time to the dispute. A resolution of the dispute is thus far quicker than in a court trial. Additionally, rules of evidence apply and, therefore, the parties' rights are better protected.[17]

16 Combined processes or hybrid processes

As ADR processes have developed over the years, the inherent flexibilities in the system have led to a combination of processes to suit the nature of the dispute. The most common combined processes are the mediation/arbitration or arbitration/mediation, which are nothing more than a combination of mediation and arbitration.

(a) Mediation/arbitration and arbitration/mediation

Naturally, not all mediations result in a final resolution. Consequently, two hybrid processes called mediation/arbitration (med/arb) and arbitration/mediation (arb/med) have developed.

In med/arb, the neutral third party begins the process in the role of a mediator. If the mediation does not result in a resolution, the mediation ceases and the mediator becomes an arbitrator, who then renders a binding decision.

In an arb/med, the disputants present their cases to the neutral third party who, acting as an arbitrator, prepares a decision. The decision is not shared with the parties immediately. The arbitrator then becomes a mediator and attempts to facilitate a resolution between the disputants. If the disputants are able to reach a resolution during the mediation, the decision prepared by the neutral third party is destroyed without being shared with the disputants. If the disputants are not able to reach a resolution during the mediation, the decision of the neutral third party, made in the arbitration, is released to the disputants and they are bound by the decision.

---

16 For example, see Shapiro, DS, 'Private Judging in the State of New York: A Critical Introduction' (1990) 23 Colum JL & Soc Probs, pp 275 and 293.

17 For a detailed explanation of California's private judging rules, and criticisms and defences of the practice, see Chernick, R, 'The Rent-a-Judge Option', *Los Angeles Lawyer*, October 1989, 18; and 'What's Wrong With Private Judging?', *ibid*, November 1989, appendix 19. These articles are reprinted in Center for Public Resources, *CPR Practice Guide: ADR Use in Federal and State Courts*, 1990, pp A267 to A278. For a court-sponsored report on private judging, see Judicial Council of California, *The Report and Recommendations of the Judicial Council Advisory Committee on Private Judges*, 1991.

(b) Mini-trial

Another hybrid process is the mini-trial, described under paragraphs 6 and 7 above. This hybrid is used primarily in large corporate litigation. This is a hybrid of negotiation, mediation and case evaluation. Used primarily in businesses, the mini-trial has, as its philosophical basis, the realisation that mutual benefit may be gained by each corporation or company in resolving disputes without protracted litigation. Continued business dealings will enhance each company's profitability. Therefore, preservation of the business relationship is a key element in the resolution. It is imperative that a high level corporate decision maker attends the process. The attorneys and corporate executives meet with an expert third party advisor and all sides present their 'best case'. Direct negotiation by the corporate executives, usually without the attorneys or the neutral present, follows. If unsuccessful after a predetermined amount of time, the expert advisor provides a non-binding opinion or evaluation regarding the merits of the case. Thereafter, the executives, armed with this additional information, negotiate again. If a resolution is not reached, the neutral third party may act as a mediator.

(c) Jury determined settlement

Another recently developed hybrid process is the jury determined settlement (JDS). It is a blend of summary jury trial and arbitration. In the jury determined settlement proceeding, the jury is empaneled, and the trial proceeds similarly to a summary jury trial. However, at the conclusion of the JDS, the jury provides a binding settlement rather than a verdict.[18] Moreover, the parties are more directly active in the process, and set limits of the settlement in advance through the use of a high-low agreement.

17 Trial

Finally, there is the trial, against which all else is measured. But lest it be forgotten, a trial has some very positive advantages over ADR and is suited to certain types of cases, such as constitutional motions.

Among those advantages are the following:

(a) the parties receive a binding decision;

(b) the decision becomes a binding precedent;

(c) a trial provides procedural safeguards designed to ensure that a fair and just result is obtained;

(d) a decision is handed down by a judge who is a trained and experienced professional;[19]

(e) there is the protection of people's legal rights; and

(f) jurisprudence is built through the system of judicial precedents.

The advantages must be contrasted with the disadvantages, some of which were identified earlier, and which include the following:

---

18 Vidmar, N and Rice, J, 'Jury-Determined Settlements and Summary Jury Trials: Observations About Alternative Dispute Resolution in an Advisory Culture' (1991) 19 Fla St UL Rev, pp 89 and 98.

19 This statement needs to be qualified because the *Alcalde's* Court in Belize, JP's jurisdiction in Jamaica and magistrates' courts in England all seem to be exceptions.

(a) cost;

(b) public nature of the trial, that is, no privacy except in the case of minors;[20]

(c) delay in reaching a decision;

(d) relative uncertainty as to what the result will be;

(e) the rigidity of the trial process;

(f) compulsion to fit a case within the rules of pleadings;

(g) potential to destroy a relationship between the parties;

(h) parties have very limited control over the process;

(i) no choice in the selection of the judge; and

(j) no control over the outcome.

CASELOAD MANAGEMENT[21]

As an off-shoot of access to justice reforms, ADR is now featuring prominently in caseload management in the practice rules in the courts. Such rules are currently operational in the Organisation of Eastern Caribbean States (OECS) jurisdictions, as well as in Trinidad & Tobago and Jamaica. Barbados is consulting widely on similar rules, pioneered by Chief Justice Sir David Simmons when he was Attorney General.

If properly applied, case management processes are designed to eliminate some of the glaring criticisms against litigation.[22]

So that the civil trial system may achieve justice with speed, there has to be a systematic change to reflect the following objectives:

(a) to put the parties before the court on an even footing;

(b) to save or cut down on expense;

(c) to allocate court resources in proportion to the subject matter of the trial;

(d) to be expeditious; and

(e) to be fair.

In order to achieve these aims, three things ought to happen. First, the present lawyer-driven litigation management process needs to be changed to a system of judge-driven case management. Secondly, the court management process needs to be improved and, thirdly, the standards of the Bench and Bar need to be raised.

In the OECS states, there is a quiet ongoing revolution taking place along these very lines. This systemic change requires a complete transformation in the culture of litigation, as it is known today. Under the caseload management system, it is the court, and not the lawyer, that assumes responsibility for the litigation before it. This system is also designed to water down the concept of adversarial litigation and trial by ambush. It imposes a duty of disclosure on litigants, to one another as well as to the court. This change also requires a paradigm shift in the ethical values of the Bar from simply a duty to the client to a duty to both the client and to justice.

---

20 See s 18(9) of the Constitution of Barbados. Similarly, cases of national security would require privacy.

21 Caseload management is discussed more fully in Chapter 8.

22 Fiadjoe, A, 'The Independence of the Judiciary' (2001) 6(1) Caribbean Law Bulletin 8.

The case management system is also useful in filtering cases, identifying those that are susceptible to mediation and ADR processes and leaving them in that pigeonhole for resolution. At the case management conference, the case is scheduled to trial and timescales are fixed, all within 90 days of the filing of a writ. So far, this is the timescale adopted by the OECS jurisdictions and Jamaica, which currently apply case management. Naturally, case management works best in the context of some form of automation and the use of technology and contemporary systems. Studies have shown that merely by improving management systems, through the use of technology, there have been improvements in the quality of justice of between 50% and 75%.

SOME CRITICAL ISSUES

Despite the wide receptability and application of ADR, it would be wrong to see ADR as the panacea to all the ills of litigation. In fact, the introduction of ADR poses some tough challenges when compared to the existing processes of courtroom litigation. A list of some of these challenges would be as follows:

(a) how to safeguard the system of justice;

(b) how to assure the equity and quality of ADR initiatives;

(c) quality control;

(d) budgetary control;

(e) management issues;

(f) competing policy issues, such as the confidentiality of ADR versus the traditionally public nature of the courts;

(g) in court annexed ADR, co-ordinating the role of the Bench and Bar;

(h) designing appropriate ADR programs;

(i) problems of training and program administration;

(j) difficulties in matching cases to suitable ADR methods, etc;

(k) the constitutionality of ADR, if compulsorily annexed to the court system;

(l) the uncertainty of outcomes in ADR;

(m) the privacy of ADR; and

(n) a legal system founded on case law which could be undermined by ADR.

The lesson is that cheaper and faster is not necessarily better. Also, there are conflicting impulses and purposes behind ADR, which need further elaboration and exploration.

Lord McKay, in the Hamlyn Lecture Series,[23] has argued that good governance requires that the provisions of a civil system should advance the rule of law, secure and enforce legal rights, and must possess the qualities of finality and certainty. Tested against these criteria, ADR fails the test. Lord McKay was not in favour of court annexed ADR because it would entail second guessing the judge, lead persons to question the integrity of the judge when acting as a mediator, introduce compulsion in a seemingly voluntary process and it could compromise the legal rights of litigants.

In similar vein, while Lord Woolf also extols the virtues of ADR, he is not in favour of anything but 'encouragement' to the parties to use ADR. However, in deciding on

---

23 *The Administration of Justice*, 1994, Sweet & Maxwell, pp 69 *et seq*.

the future conduct of a case, the judge should be able to take into account a litigant's unreasonable refusal to attempt ADR.

As noted by Professor G Woodman, the advancement of alternative dispute resolution has been criticised on the basis of the values of the liberal democratic state. He contends that insofar as 'critics claim that alternative dispute resolution is inimical to the rule of law, their analysis may be questioned'. His paper argues that these processes may be inimical to the rule of law of state adjudication, but 'in accord with the rule of other laws'.[24] Other criticisms have focused on the argument that alternative dispute resolution tends to increase the disadvantages of already disadvantaged groups and provides more openings for the influence of social prejudices.[25] In response, Professor Woodman says that these criticisms generally compare ADR processes with adjudication in the regular state courts and that the scope of the debate is thus limited. He has some firm support from Galanter who states that 'far more disputing is conducted within ... indigenous [ie, non-state] forums than in all the free-standing and court-annexed institutions staffed by arbitrators, mediators and other ADR professionals'.[26]

So the debate is on.

With respect to court annexed ADR, some of the issues to consider are, from the perspective of the developing world:

(a) What values should a court institutionalised ADR device serve?

(b) Who should pay for it?

(c) Who should have access to it?

(d) What are the consequences of using ADR devices for the rest of the system?

(e) When should a public system subsidise private arrangements?

(f) What are the politics of ADR?

(g) How should the quality of justice be measured?

(h) What processes are appropriate for settling cases?

(i) How are the financial and human resource implications of ADR addressed?

At the end of the day, there is agreement with Menkel-Meadow[27] that there are some larger issues of general concern in the introduction of ADR to the legal system. 'In the end, truth is almost found on both sides. The key is not to compromise, but to work toward a principled and fair resolution of these issues.'

---

24 Woodman, G, 'The Alternative Law of Alternative Dispute Resolution' (1991) 32 Les Cahiers de Droit 30–31. See also Nader, L, 'Disputing Without the Force of Law' (1979) 88 Yale LJ 998; Young, R, 'Neighbour Dispute Mediation: Theory and Practice' (1989) 8 Civ Just Q 319.

25 Economides, K, 'Small Claims and Procedural Justice' (1980) 7 British JL & Soc 111; Delgado, R, et al, 'Fairness and Formality: Minimizing the Risk of Prejudice in Alternative Dispute Resolution' (1985) Wis L Rev, p 1359; Nailey, MJ, 'Unpacking the 'Rational Alternative': A Critical Review of Family Mediation Movement Claims' (1989) 8 Can J Fam L 61; Bush and Luban et al, 'Defining Quality in Dispute Resolution: Taxonomies and Anti-Taxonomies of Quality Arguments' (1989) 66 Denver ULR 335–562.

26 Galanter, M, 'Compared to What? Assessing the Quality of Dispute Resolution' Denver ULR xi.

27 Menkel-Meadow, C, 'Pursuing Settlement in an Adversary Culture: A Tale of Innovation Co-Opted or "The Law of ADR"' (1991) 19 Fla St UL Rev 1.

Or, as Lord Bingham of Cornhill put it, 'conventional litigation processes and ADR are not enemies, but partners. Neither can ignore developments in the other'.[28]

Many more issues could be raised. The important thing is to design an ADR system, which is effectively funded, while balancing all of the competing interests. That will not be easy. The bottom line is that it must be recognised that considerable savings accrue to the judicial and legal system if parties settle their litigation at an early stage of the proceedings. All of these interests call for a careful study as to what would be in the best interests of each Commonwealth Caribbean territory.

In the context of the developing world, the reality has to be faced that a large number of the processes in the ADR spectrum may not be feasible due to human resource capacity reasons. The application of the full spectrum will be a matter of time. It will be some time before the region implements a policy of say, renting a judge or introducing a judicial mini-trial.

SKILLS TRAINING/UWI FACULTY OF LAW/ CARIBBEAN LAW INSTITUTE APPROACH

One of the greatest benefits of ADR is that it has not only changed the face of legal training, it has also provided an avenue for skills training in dispute resolution and management.

At the University of the West Indies (UWI), the ADR syllabus is a mix of theoretical and practical skills training. UWI students go through various texts, do role plays, watch video films of negotiation, mediation and arbitration, draw important lessons therefrom and elicit from them guiding principles. Thereafter, the students try to replicate the situations in which skills training as ADR practitioners can be applied.

The skills training provided at the UWI is based on the seven elements of 'principled negotiation' developed by the Harvard dispute resolution team of professors. Those principles focus on the interests of the parties rather than on their positions, developing relationships, effective communications, the generation of options for mutual gain, the establishment of objective criteria and a commitment to a deal which is better than each party's best alternative to a negotiated settlement.

At the regional level, the Caribbean Law Institute was working on model rules for the introduction of ADR.[29] The Institute was very much at the advisory stage of its work but the general thinking was that it should move towards a system of court facilitated ADR and that this should be supported by some form of legislation that gives the judge the discretion to offer ADR to the disputants.

This would be consistent with the multi-door approach to litigation whereby all possible avenues of a resolution remain open to the parties.

ADR will then turn out in its new garb of *appropriate dispute resolution*.

---

28 *The ADR Practice Guide: Commercial Dispute Resolution*, 2000, Butterworths, p v.
29 The project has unfortunately been adjourned *sine die* for lack of funding. (The funding was diverted to training by the USAID.)

CHAPTER 3

PRINCIPLES OF NEGOTIATION

THE BASICS

Negotiation, like conflict, is a fact of life. Whether we realise it consciously or not, we all are called upon to conduct negotiation, in one form or other, in our lives on a daily basis.

Discussions about a pay rise in employment or agreement on price with a vendor or decisions on where the anniversary dinner should take place are all forms of negotiation. Similarly, collective agreements by trade unions represent the end result of negotiations. So, also, may we conclude when states engage in discussions with the objective of promoting peace, as happened in 1993 at Camp David, USA, between Israel and Palestine during the administration of President Clinton. In dramatic conflict situations, such as hijackings, the principal tool required for diffusing tension is negotiation. So, negotiation is, thus, a versatile, universal tool in diffusing conflict.

That apart, the basic assumption that is made is that everyone is, indeed, a good negotiator, even though they have neither received formal training nor given thought to any notion of planning. But it is also known that, for example, no one undertakes litigation without considerable thought, planning and investment in time and money. While it could be said that negotiation is, thus, pragmatic, it is being realised more and more that the acquisition of certain basic skills may be helpful to effective negotiation. Among such skills would be:

(a) effective communication in its various manifestations;

(b) importance of privacy;

(c) recognising and addressing 'iceberg' factors in a dispute;

(d) identifying conflict fuelling indicators;

(e) building capacity in the disputants to see different points of view;

(f) recognising communication blockers; and

(g) learning to handle difficult conversations.

The appreciation and identification of these factors represent skills which can be learnt. Debunking the unscientific theory that negotiating skills cannot be learnt, the negotiation manual of the Inns of Court School of Law in the UK says:

> Negotiation is an intellectual skill. It combines thinking and doing. The more you understand about the skill, the more you will understand how you and others operate and see the ways in which you can become more skilled. Just practising negotiation without any understanding of the theory means you merely reinforce your existing methods of negotiating, probably ingrained from childhood. You do not extend your range of techniques and may well reinforce bad habits.[1]

---

1 *Negotiation 1999/2000*, 1999, Blackstone, p 4.

It says, therefore, that a negotiator needs to have a theoretical framework in which:

> ... to understand the different types of negotiation, what happens in any negotiation, the peculiar characteristics of legal negotiations, the different strategies and tactics which are often used and some of the cognitive influences and ethical considerations in negotiations.

What then is negotiation? Roger Fisher and William Ury[2] define negotiation as a 'back-and-forth communication designed to reach an agreement when you and the other side have some interests that are shared and others that are opposed'. It is an interactive process which covers shared interests, common concerns and those in conflict. It may be used as a tool to handle a multiple variety of disputes. A negotiation may be about a single issue or a multiple set of issues, be personal or impersonal, one-off or otherwise, involve a single party or multiple parties, be distributive or zero-sum, representative or for oneself.

TYPES OF NEGOTIATION

While it is acknowledged that negotiation may be applied to a multiplicity of situations, it is generally agreed that there are three strategies that fall to be discussed. These are the competitive, co-operative and principled approaches, explained by Fisher and Ury in this way:

> People find themselves in a dilemma. They see two ways to negotiate: soft or hard. The soft negotiator wants to avoid personal conflict and so makes concessions readily in order to reach agreement. He wants an amicable resolution; yet he often ends up exploited and feeling bitter. The hard negotiator sees any situation as a contest of wills in which the side that takes the more extreme positions and holds out longer fares better. He wants to win; yet he often ends up producing an equally hard response which exhausts him and his resources and harms his relationship with the other side. Other standard negotiation strategies fall between hard and soft, but each involves an attempted trade-off between getting what you want and getting along with people.

> There is a third way to negotiate, a way neither hard nor soft, but rather both hard *and* soft. The method of *principled negotiation* developed at the Harvard Negotiation Project is to decide issues on their merits rather than through a haggling process focused on what each side says it will and won't do. It suggests that you look for mutual gains whenever possible, and that where your interests conflict, you should insist that the result be based on some fair standards independent of the will of either side. The method of principled negotiation is hard on the merits, soft on the people. It employs no tricks and no posturing. Principled negotiation shows you how to obtain what you are entitled to and still be decent. It enables you to be fair while protecting you against those who would take advantage of your fairness.[3]

---

2   *Getting to Yes*, 1991, Penguin, p xvii. See also Maddux, R, *Successful Negotiation*, 2nd edn, 1999, Course Technology PTR, p 5.
3   *Ibid*, p xviii.

Competitive/hard negotiating style

As the name suggests, a competitive style is tough, bullying, unco-operative, hard and inflexible. It makes unrealistic demands and very few concessions. It accuses, bluffs, misleads and tries to outmanoeuvre the other side. It is a strategy which works on the psychology of the other party and tries to wear them down. At the bottom of it, it is designed to achieve victory at the expense of the other side. These observations notwithstanding, it is a style that may have its advantages. Among these are the following:

(a) walking away with a better substantive deal;

(b) taking the initiative in negotiation;

(c) not yielding to manipulation from the other side; and

(d) gaining a tough reputation.

Among its disadvantages are the following:

(a) prevention from reaching a mutually beneficial deal;

(b) failing to take advantage of the full range of possibilities on the table;

(c) creation of misunderstandings;

(d) infliction of damage to relationships;

(e) non-sustainability of solutions arrived at; and

(f) poisoning the atmosphere for future negotiations.

Co-operative/soft negotiating style

A co-operative style, on the other hand, is friendly, courteous and concessionary. It focuses on building trust and promoting relationships. It is tactful and conciliatory, always trying to reach a deal. It shares information and appeals to the reasonable instincts of the other side. Its primary objective is to achieve some sort of fair agreement.

Among its principal advantages are:

(a) reaching a conclusion quickly;

(b) reaching a conclusion which is fair;

(c) building long-term relationships; and

(d) building up a good reputation and image.

Some of the problems associated with this style of negotiation are:

(a) the failure to get a good deal;

(b) the possibility of manipulation by the other side;

(c) the acquisition of a reputation for being soft; and

(d) a reluctance to walk away from the table.

Principled/problem solving negotiation style

Two influences lie behind this negotiation style. One is the 'principled' approach developed by Fisher and Ury of the Harvard Negotiation Project. The other is the 'problem solving' approach attributed to Carrie Menkel-Meadow.[4] Both terms are used here interchangeably, for the same theory underlies the strategies behind them, though their goals are slightly different. Both assume that through collaboration, the parties can reach agreement by explaining each other's underlying interests and creating options for mutual gain. The point of differentiation is that both use different standards to measure the outcome reached. The problem solving strategy tries to measure the settlement against the real interests of the parties, while the principled strategy measures the results by reference to some objective standard which may be external to the parties. There is no need to be detained by this very fine dividing line.

A great deal of emphasis is placed on the 'principles' which underpin 'principled negotiation'. Fisher and Ury have claimed that it is an all-purpose strategy that overcomes the disadvantages in the two other strategies. The justification for it, they say, is that:

> ... principled negotiation can be used whether there is one issue or several; two parties or many; whether there is a prescribed ritual, as in collective bargaining, or an impromptu free-for-all, as in talking with hijackers. The method applies whether the other side is more experienced or less, a hard bargainer or a friendly one. Principled negotiation is an all-purpose strategy.[5]

Before evaluating principled negotiation, it might be useful to set out that strategy. Its principles are as follows:

(a) Interests – that is, don't bargain over positions.

(b) Relationships – that is, separate the people from the problem.

(c) Communications – that is, stress the importance of communication and persuasion with reasoned arguments.

(d) Options – that is, invent options for mutual gain.

(e) Legitimacy – that is, insist on using objective criteria.

(f) Alternatives – that is, develop a BATNA – best alternative to a negotiated agreement.

(g) Commitment – that is, accepting a deal which is usually better than the BATNA.

Each principle speaks to a strategy which needs some amplification.

With respect to interests, the strategy is to avoid bargaining over positions. The explanation for this is that positions can only be satisfied in *one* way, but interests can be satisfied in a multiplicity of ways. Generally, in negotiations, most people present positions which, in turn, invite counter positions. What principled negotiation mandates is that instead of going through the futile process of positional bargaining, it is better to uncover the interests underlying the positions. Positions reflect the basic demands of disputants. Interests, on the other hand, reflect the reasons behind those demands.

---

4   'Toward Another View of Legal Negotiation: The Structure of Problem-Solving' (1984) 31 UCLA Law Review 754.

5   *Getting To Yes, op cit*, fn 2, p xix.

To uncover the underlying interests, questions must be asked to discover the reasons behind those positions. This is why sharpened communication skills are an undoubted asset to a negotiator.

With respect to relationships, the principle is to separate the people from the problem. It is obvious that personality and attitudinal differences can easily derail a negotiation by deflecting the parties away from the real problems in issue. This principle, therefore, urges that the parties be *soft* on each other but *hard* on the problem.

Communication remains a critical tool in any form of negotiation. Good negotiators apply skills of active listening, paraphrasing and summarising to encourage back and forth communication. Through reasoned arguments, a party stands a better chance of addressing the underlying interests behind a problem. Listening skills also play a vital role in negotiation. Nothing promotes a dialogue better than for the other side to know that they have been heard and understood. Similarly, non-verbal communication plays a vital role in negotiation. The ability to appreciate and interpret the several ways in which we communicate through our behaviour is a critical skill. Communication through body language, facial expression, hand gestures, posture, smile, grin or frown can affect the outcome of a negotiation. Even more complex is how to interpret these forms of non-verbal communication. Communication is, therefore, not just the spoken word. It is consideration of the spoken word, the interpretation of what is said and the behaviour of the individual.

In the midst of all these influences is how our own behaviour and cultural programming affect the negotiation.

Option generation is one of the most important stages in any negotiation. Here, the parties are encouraged to generate as many options as possible to satisfy their interests without making an initial determination as to their suitability. So, the parties are encouraged to create and invent options without restriction, without criticism and without commitment. That way, the parties become more creative than usual. It is not unknown that what starts off as a 'bad' option may turn out to be a 'good' option. In thus 'expanding the pie', the win-lose dynamic is jettisoned in favour of a win-win philosophy.

In evaluating the options, it is best to rely on objective criteria as a way to establish the legitimacy of the selected option. This way, the settlement is based on an objective yardstick, standard or custom, which supercedes the opinion or will of another party. It is claimed that this is one of the manifest advantages which principled negotiation has over the other styles of negotiation.[6] Examples of objective criteria could be:

(a) market value;

(b) the terms of a contract;

(c) expert opinion;

(d) scientific standard;

(e) cost of living index; or

(f) rate of inflation.

---

6   Condlin, RJ, 'Bargaining in the Dark: The Normative Incoherence of Lawyer Dispute Bargaining Role' (1992) 51 Maryland Law Review 1.

Before a party makes commitment to a deal, it is advisable to have regard to their BATNA. Essentially, BATNA answers the question: what alternatives are there should the parties not reach a deal and have to walk away from the table? BATNA is, thus, the concept which informs each party as to what the best outcome would be if the issues are not settled through negotiation. It is, indeed, a reality test. The advice is for a negotiator only to commit to a deal which is better than their BATNA. It helps the negotiation where the disputants are aware of their own and the other side's best and worst alternatives to a negotiated settlement.

Similar to principled negotiation is problem solving negotiation. Like the former, the latter goes beyond the stated aspirations of the parties and tries to assess underlying needs and preferences. Carrie Menkel-Meadow is a leading exponent of the problem solving strategy, the very elements of which are:

(a) exploring shared interests;

(b) identifying differences;

(c) identifying objectives of both parties;

(d) creating solutions which meet the parties' needs; and

(e) expanding the options available to the parties.[7]

While both strategies focus on the full exploitation of the parties' interests, the key difference is that principled negotiation divides the pie on the basis of objective criteria external to the parties, while the problem solving strategy seeks a solution which is fair and just to the parties.[8]

Irrespective of whichever strategy is adopted, negotiation is the base unit of conflict resolution. Its conduct requires foundation skills.

INTERNATIONAL NEGOTIATIONS[9]

As stated earlier, these skills can be applied to several disparate situations. But, from the viewpoint of the developing countries of the Caribbean Community and Common Market (CARICOM), it is proposed to address the conduct of negotiations on the international scene.

In the domestic context, the point has been made that there are several causes of conflict and that the failure to manage conflict could lead to disastrous consequences. The same is true of international conflict. So, abuse of power, unfulfilled needs and other differences of opinion must be managed if international conflict is to be avoided. Nevertheless, international negotiations are qualitatively different from domestic negotiations because of two additional dynamics. First, a failure to manage a conflict with international ramifications could lead potentially to a threat to international

---

7   *Op cit*, Menkel-Meadow, fn 4.

8   *Op cit*, Menkel-Meadow, fn 4, 813.

9   Because of the obvious focus of this chapter on the negotiating capacity of CARICOM states, no discussion has been conducted of the legal technicalities of negotiations in international law (such as in the *North Sea Continental Shelf Cases*) and of the impact of the MFN principle and the difference between the various kinds of national treatment obligations in goods and services in the WTO negotiation process. As to how non-CARICOM players operate without the deficiencies which been identified in this chapter, see, for example, Binnendijk, H, *National Negotiating Styles*, 1987, Diane Publishing, chapters on China, Japan, France; Adler, NJ, *Negotiating with Foreigners*, 1993, PWS-Kent Publishing, Chapter 7, fn 9.

peace and security and, secondly, a failure to recognise the importance of cross-cultural differences could easily lead to botched-up negotiations.

Today's world places enormous stress and emphasis upon 'security' and global trade. In both areas, negotiation skills are very necessary.

With respect to security, states usually provide mechanisms for dealing with security threats in treaties negotiated up front.[10] These threats can arise from political instability or disequilibrium in trade. From a developing world perspective, the difficulty is that the full weight of these countries is not deployed towards shaping the outcome of the discussions *before* the enactment of the treaties and protocols. The end result is that these states get sucked into a political and economic regime which is shaped largely by others. Such is the story behind the World Trade Organization (WTO), for example, and the current negotiations towards the Free Trade Area of the Americas (FTAA) treaty. Is CARICOM negotiating with one voice on critical areas of concern to the Caribbean? It is impossible to say, as each territory still maintains a voice in the preparatory meetings, despite the establishment of a CARICOM Regional Negotiating Machinery (CRNM).[11]

It is difficult, therefore, to make a meaningful assessment as to how effective the negotiations are that are being made on behalf of CARICOM. It would be interesting to find out whether the negotiators do have formal training in negotiation skills beside their enormous diplomatic skills. A considered assessment must await further and better particulars from both the CRNM and CARICOM.

It is in the area of trade that critical negotiating skills are called for, from the perspective of developing countries.

The publicly disclosed aspect of the work of the CRNM reveals that it is a strategic arm of CARICOM, with a specific mandate to advance a cohesive and effective framework for the co-ordination and management of the Caribbean region external negotiating resources and expertise.

As set out by the Director General, Ambassador the Honourable Dr Richard Bernal:

> At present the Caribbean Region is involved in a packed agenda of trade negotiations. The Caribbean (which in recent years has also become involved in bilateral negotiations with individual countries or groups of countries through Latin and most recently Central America) is engaged in its most formidable negotiations of the post-independence period, both in respect of scale and complexity at the hemispheric and multilateral levels.
>
> Caribbean Governments recognize the complexity and importance of these negotiations which together have implications for regional trade in goods and services. The results of these negotiations will impact the long-term development prospects of the Region. Against this backdrop, the [C]RNM continues to discharge the mandate given it by the Conference of Heads of Government of CARICOM to develop, advance and execute an overall and cohesive trade negotiating strategy for the Region. The [C]RNM's responsibility in this regard is critically important seeing as

---

10   See examples in the UN Charter, the WTO, the Caribbean Basin Initiative (CBI) Treaty, the EU, etc.
11   The Regional Negotiating Machinery remains the 'secret' tool of CARICOM governments. All attempts to obtain a simple write-up on the outfit were unsuccessful. Furthermore, research disclosed that its work was confidential to the heads of CARICOM.

trade accords have emerged as one of the central catalysts of the global organization of production, investment and trade. Indeed, it is fair to say that the commercial success and economic welfare of nations are leveraged on trade agreements. This is because such accords influence government policy and regulatory decisions that affect their countries' role in global trade and ability to attract foreign investment.

The press kit issued by the CRNM reveals that the it was created by CARICOM governments to develop and execute an overall negotiating strategy for various external trade related negotiations in which the region is involved, as well as to co-ordinate its position in negotiations. Formally established on 1 April 1997, the CRNM received its mandate from the Conference of Heads of CARICOM. This mandate came against the background of a global economic environment increasingly based on free trade and moving away from the traditional preferential arrangements that have benefited many Caribbean economies.

A major task of the CRNM is to bring a systematic and focused approach to new pressing international issues. Its structure, which taps into the regional pool of talent, provides a mechanism through which the limited human and financial resources of individual territories can be combined and co-ordinated to represent regional interests effectively. The ultimate goal is to ensure that Caribbean development is not impeded by changes in global trade arrangements and that maximum benefit can be secured.

The CRNM works to develop a cohesive and effective framework for the co-ordination and management of the Caribbean region's negotiating resources and expertise.

Its principal function is to assist member states in maximising the benefits of participation in global trade negotiations by providing sound, high quality advice, facilitating the generation of national positions, co-ordinating the formulation of a unified strategy for the region and undertaking/leading negotiations where appropriate.

The CRNM has been described as the primary catalyst and agent of change leading the process through which the region maximises the benefits available from trade in the new, challenging, global economic order.

The CRNM reports to the CARICOM Prime Ministerial Sub-Committee (PMSC) on External Negotiations, which is currently chaired by Prime Minister Patterson of Jamaica, and through this body to the full Conference of Heads of Government of the Community. It also seeks the advice of and reports to the Council for Trade and Economic Development (COTED) of the Community.

Addressing the new trade involvement, the CRNM says that:

The Caribbean is engaged in its most formidable external trade negotiations of the post independence period both in respect of scale and complexity. For many years, the Region has benefited from non-reciprocal trade preferences allowing access to major markets of the world including the United States of America, Canada and the European Union. These arrangements have enhanced the competitive position of qualifying regional products and in the case of the Lomé Convention/Cotonou Agreement, have also provided considerable development assistance. However, in recent years, reciprocal trading arrangements have become the norm the implications of which are far reaching for national economies and standards of living in the Region.

In this context, Caribbean governments are now engaged in trade negotiations as follows:

(a) at the multilateral level within the framework of the WTO (Doha Agenda negotiations targeted conclusion set for 1 January 2005);

(b) at the inter-regional level in devising an Economic Partnership Agreement (EPA) with the EU by January 2008;

(c) at the hemispheric level in negotiations relating to the FTAA to be concluded by 31 December 2004; and

(d) bilateral negotiations between the Caribbean and individual countries or groups of countries, for example, CARICOM and Costa Rica.

Caribbean governments recognise the complexity and importance of these aforementioned negotiations. The results of these negotiations will be very influential factors in the long-term development prospects of the region.

Against this backdrop, the CRNM has been mandated by the Conference of Heads of Government of CARICOM to develop and advance a cohesive trade negotiating strategy for the Caribbean region. While the major focus has been the WTO, FTAA and EPAs, the remit of the CRNM is dynamic. It has expanded to reflect various aspects of the region's bilateral negotiations and issues such as the concerns of small states within the context of the Commonwealth Secretariat/World Bank initiatives being led by the Prime Minister of Barbados, the Right Honourable Owen Arthur.

The overall mandate, as expressed in the responsibilities of the head of the CRNM, is to:

(a) develop and execute an overall negotiating strategy for the various negotiations in which the region is involved;

(b) lead the region's negotiating team and be the main spokesperson in the conduct of the negotiations, especially those at the decision making level;

(c) develop and fine-tune the strategy for the various negotiations within the timetable identified for the particular area; and

(d) maintain regular contact with sectoral negotiators and work with them in the identification of issues and the development of appropriate responses.

The objective of the regional negotiating strategy is to ensure that the region derives the maximum benefits possible from major international trade negotiations. In pursuit of its mandate, the CRNM is required to undertake the technical studies needed to shape regional positions on trade issues. The CRNM also organises technical working groups, reflection groups and consultations with member state government officials, the private sectors and civil society groups. Ultimately, this consultative approach enables the emergence of the most technically sound and widely discussed negotiating positions, which have the participation and support of a variety of stakeholders. The involvement of all stakeholders gives legitimacy and ownership of the negotiating positions to those whose interests they are intended to advance.

As the entity representing the trade interests of the Caribbean Region, the CRNM is confronted by both institutional and negotiating challenges. These include:

(a) coping with an ever-expanding negotiating agenda, diversified and increasingly complex, with many of the subjects entirely new to CARICOM's trading regime;

(b) ensuring that the particular problems facing small and vulnerable economies are factored into the new trading arrangements;

(c) ensuring consistency in positions taken by the region in the various negotiating theatres;

(d) responding to the technical requirements of current trade negotiations as these evolve beyond a focus on broad frameworks and parameters to areas requiring highly specialised knowledge;

(e) obtaining the technical and statistical data required for effective participation in the negotiation process, given the absence in many territories of information/databases needed to support the negotiations; and

(f) deploying limited human and financial resources to execute effectively its multifaceted mandate.

Within CARICOM, regional trade is riddled with serious problems. At the bottom of it all, regional trade is in competition, rather than in co-operation, with each other. Trade revolves around similar goods and services (bananas, sugar and tourism), and export trade is founded on one-way preferential trade arrangements with the USA, Canada and the EU. These preferential trade arrangements are being phased out in keeping with the terms of the WTO. Sugar, bananas and rum are being choked out of existence by external pressure and none of them are able to take advantage of economies of scale. Some of the region's best exports, such as garments and rum, are not on the preferential list and, of course, transportation and labour costs are high.

The resolution of these enormous challenges will call for the greatest skills and dexterity in negotiations by the CRNM. The CRNM has recently established a website (www.crnm.org) where information of a general nature may be found about its mandate, policies and practices.

DISPUTE SETTLEMENT IN CARICOM

If, as seems to be the case, the Caribbean region is going to find it more and more problematic to be competitive in the global trade regime imposed by the WTO, then a simple survival kit for CARICOM would be to promote and enhance intra-Caribbean trade. Trade among nations inevitably leads to trade disputes. This is where the CARICOM protocol on dispute settlement becomes relevant.

Chapter 9 of the Revised CARICOM Treaty (Revised Treaty of Chaguaramas) provides a broad scope for dispute settlement. The relevant Article for present purposes being Article 187(b):

(b) allegations of injury, serious prejudice suffered or likely to be suffered, nullification or impairment of benefits expected from the establishment and operation of the CSME;[12]

Article 188 of the revised CARICOM Treaty stipulates that such disputes shall be settled only by recourse to one of the following modes for the settlement of disputes,

---

12 Other grounds for involving the dispute settlement clause are:
   • allegations that an actual or proposed measure of another Member State is, or would be, inconsistent with the objectives of the Community;
   • allegations that an organ or body of the Community has acted *ultra vires*; or
   • allegations that the purpose or object of the Treaty is being frustrated or prejudiced.

namely good offices, mediation, consultations, conciliation, arbitration and adjudication. These processes require some elaboration. Article 188(4) makes it clear that, without prejudice to the exclusive and compulsory jurisdiction of the Caribbean Court of Justice, parties to a dispute may employ any of the voluntary modes of dispute settlement provided for in the CARICOM Treaty, these being good offices, mediation, consultations, conciliation or arbitration. These processes may be employed interchangeably. Even in the case of arbitration or adjudication, the parties may agree, pending settlement, to have recourse to good offices, mediation or conciliation in order to arrive at a settlement.[13]

CARICOM member states party to a dispute may agree to employ the good offices of a third party, including those of the Secretary General, to settle the dispute. Good offices may begin or be terminated at any time. Subject to the procedural rules applicable in respect of arbitration or adjudication, good offices may continue during the course of arbitration or adjudication.[14]

Article 193 deals with the obligation of member states to enter consultations. A member state shall enter into consultations upon the request of another member state where the requesting member state alleges that an action taken by the requested member state constitutes a breach of obligations arising from or under the provisions of this Treaty. Where a request for consultations is made, the requested member state shall enter into consultations within 14 days of the receipt of the request or a mutually agreed period.

Article 193 also mandates that the request for consultations shall state the reasons for the consultations and identify the measure at issue and the legal basis for the complaint. The Secretary General shall be notified of any request for consultations.[15] Consultations shall be confidential and without prejudice to the rights of the member states in any further proceedings. However, before resorting to further proceedings, the member states shall employ their best endeavours to settle the dispute.[16]

Conciliation, which is well-known in international law, is provided for as an alternative dispute resolution mechanism under the Treaty. The term in international law is much narrower than in domestic municipal law, being applied as a method of amicably settling disputes in the context of international relations.

It is pertinent to observe that CARICOM preferred to write its own conciliation rules in preference to the conciliation rules of the United Nations Commission on International Trade Law (UNCITRAL), to which the Commonwealth Caribbean countries have access by virtue of being UN members.

Initiation of conciliation proceedings in CARICOM is by notification addressed to the other party or parties to the dispute.[17]

Article 196 provides that a list of conciliators shall be established and maintained by the Secretary General. Every member state shall be entitled to nominate two conciliators, each of whom shall be a person enjoying the highest reputation for fairness, competence and integrity. The names of the persons so nominated shall

---

13 Article 188(3).
14 Article 191.
15 Article 193(5).
16 Article 193(6).
17 Article 195.

constitute the list. If at any time the number of conciliators nominated by a member state is fewer than two, the member state concerned shall be entitled to make such nominations as are necessary to increase their nominees to two. The name of a conciliator shall remain in the list until withdrawn by the member state which made the nomination and, where a conciliator has been appointed to serve on any mediation or conciliation commission, the conciliator shall continue to serve on such commission until the completion of the relevant proceedings. The term of office of a conciliator, including a conciliator appointed to fill a vacancy, shall be five years and may be renewed.

A conciliation commission shall be constituted from time to time and its function shall be to hear the member states' party to disputes, examine their claims and objections, and make proposals to the parties with the aim of helping the parties to reach amicable settlements. The conclusions or recommendations of a conciliation commission, however, shall not be binding upon the parties.

The conciliation proceedings shall be deemed to be terminated when the parties have accepted, or one party has rejected, the recommendations of the report by notification addressed to the Secretary General, or when a period of one month has expired from the date of transmission of the report to the parties.[18]

Finally, mention must be made of Article 223, which provides that member states shall, to the maximum extent possible, encourage and facilitate the use of arbitration and other modes of alternative dispute settlement for the settlement of private commercial disputes between nationals of member states, as well as between nationals of member states and nationals of other states.

All the processes mentioned in the Treaty, from good offices to arbitration, require negotiation skills.

The CARICOM single market and economy espoused in the Treaty requires a Caribbean dispute resolution mechanism. That is currently embodied in the original jurisdiction of the Caribbean Court of Justice in Article 211, which provides that:

> The Court shall have compulsory and exclusive jurisdiction to hear and determine disputes concerning the interpretation and application of the Treaty, including:
>
> (a) disputes between the member states parties to the Agreement;
>
> (b) disputes between the Member States parties to the Agreement and the Community;
>
> (c) referrals from national courts of the Member States parties to the Agreement;
>
> (d) applications by persons in connection with Article 222, concerning the interpretation and application of this Treaty.

At the moment, there is no clear evidence of CARICOM's intervention in training and education in the primary areas of critical negotiating skills which must underpin the success of these laudable provisions. This is not a point to be minimised, for access to the WTO dispute resolution mechanism is not going to be easy, cheap or accessible to CARICOM states.[19] CARICOM's first line of dispute resolution must remain in the Caribbean region.

---

18   Article 202.
19   See Chapter 6 on the WTO.

Two other equally important points need to be made. One is that global trade requires big players. This means that CARICOM states ought to be investing time and energy in strategic alliances and joint ventures. Evidence of this happening is not easily apparent.[20]

The other is that the successful conclusion of a negotiated deal translates, usually, into a contract. Is it a requirement that CARICOM negotiators must be versed in the essential elements of contract law? Is it a requirement that CARICOM negotiators must be versed in the language and culture of its trading partners? This *cri de coeur* is for a process which unites in CARICOM negotiators expertise in law, trade issues and knowledge of the languages and cultures of its trading partners.

The global market, together with information technology, shows vividly the universality of the world. But the fact that globalised treaties, such as the WTO, the North American Free Trade Agreement (NAFTA) and the imminent FTAA, provide an unequal framework in which developing countries may negotiate is not too easily apparent. The vicissitudes of the sugar and banana trade show the uphill nature of the task of negotiation in both the regional and global economy.

Wherever there is trade, there is a great deal of negotiation and, most likely, trade disputes as well. Clearly, the volume and intensity of trade, as a result of free enterprise and open markets, means that no one negotiator may confine their skills to their national boundaries. The Internet has already provided us with the notion of the 'geography of nowhere'. If the survival of the nation state is dependent upon free and fair trade, then there is a great role cut out for skillful negotiators.

It is important to appreciate that the protection of trade, services and intellectual property involves, from the negotiating perspective, face-to-face meetings. This requires the interface of people from different cultures and countries. Effective communications were identified as one of the most important tools in any form of negotiation. Transnational transactions require communication with members of different cultures. What is not disputed is that there are several different negotiating styles and behaviours throughout the world. It should be expected that China would have a different negotiating style from Latin America, Japan, Canada, the USA, Africa or the Caribbean.

Which countries have hard, competitive bargaining strategies? Which ones aim for short-term relationships only? Which ones make few concessions? Which ones opt for objective facts? Which ones inject emotionalism into their negotiation strategies? It may well be accurate to say that all international negotiations are cross-cultural and complex because of the added dimension of cultural diversity, which is an extremely difficult issue. This translates into the need for professional preparations for international negotiations. Fuller, in *The Negotiator's Handbook*,[21] lists among the skills required of the international negotiator:

(a) planning as to location/site for the negotiations;

(b) overcoming language barriers;

(c) familiarity with the other country's customs;

---

20 On the advantages and issues of strategic alliances and joint ventures, for example, see Bleeke, J and Ernst, D, 'The Way to Win in Cross-Border Alliances' in *Collaborating to Compete*, 1993, John Wiley, pp 145–63.

21 1991, Prentice Hall, pp 222–23.

(d) knowledge of the cultural differences, including factors such as the degree of formality/informality at meetings, authority of the negotiator and the extent of socialising;

(e) detailed knowledge of the other country;

(f) knowledge of the operative legal system; and

(g) understanding local business protocol of the other country.

At the bottom of international negotiations, is a fairly basic issue: how does a person influence and communicate with members of cultures different from their own? While vast differences persist in the world, the basic tenets of pulling together people, problems and processes still hold true. That being the case, the foundational principles in principled negotiation hold true. But, in addition, the international negotiator needs to harness the additional qualities of:

(a) preparation and planning skill;

(b) quick thinking;

(c) wise judgment;

(d) integrity;

(e) language competence; and

(f) product knowledge.

Additional issues which must be factored into the overall plan include:

(a) settling the location for the negotiations;

(b) physical arrangements;

(c) team selection;

(d) importance of time limits;

(e) knowledge of the legal regulatory framework; and

(f) the interpretation of cultural norms.

In the context where cultural norms are volatile, as, for example, where women are subjugated in society, or where bribery is the norm in arriving at deals, or where there is no regard for time limits, the answer seems to lie in a vigorous application of the essential elements of principled negotiation:

(a) interests;

(b) relationships;

(c) communication;

(d) option generation;

(e) legitimacy; and

(f) alternatives.[22]

---

22 The literature on international negotiations is legion. The following is a sample:
    Casse, P, *Training for the Cross-Cultural Mind*, 2nd edn, 1981, Society for Intercultural Education, Training and Research.
    Cohen, I, *You Can Negotiate Anything*, 1990, Lyle Stuart.
    Fayweather, J and Kapoor, A, 'Simulated International Business Negotiations' (1972) 3 Journal of International Business Studies 19–31.
    Fisher, G, *International Negotiations: A Cross-Cultural Perspective*, 1980, Intercultural Press.
    Glenn, ES, Witmeyer, D and Stevenson, KA, 'Cultural Styles of Persuasion' (1977) 1(3) International Journal of Intercultural Relations 52–66.

In both domestic and international negotiations, the following basic tenets need to be emphasised:

(a) focusing on the problem and not the people;

(b) identification of underlying causes;

(c) creative solutions;

(d) ownership of those solutions;

(e) win-win outcomes;

(f) maintenance of relationships;

(g) use of objective criteria; and

(h) creative deployment of BATNA.

SOME CRITICAL CHALLENGES TO CARICOM'S NEGOTIATION SKILLS

Within CARICOM there is no shortage of situations which call for critical negotiating skills. Long-standing border conflicts afflict Guyana (with Venezuela) and Surinam and Belize (with Guatemala). In December 2001, a long-standing fishing dispute,between Barbados and Trinidad & Tobago flared up when Barbadian fishermen were harassed, arrested and charged by Trinidad & Tobago, for 'illegal fishing', off the waters of Tobago. Barbados repeatedly threatened retaliation as follows:

(a) a threat to deport Trinidadians living illegally in Barbados;

(b) a review of imports of Trinidadian goods into Barbados;

(c) a review of the relationship between Barbados' government departments and Trinidad & Tobago; and

(d) a reference of the fishing dispute to CARICOM under Protocol 9, since 'Trinidadian authorities were certifying the Taiwanese fishing vessels and allowing them to fish and export their catch to Barbados'.[23]

In 2004, the same dispute flared up again. This time Barbados imposed limited trade sanctions against Trinidad & Tobago and referred the question of the delimitation of national boundaries to arbitration under the law of the Sea Convention.

Making the important linkage between the fishing dispute and the Caribbean Single Market and Economy (CSME), the editorial of the *Daily Nation* newspaper had this to say:

> Taking action against nationals of Trinidad and Tobago who are illegally in Barbados is one thing. Expediting the process for resolving the protracted fishing dispute is another. But moving precipitately on the trade and economic front in a tit-for-tat approach could have serious consequences.

> And not negative consequences just for Barbados-Trinidad and Tobago relations but for current efforts to transform CARICOM into the much canvassed Caribbean Single Market and Economy (CSME).[24]

---

23 (2001) *Barbados Sunday Sun*, 16 December.
24 (2001) *Daily Nation*, 18 December.

Clearly, a failure to resolve the immediate impasse through negotiations could weaken CARICOM as an economic integration movement. One commentator provided a critique and a creative solution as follows:

> It is really ridiculous, that two countries that share so much in common, face such serious common external challenges to their continued survival, that bear such great responsibility for taking the Caribbean forward, can do nothing better to do with each other than to contend and row over such a simple and straightforward matter.
>
> Clearly, Barbadian fishermen fishing in Trinidad's 'exclusive economic zone' could never be an issue. Indeed, we could have gone far beyond that primary stage a long time ago, and the two countries should by now have led the way in creating a modern, collectively owned Caribbean fishing industry.
>
> I am therefore saying that the government and private sectors of the various Caribbean nations need to come together and jointly invest in the development of a modern fishing industry consisting of a boat-building capacity, a modern fishing fleet, one or more canning plants, an efficient marketing mechanism, and the educational programmes that would be required to support such an initiative.[25]

In one sense the fishing dispute between Barbados and Trinidad & Tobago is illustrative of the kinds of intra-CARICOM negotiations which must be conducted at regular intervals in order to create a 'new dimension of togetherness'. That togetherness is reflected, for example, in the creation of a Caribbean Court of Justice, the establishment of the CARICOM Single Market and Economy, the Charter of Civil Society and the free movement of citizens. These efforts ought to coalesce into a CARICOM which speaks with one voice in the councils of the world. That should augur well for CARICOM's negotiating position as it takes on the following negotiations:

(a) With the EU, within the African Caribbean and Pacific group (ACP), as a suitable successor agreement to the Lomé Convention and the Cotonou Agreement is worked out. Already, the EU has made clear its intention to negotiate separate regional free trade agreements.

(b) With the WTO, post-Doha. The feeling in the developing world was that the Uruguay Round, leading to the WTO, did not take into account the needs and interests of those countries. The only way the developing world can have any effective voice would be to participate actively in the negotiations before, and not after, the new rules have come into force. New areas to be negotiated are services, agriculture and specific areas of international concern, such as education.

(c) With the Free Trade Area of the Americas (the FTAA). These negotiations are currently ongoing, designed to settle the ground rules for trade in the Americas from 2005. The FTAA will establish a free trade zone in the Americas from the Arctic to Argentina by 2005, linking some 800 million people who produce over USA$11 trillion dollars in goods and services. These would range from the world's largest economy – the USA – to some of the smallest. The WTO has one set of pincers directed against the Caribbean. The FTAA will produce another set, unless Caribbean negotiators make effective and creative use of the life line in the foundational protocol which recognises 'special and differential' treatment for small, developing countries. Unless that avenue is vigorously pursued, it is clear that the FTAA could drown the tiny economies of the Caribbean nations.

---

25 Commissiong, D, 'Seeking Reality' (2001) *Daily Nation*, 18 December.

Two approaches are open to the Caribbean. One takes the form of appeals to the big powers for help, recognising that the life line to give 'special and differential treatment to small economies' would be hollow in the FTAA since the final pact has to comply with WTO standards.[26]

The other approach is for the Caribbean, through its Regional Negotiating Machinery, to show that notwithstanding its small population of approximately six million, it is the sixth largest market for US goods, greater than that of Russia, China and India combined, and that it has tremendous strengths to enrich the culture of the Americas through the products of its peoples' creative imagination, the literary arts, drama and music.

The road to that goal of negotiating viability looks forlorn for now. The following quotes from knowledgeable opinion leaders in the Caribbean region speak for themselves:

Chris Sinckler, Executive Co-ordinator of the Caribbean Policy Development Centre, says:

> ... teams to meetings of the World Trade Organisation, the Free Trade Area of the Americas and the Caribbean Single Market and Economy should go beyond a minister 'and a few public servants'.

> ... challenges in the face of globalisation and trade liberalisation are many and varied, and we cannot afford the luxury of having a divided foreign policy.

> We have to draw on all of the expertise and talent we have in our country and ensure we get the best possible policies. I would like our foreign affairs policy, economic and political, to be more participatory and inclusive ...

> ... limiting negotiating trade teams to a handful of civil servants who have in many instances to cover so many different briefs, could stretch resources thin.[27]

David Jessop, Executive Director of the Caribbean Council, says as follows with respect to the WTO organisations:

> Despite the extraordinary efforts of the six Caribbean resident diplomatic missions in Geneva (Jamaica, Barbados, St Lucia, Trinidad and the Dominican Republic) there is a danger that the Caribbean's position may go by default. The reason is that both the public and private sectors in the region, seemingly unaware of the finite and far reaching nature of the WTO negotiating process, are failing to provide the practical inputs necessary to ensure a chance of success.

---

26 At a heads of government meeting of the Association of Caribbean States (ACS) held in Porlamar, Venezuela in December, 2001 the Prime Minister of Barbados was reported in the *Daily Nation*, 13 December 2001 as having said:

The WTO didn't give 'special and differential treatment to small economies' its blessing, the calls for such special consideration for Caribbean and Central American nations in the FTAA would turn out to be rhetoric. That's because when the FTAA pact was concluded it still must meet WTO standards.

What I am suggesting as the way out of the paradox, is for the governments of the Americas, led by the United States, Canada and Mexico to agitate vigorously for special and differential treatment for the smaller economies within the WTO.

You cannot espouse one set of principles in the Americas and not pursue them elsewhere. Otherwise the lofty calls for special consideration within the FTAA will remain nothing but rhetoric. In other words, a sham.

27 (2002) *Weekend Nation Extra*, 26 April.

No one would deny that to most the WTO process is numbing and arcane. Nevertheless, what is being discussed will determine the long term viability and competitiveness of virtually every Caribbean industry.

Put another way, it may well be that by the time that the detailed EU/ACP trade negotiations for economic partnership agreements takes place, what really matters will have already been decided in Geneva at the WTO.

To explain: the first phase of negotiations for the EU/ACP Economic Partnership Arrangements will begin in September of this year but it is widely accepted that the ACP will not be in any position to begin a serious discussion of general principles until late 2003. This first phase is expected to last to at least the end of 2004 although most EU member states privately concede that delays will occur. This in turn means that the earliest that any industry specific discussion negotiations might occur would be in 2005 with the objective that a final overall ACP/EU agreement on EPA's might be achieved by late 2006 for implementation from 2008 on. In contrast the WTO process anticipates that significant progress will have been made in most areas of agriculture and services by the time of the next WTO ministerial meeting in September or October of 2003.

For example, while the sugar industry, is preparing for a tough negotiation with Europe as to the future of the legally binding ACP/EU sugar protocol, the industry's viability could be swept away much earlier in the WTO process. For a number of technical reasons relating to previous negotiations, a so called WTO peace clause on agriculture will expire as this year goes on. The result may well be a challenge from nations such as Brazil or Australia to European agricultural subsidies and by extension to the guaranteed price paid for ACP cane sugar.

In Geneva negotiations that affect every single industry occur daily in small working groups, in corridor deals and on paper through a process of requests and responses once a general framework for negotiations has been agreed. This has serious implications for the future for sugar, bananas, rum, financial services, poultry, fisheries, tourism, free zones, textiles, export incentives, investment provisions and so on.

Despite this, Caribbean industries hardly ever visit Geneva and most have no WTO negotiating position. Worse still many governments try to cover the daily process of negotiations either from capitals or though occasional visits by Ministers, diplomats and officials.

The problem is that the WTO process is not as accessible as other trade negotiations. Instead of focussing on specific industries and sectors it deals with general principles and crosscutting themes that cause member states to act in coalitions that vary depending on the issue to be discussed.

To illustrate in concrete terms the seriousness of what is being determined in Geneva, a few simple but practical questions will suffice.

Have Caribbean governments a clear negotiating response to proposals in the agriculture round that would require every state to reduce certain import tariffs in a manner that would see sudden and substantial falls in government revenues? What will Caribbean governments say when they are told for reasons related to factory fishing that their own small fishermen can no longer have their fuel subsidised?

Where are the positions of the Caribbean rice sector on agricultural negotiations; the coffee growers on geographical indications; or the energy sector of the liberalisation of energy related services. Has the Association of Indigenous Banks yet prepared a memorandum for the Regional Negotiating Machinery on the ways in which the services negotiations may affect the Caribbean financial sector? Has the Poultry Breeders Association identified how Caribbean poultry producers might continue to defend their domestic markets against poultry from let us say the United States?

Has anyone undertaken an assessment of the likely impact of negotiations in the services sector at the WTO on manufacturing in free zones? Is anyone thinking about the ways in which the region's tourism industry might use the negotiations to ensure that the regional industry is better able to receive a greater part of the income that presently flows to external tour operators?

These comments are not meant to be critical of the institutions named. Instead they are intended to point to the fact that urgent activity is required if those in Geneva who have to negotiate on behalf of the region are to stand any real chance of ensuring the region's interests are defended and advanced.

None of this requires an academic or theoretical approach. Rather it points to the development of a coherent set of documentation making the case of every industry. This is essential if the Caribbean's very able but under resourced and sometimes forgotten representatives in Geneva are to make a difference.[28]

Owen Arthur, Prime Minister of Barbados has also stated as follows:

The creation of the Caribbean Single Market and Economy (CSME) would require significant private sector reform but this was not sufficiently well appreciated nor acted upon.

The regional private sector institutions now available to support the development of private sector activity are generally unrepresentative of the sector itself, poorly funded, lack institutional depth and cannot adequately help in carrying out the changes contemplated by the CSME, far less those under the FTAA (Free Trade Area of the Americas) and WTO (World Trade Organisation).

In the face of these momentous challenges, some hope of a solution must lie along the lines of one of the suggestions coming out of a seminar on Caribbean Economic Integration held to commemorate the 30th anniversary of the Central Bank of Barbados.[29] The idea is modelled on a Caribbean think tank, to be composed of some of the best regional minds, from all sectors, to be at the service of the Caribbean, on an as needed basis for specific assignments/missions, with the public and private sectors contributing to a special fund to make it a functional project. Linked to that is the establishment of a regional skills bank in the field of negotiation, to be available to CARICOM and the CRNM on an as needed, when needed basis.

28 (2002) *Trinidad Express*, 9 May.
29 Commented upon in the *Daily Nation*, 23 May 2002.

CHAPTER 4

MEDIATION PROCESSES AND SKILLS ACQUISITION

Beyond negotiation, mediation is the other big and popular process used under the umbrella of ADR. Mediation is an old form of dispute resolution process. It has been practised for centuries in Africa, China, the Far East and now, recently, in the western world. H Alves had this to say about the origins of mediation:

> Mediation had its genesis in traditional decision making procedures used at some stage in the history of almost all cultures of the world. The Hindu villages of India which have traditionally engaged the panchayat justice system, (and which system, in traditional times, was also used in Trinidad and Tobago as a means of dispute resolution). In traditional African societies, respected notables were often called to mediate disputes between neighbours, and Islamic traditional pastoral societies in the Middle East also established mediation methodologies. In the Jewish culture, a form of mediation was, in Biblical Times, practised by both religious and political leaders. Mediation has also been widely practised in Japan and a number of other Asian societies. The Christian religion has as well, traditionally used mediation among its members.

> Whilst factors such as cultural values, beliefs, self concepts, the relationship between the parties will affect the process used, the introduction of an impartial third party to the resolution process appears to transcend these differing factors.

> Despite the established historical background of mediation, it has only been since the mid-1990s that the process has become formalized, and, only within the last twenty-five years that the process has gained ground as an institution and as a developing procession.[1]

This quotation reinforces the point made in Chapter 1 to similar effect.

According to CW Moore,[2] 'mediation has a long and varied history in almost all cultures of the world. Jewish, Christian, Islamic, Hindu, Buddhist, Confucian and many indigenous cultures all have extensive and effective traditions of mediation practice'.

In Africa, for example, mediation has been utilised in the resolution of disputes, using elders, councillors, headmen and tribal chiefs as mediators.

Today, mediation is in use in a multiplicity of conflict situations. It is used in the resolution of inter-personal conflicts, in labour, management, commercial, ethnic community, education and international disputes. Its growth and popularity stem from the deep disaffection with the litigation alternative,[3] the lack of involvement of the parties in crafting creative solutions to their problems and the shift from a focus on 'rights' to a focus on 'interests'.

In the Caribbean, mediation has been employed in the resolution of disputes in the following areas:

---

1 'Mediation: A Method of Alternative Dispute Resolution' (2000) 36 Hugh Wooding Law School Journal 37.
2 *The Mediation Process*, 2nd edn, 1996, Jossey-Bass, p 20.
3 See Chapter 1 for some of these reasons.

(a) landlord and tenant;

(b) personal injury;

(c) employment contracts;

(d) student disputes;

(e) land disputes;

(f) commercial contracts;

(g) matrimonial property;

(h) wills and estates; and

(i) parenting issues.[4]

According to Brown and Marriott, mediation has been employed in the UK in the following fields:

(a) commercial and civil disputes;

(b) industrial and labour disputes;

(c) family disputes, including issues arising on separation and divorce;

(d) community and neighbourhood issues;

(e) public policy and social conflict; and

(f) international issues.[5]

They state, further, that there are many other fields into which mediation has extended in other countries, for example, in academia, in the church, in hospitals and health care systems, in consumer disputes, for gender, race and ethnic issues, in assessing claims for asbestos injuries, in dealing with farmer/lender debt issues, in dealing with prison grievances and for many other disparate purposes, even the mediation of gang warfare and complaints by patients about doctors.

These lists show the versatility of mediation as a dispute resolution tool. It can be used in the court system, in community centres, in educational settings and in law enforcement by the police.[6]

MEDIATION: COMMON FEATURES

Simply defined, mediation is a consensual process in which a neutral third party helps others to negotiate a solution to a problem. The mediator has no authority to make binding decisions for the disputants. What the mediator does is to use certain procedures, techniques and skills to help the disputants to arrive at a resolution of their dispute by agreement without adjudication.

The need for the acquisition of skills and techniques was stressed in relation to negotiation. That point takes on added significance once it is appreciated that mediation is an extension of negotiation. A mediation normally occurs when the

---

4   'Mediate Don't Litigate', 2002, Council of Legal Education Hugh Wooding Law School, Legal Aid Clinic Mediation Centre Pamphlet.

5   *ADR Principles and Practices*, 1999, Sweet & Maxwell, p 125.

6   For further reading on this point, see *The Mediator Handbook: A Training Guide to Mediation Techniques & Skills*, prepared by the Centre for Dispute Resolution, Capital University Law & Graduate Centre, Columbus, Ohio, for the Dispute Resolution Foundation of Jamaica, March 1999.

parties come to the realisation that they cannot resolve their dispute on their own and that they need the help of third party intervention.

This neutral third party, called a mediator, is essentially a *facilitator* only. Apart from that, all the essentials of the negotiation process are preserved.

The mediator has no role or function to make a decision for the parties. This is the most important difference between a mediator and an arbitrator. The role of an arbitrator is to consider the issues and then to make a decision which determines the issues. An arbitrator's decision is binding on the parties.

It is important to underscore the fact that the mediator's duty goes beyond what facilitation may, at first glance, suggest. It is the mediator's duty to assist the parties to examine their mutual interests and promote a lasting relationship. Indeed, the fact that the mediator lacks decision making authority makes it attractive to disputants, who retain ultimate control of the outcome as the decision makers. But this point should not mask the reality that mediators do have influence and authority. In the words of CW Moore:

> The mediator's authority, such as it is, resides in his or her personal credibility and trustworthiness, expertise in enhancing the negotiation process, experience in handling similar issues, ability to bring the parties together on the basis of their own interests, past performance or reputation as a resource person, and in some cultures, his or her relationship with the parties. Authority, or recognition of the right to influence the outcome of a dispute, is granted by the parties themselves rather than by an external law, contract, or agency.[7]

Mediation is a flexible process, subject only to a few essential rules. It may take a variety of turns. For example, the mediator in a commercial dispute may adopt approaches which may be very different from the mediator in a family law setting or from a labour or industrial relations setting. That notwithstanding, there are certain fundamental principles and core skills associated with being a mediator. Among the common features of a mediation are the following points:

(a) Neutrality of the mediator. The neutrality and impartiality of the mediator are of fundamental importance to this process.

(b) Nature of the mediator's authority. The mediator has no authority to impose a settlement on the disputants. The mediator is only a facilitator of the process, whose primary role is to assist the disputants to settle their differences through a negotiated agreement. Mediation involves some element of facilitation and assistance so that the disputants can negotiate with one another .

(c) Consensual resolution. Mediation is consensual. So, the only binding outcome of mediation is one with which all the parties agree.

(d) Maximisation of interests. The objective of a mediated settlement, unlike an adversarial trial, is to maximise the interests of all parties.

(e) Provision of secure environment. It is the mediator's responsibility to create conditions, which are conducive to discussion and the exploration of settlement options and possibilities. This applies not only to the physical arrangements and the ambience, but also to ground rules regulating the process.

---

7   *Op cit*, fn 2, p 18.

(f) Offer of confidentiality. Mediation is, by its very nature, a private and confidential process. The mediator must first offer confidentiality to the parties, who may also agree to mutual confidentiality.

(g) Inability to offer independent advice. Because in mediation the parties are responsible for their own decisions, a mediator is not supposed to offer advice to the parties. Where appropriate, the disputants may take advice from independent sources, but they may not do so from the mediator.

(h) Empowerment of the parties. This enables the parties to make their own decisions, with little dependence on third party advisers.

(i) Maintenance of relationships. The containment of escalation in a controlled atmosphere promotes communications between the parties and aids the maintenance of relationships.

These basic features also reflect some of the main advantages claimed for mediation over other forms of dispute resolution, especially litigation. Mediation is faster, cheaper and more satisfying to the parties than litigation. The process is private and confidential, consensual and non-adversarial. It employs co-operative, problem solving approaches and enhances communication between the parties. Most importantly, the parties take responsibility for crafting creative solutions to their problem.

As a neutral facilitator, the mediator is uniquely placed to assist with, or do, the following:

(a) win the trust of all parties;

(b) facilitate communication;

(c) focus the parties on the problem;

(d) overcome emotional blockages;

(e) help one party to understand the other party's case;

(f) probe each party's case for interests, positions, strengths and weaknesses;

(g) help parties realistically assess their own cases;

(h) suggest new avenues to explore;

(i) overcome deadlock and help save face;

(j) explore settlement proposals in depth;

(k) assess realistically the chances of settlement; and

(l) win approval for settlement proposals.[8]

The Mediation Training Course Handbook of the Centre for Excellence in Dispute Resolution (CEDR) lists the following as cornerstone principles which delimit a mediator's responsibilities:

(a) check (and re-check) confidentiality;

(b) let the parties own the problem and the solution;

(c) resist imposing the mediator's own solution;

(d) be neutral and do not offer an opinion;

(e) be impartial and give equal value to everyone;

(f) avoid stereotyping;

(g) check own assumptions;

---

8   *Op cit*, fn 6.

(h) always show respect;

(i) develop and demonstrate understanding;

(j) be open and honest (with oneself and with others); and

(k) be flexible.[9]

CLASSIFICATION

In terms of general classification, mediation may be rights-based or interests-based.

Rights-based mediation

A rights-based mediation occurs where the parties to a dispute want a neutral third party to provide them with an independent assessment of the likely outcome of the case, if there is no settlement at the mediation. The mediator provides an assessment of the legal and equitable rights of the parties.

It is then left to the parties to choose to accept or reject or modify the assessment provided. It must be obvious that, in a rights-based mediation, only a person with some real expertise in the substantive area of the dispute may be chosen to provide the assessment of rights.

It is not uncommon for the mediator to use their personality and expertise to browbeat one party to change their position and adopt the mediator's proposal. For this reason, rights-based mediation is sometimes referred to as 'muscle mediation'.

A rights-based mediation may be employed where the parties believe that one side has an unrealistic assessment of the outcome of the case, and where that position could be influenced by the opinion of the mediator. Also, some lawyers employ rights-based mediation where they believe that their own clients have an unrealistic assessment of their case and are intransigent.

Interests-based mediation

This is the more popular form of mediation. Indeed, when people talk of mediation, it is this type of process to which they refer.

This type of mediation focuses on the underlying interests, goals and needs of the parties, rather than on the perceived outcome of the litigation

This approach to mediation is, again, attributed to the Harvard Negotiating Team.[10]

In an interests-based mediation, the mediator attempts to determine the interests behind the positions adopted by the parties, encourages them to generate options that satisfy those interests and helps them to choose their own solutions. To the extent that mediation brings together people, their problem and a process of resolving those problems, the interests-based mediator controls the process of the mediation and assists the parties and their advisors to resolve the substantive issues.

---

9   Extracted from CEDR Mediation Training Course Handbook, 1997, p 54.

10 Fisher, R and Ury, W, *Getting to Yes*, 1991, Penguin.

The mediator need not be an expert in the substantive areas of the dispute. This is because the interests-based mediator is supposed to be a process expert who can leave the substantive issues to the parties, who would normally have a greater familiarity with the facts than the mediator.

COMMENCEMENT OF MEDIATION

A mediation may be commenced in a number of ways. The most common form is by agreement of the parties. That agreement may contain the mechanism for the selection of a mediator. Failing that, it is not unusual to have an independent organisation choose the mediator for the parties.

A second way to get a mediation started is by providing for the process in a mediation clause within an existing agreement. Such a clause would stipulate that the parties agree to attempt mediation prior to engaging in a binding form of dispute resolution. When the dispute arises, the parties will then be required to follow the procedures set out in the contract.

Yet another way to get to mediation is to be required by the law to attend a mediation session. In that case, the mediator is usually chosen for the parties by the law. An example may be found in s 8 of the Family Law Act of Barbados 1985 (Cap 214). It provides that:

(8) Where an application for the dissolution of a marriage discloses that the parties have been married for less than 2 years preceding the date of the filing of the application, the court shall not hear the proceedings unless the court is satisfied that:

(a) the parties have considered a reconciliation with the assistance of a marriage counsellor, an approved marriage counselling organisation, or some suitable person or organisation nominated by the Registrar or other appropriate officer;

It thus makes the exhaustion of some form of a mediation process a pre-condition for pursuing litigation.

Where the parties come to a mediation voluntarily and by a consensual process, it is reasonable to provide the terms and conditions in a mediation agreement.

THE MEDIATION AGREEMENT

There is no standard mediation agreement, as the parties are free to adjust the terms to suit their interests and the nature of the issues to be mediated. It is advisable that certain basic ideas be reflected in the mediation agreement. They represent the basic rules of the game and speak as to the legal protections that may be afforded to a mediator and his notes.

Below is a basic type of mediation agreement that may be adapted, as appropriate, to the demands of a specific dispute.[11]

---

11 This sample agreement has been adapted from Noone, M, *Mediation*, 1996, Cavendish Publishing.

AGREEMENT TO MEDIATE

BETWEEN: (party)
AND: (party or parties)
AND: (mediator)

1   *Appointment of mediator.* A dispute having arisen between the parties, they [and their legal representatives] have agreed to attend a mediation to resolve this dispute and the signing of this agreement is evidence of the parties having appointed the mediator and having the intention to participate in the mediation in a *bona fide* and forthright manner, to explore alternative solutions, consider compromises and accommodations and to make a serious attempt to resolve this dispute.

2   *Conflicts of interest.* Prior to the mediation, the mediator will disclose to the parties any prior dealings she or he has had with any or the parties and any interest he or she has in the dispute.

3   *Co-operation.* The parties shall co-operate with each other and the mediator during the mediation.

4   *Authority to settle.* The parties or their appointed representative have full authority to settle this dispute at the mediation.

5   *Conduct of the mediation.* (i) The mediator will be impartial and neutral. (ii) The mediator will not provide legal advice to any party. (iii) The mediator will not make decision for any party. (iv) The mediator may hold joint and private sessions.

6   *Confidentiality.* (i) The parties and the mediator will not disclose to anyone not involved in the mediation any information or document given to them during the mediation unless required to do so by law. (ii) Any information disclosed to a mediator in private is to be treated as confidential by the mediator unless the party making the disclosure states otherwise.

7   *Privilege.* The parties shall not rely on or introduce as evidence in any subsequent arbitral or judicial proceedings any views expressed, or suggestions made, by the other party in respect of the possible settlement of the dispute, or any admissions made by the other party in the course of the mediation, or the fact that the other party had indicated a willingness to consider or accept a proposal for settlement, or any statement or document made by the mediator. Parties will not subpoena or otherwise require the mediator to testify or produce records or notes in any future proceedings. All notes and records of the mediation will be destroyed at the end of the mediation.

8   *Subsequent proceedings.* The mediator will not accept appointment as an arbitrator or act as an advocate in or provide advice to a party to any arbitral or judicial proceedings relating to this dispute.

9   *Termination.* The mediation may be terminated at any time by a party or the mediator. The mediation is automatically terminated upon execution of a settlement agreement.

10 *Settlement.* Where a settlement is reached, the terms will be written down and signed by the parties before they leave the mediation and the parties will carry out the terms of the settlement as soon as possible. Any party may enforce the terms of the settlement by judicial proceedings.

11 *Exclusion of liability.* The mediator will not be liable to a party for any act or omission in performance of the mediation unless the act or omission is fraudulent.

12 *Indemnity.* The parties will indemnify the mediator against any claim for any act or omission in performance of the mediation unless the act or omission is fraudulent.

13 *Length of mediation and fees.* The parties will agree an estimate of the length of the mediation and also signal their consent to the mediator's fees.

DATED at _____ on the _____ day of _____ 200_

Party 1   Party 2   Mediator

What basic features emerge from the above draft? These are:

(a) a common desire to settle the dispute by mediation;

(b) a pledge to act in good faith;

(c) a stipulation of confidentiality for the mediator, as well as the parties;

(d) a 'without prejudice' clause so that the comments made in the mediation may not be used outside the mediation, nor in any future proceedings;

(e) inability to call the mediator as a witness at future proceedings, nor will the mediator's notes be subpoenaed;

(f) the name of the mediator, the length of the mediation and the fee for the mediation; and

(g) the right of the parties to withdraw from the mediation at any time.

In addition to these basics, it is advisable to have regard to issues such as who may attend the mediation in an advisory capacity, who has final authority to settle a deal and whether a written summary of the parties' cases ought to be supplied to the mediator in advance of the mediation.

Power imbalances remain a big problem in any form of discussion. So it is desirable to decide beforehand who may attend the mediation, especially in the case of professional advisers, and to include this in the mediation agreement.

A person is said to have authority to settle if that person can agree to a proposed resolution without first getting approval from a third party. If the parties do have the authority to settle at the mediation, the mediation can conclude with a signed agreement.

But there are situations, however, especially in mediations where corporations are involved, where the ultimate decision maker cannot be physically present at the mediation. In that situation, the limitations on the authority of those in attendance at the mediation should be set out in advance of the mediation.

There may also be a situation where one party has the authority to settle while the other party does not. It is advisable to decide prior to the mediation whether both parties will have a specified period of time to consider and approve a tentative deal, or whether only the party without authority will have time after the mediation to ratify the tentative deal.

THE MEDIATION PROCESS

It is customary to begin the actual mediation process by 'setting the table'. This involves confirming the names of the parties, determining how the parties want to be addressed, determining whether the parties have been at a mediation before, and providing information about the facilities for, and timing of, the mediation. It is important for the mediator to discuss his role, which is that he is an impartial neutral with no power to impose an outcome on the parties. Rather, the parties are supposed to persuade each other.

The mediator will remind the parties that the mediator is not a legal adviser to the parties and, therefore, will not give legal advice to the parties.

The mediator will review the terms of the agreement to mediate, and ensure that it is signed.

It is also important that the mediator sets out the ground rules for the mediation. Among such rules would be:

(a) that only one person speaks at a time;

(b) that the rules agreed upon are to be followed and respected;

(c) that only civil language may be used and personal verbal attacks are to be avoided;

(d) that the parties may leave the mediation at any time; and

(e) that the overriding purpose is to make the parties comfortable with the process.

OPENING REMARKS

After the mediator's introduction, the parties or their counsel usually provide a brief summary of each party's views on the issues in dispute.

The mediator may then ask questions of a clarifying nature to ensure that each party's case is well understood by the other side.

Disputes involve a lot of steam: so the mediator allows the parties opportunities to let off steam and express strongly held emotions, keeping a benign eye to ensure that the mediation does not deteriorate out of control.

Thereafter, the mediator then identifies the issues that are in dispute and need to be resolved. Critical to the process is the next stage, generating options that satisfy the interests of both or all of the parties. The options developed should seek to resolve the issues in innovative ways.

This is a critical stage in the mediation, which should not be rushed. The parties must be encouraged to feel comfortable in each other's company and to share information and ideas. It is only in a collaborative environment that problem solving can be mutually pursued. The mediator then explores with the parties the options which have the potential to resolve the issues, and the parties can refine the options which have been generated.

Because most people approach problems from a final position which they may have come to, they also see the solution in one-dimensional terms. To shift the parties to explore a range of possible solutions requires the mediator's skills to shift the parties' focus from positions to interests. By that process, the parties themselves bring up suggestions to satisfy their interests, thus reinforcing the durability of any solutions arrived at. At the option generation stage every suggestion is acceptable without comment or criticism. The single reason for this is that what may start off as a 'bad option' could eventually turn out to be a 'good option'.

In selecting appropriate options, the parties may have reference to objective criteria and follow the basic steps in a negotiation process, as, for example, settling for a deal which is better than one's BATNA. Those objective criteria revolve around relationships, communication, interests, options, legitimacy and commitment.

DEALING WITH DIFFICULT MEDIATIONS

Not all mediations proceed smoothly. Several factors, such as anger, position, plain misunderstanding or a simple miscommunication could lead to an impasse in the mediation. Below is a list – by no means exhaustive – of a few strategies that a mediator may employ to diffuse the impasse:

- Take a break from the mediation. Relaxing to reconsider a point sometimes leads to fresh thinking on a problem.
- Emphasise the areas of agreement. This enables the parties to see the commonality of their interests and the futility of walking away from the table.
- Use humour. Appropriate humour is always a good move for relaxation.
- Explore settlement in incremental stages. If a partial agreement is feasible, harp on it.
- Adjourn to another day.
- Encourage the parties. Encouragement is a good motivator to further movement and action. The mediator should acknowledge whatever progress has been made, to reinforce it.
- Change the focus of the mediation. If one topic bogs down the discussion, move to another issue and address the difficult one later.
- Use silence as a weapon. Silence is an unusual condition in a mediation. Someone may feel compelled to break it.
- BATNA. It is good strategy to remind the parties of their BATNA and their WATNA.[12]
- Validate the parties' interests. When people feel validated in their own interests, they are more willing to listen to the interests of others.
- Avoid generalisations.

---

12   BATNA and WATNA stand for the Best or Worst Alternatives to a Negotiated Settlement.

- Point out similarities.
- Learn about the parties' culture/cultures.
- Share your experiences.
- Demonstrate familiarity.
- Show a desire to learn.
- Be open to individuality.
- Practice active listening.
- Stress the positive.
- Figure out what is 'fair'.
- Admit mistakes.
- Do not trick or be overly greedy.
- Be respectful of the parties.
- Try to improve the deal after making it.
- Recognise common goals.
- Discuss difficulties/constraints.
- Use a caucus. This allows the mediator to hold separate meetings with the parties.
- Establish a personal rapport.
- Disclose relevant information.
- Be honest.
- Find out what each party wants/needs.
- Look for ways to add value.
- Create options.
- Prepare.
- Have open communication.
- Try to improve the relationship between or amongst the parties.

CAUCUSING

A caucus is a deliberate pause in the mediation, at the instance of the mediator, with a view to the mediator meeting privately with each party or combination of parties. This is a useful technique to deploy when a mediation gets stuck for one reason or the other. It provides an opportunity for the mediator to engage in separate, as opposed to, joint problem solving. The caucus is confidential and the mediator can only disclose information gathered in a caucus with authorisation. This places a singular duty on the mediator to take accurate notes, especially as to what he may disclose to the other side.

The importance of information flow to the mediation process has been stressed. A caucus may thus be used to gather additional information confidentially, upon the prompting of the mediator. This could not be done in an open mediation, lest the mediator's integrity and impartiality fall to be questioned. The caucus may also be used to assist a party to assess the strengths and weaknesses of a case, or the best and worst options available to that party. Making a realistic assessment of their case is always helpful to a party when determining whether it is worth pursuing a dispute. A mediator could, thus, use a caucus to indicate, for example, the legal fees, emotional costs and time in litigating the dispute. Also, the caucus could be used to foster greater trust and confidence in the mediator, thus inviting more forthright responses from the disputants. Finally, the caucus could also be used as an educational tool to provide explanations and clarifications about the mediation process. Of course, the diligent mediator must balance these undoubted advantages against the charge of potential 'bias' from the other party to the dispute.

MEDIATION VERSUS LITIGATION

Mediation practitioners point to a number of advantages which the mediation process has over litigation. Among the claimed advantages are the following:

(a) consensual nature of the mediation process;
(b) personal involvement of the parties in the process;
(c) the parties' participation in arriving at mutually acceptable solutions;
(d) savings in time and money;
(e) deceleration of emotional stress;
(f) creation of a less intimidating atmosphere;
(g) maintenance of a continuing relationship;
(h) risk-free involvement in the process;
(i) acceptable win-win outcomes, as opposed to win-lose outcomes;
(j) freedom to put as many issues as possible on the table;
(k) confidential nature of the process; and
(l) freedom of choice of a mediator.

It is further acknowledged that even where a deal is not reached, the process of mediation allows the parties the opportunity to clarify their interests and, thus, help with the eventual resolution of the dispute.

There are some disadvantages, too, to mediation, which should now be addressed, albeit briefly. Among the prominent ones are that:

(a) mediation does not adequately safeguard the legal rights of the disputants;
(b) it lacks the procedural safeguards which attend in court trial;
(c) a failed mediation simply adds to delay and increased costs in finally resolving the dispute;
(d) its consensual nature makes it a vulnerable process;
(e) mediation is not suitable for certain types of disputes which involve, for example, serious crimes, sexual offences and constitutional infringements; and
(f) mediation detracts from the case law jurisprudence which underpins the common law, since no precedents are established in mediations.

These are weighty points which should be borne in mind as we weigh the pros and cons of the mediation process.

Finally, does mediation apply to all disputes and when is mediation appropriate?

It is very difficult to determine in advance what type of dispute would be appropriate to mediation. The following is a sample of the situations in which mediation may be awkward:

(a) Constitutional litigation. Where a party is seeking, for example, to strike down legislation, mediation would seem to be inappropriate.

(b) Where the parties are interested in setting or creating a precedent then, again, mediation would simply not do. A good example would be in the situation where the parties put forward a test case for decision.

(c) Where the dispute has generated so much acrimony between the parties that nothing short of litigation would be satisfactory.

(d) Where the parties are not willing to deal with each other in good faith, then mediation simply would not work.

(e) Where serious criminal offences have been committed.

POST-MEDIATION PROCESSES

The most important issue after a mediation is the enforcement of the mediated agreement. Equally important is whether there is a role for a mediator after the initial agreement. These and other public policy questions will be addressed later in Chapter 9.

CHAPTER 5

PRINCIPLES OF ARBITRATION – DOMESTIC AND INTERNATIONAL

INTRODUCTION

As pointed out in the Preface, arbitration's place in ADR is not free from controversy. The argument has been made, however, that arbitration has become one of the principal means of settlement of commercial disputes, especially in international trade. What that translates into is that the Caribbean region can no longer underplay the importance of arbitration.

Even at the level of the United Nations regime, Article 33 of the UN Charter obliges parties to any dispute, 'the continuance of which is likely to endanger the maintenance of international peace and security', to seek a solution by, *inter alia*, arbitration. With the advent of mega-blocks and mega-markets generating increased trade between nations and commercial entities, it is not unreasonable to predict that this region will definitely be witnessing an unprecedented explosion of gigantic proportions in commercial arbitration.

Various reasons account for the phenomenon. As stated by Prince Ajibola:

> Several factors are responsible. The rise in economic, especially commercial activities, has necessarily resulted in the increase of commercial contracts the breach of which creates disputes which have to be resolved. These disputes being business in nature require quick resolution which the adjudication process of the Courts do not ensure. Furthermore, court procedure has become rather expensive and bogged down with procedural delay, especially with its system of appeals. These are some of the circumstances that have led to the gradual moving away from court litigation to arbitration in the area of business disputes. Other factors have also led to greater leaning towards arbitration in international transactions as we shall see shortly.

> Significantly, international transactions have grown by leaps and bounds in the post-war years. The developed nations of the world were making new advances and breakthrough in technology and inventions. More goods were produced and sold to other countries. This was a great boost for trade and commerce resulting in greater demand for bilateral and multilateral commercial agreements among nations. Simultaneously, there was the rise of new nations which were granted independence by their erstwhile Imperial or Colonial powers. These constitute what is now referred to as the Developing Countries or the so-called 'Third World'. Their attainment of political independence naturally led to their yearnings for better living through economic development. Many of their nationals were poor, needing food, shelter, good health and education. They had to depend on the developed countries for these essentials. This led to a boost in trade between the two 'worlds' in which the developing world had to depend on the investment, technology and expertise of the developed world.

> In providing these needs, very many international agreement have to be entered into. These may range from agreements for sale of goods and equipment, construction of engineering works, industrial projects investments, economic assistance programmes to the transfer of technology.[1]

---

1 'Arbitration in Developing Countries', 1987, paper presented to the 13th Conference of the Law of the World in Seoul, Republic of Korea.

The overriding importance of arbitration ought not to blind the Caribbean region to the serious problems which many commentators have with arbitration.

For one, arbitration 'has for all intents and purposes fallen into disuse'[2] in this region. F Clarke lists the following among the reasons accounting for the lack of use of arbitration in the region.[3]

The reluctance of the commercial communities in the CARICOM countries to use arbitration and other methods of alternative dispute resolution may be due to several reasons, including:

(a) unfamiliarity with the arbitration and mediation processes;

(b) the non-existence of a pool of skilled and qualified persons to act as neutrals, namely arbitrators, conciliators and mediators;

(c) the lack of confidence in these communities generally in arbitrators who are not either members or former members of the judiciary;

(d) the fact that arbitrations are conducted in a no less complex manner than lawsuits; and

(e) many arbitration statutes allow for applications by the parties to the Law Courts with regard to matters which may arise in the course of the arbitration proceedings.

Commenting on some of the drawbacks to arbitration from the perspective of developing countries, the author had this to say:

> Arbitration is somewhat more worrisome and its advantages over the court process not always obvious. In fact, for the developing countries of the region, its advantages are somewhat dubious. This is so because most donor countries and foreign enterprises refuse to invest in a country unless the grant stipulates a condition, which denies the local courts jurisdiction to arbitrate. The net effect of this stipulation has been to import into such commercial contracts, arbitrations conducted under the auspices of the International Chamber of Commerce or the American Arbitration Association. Some of the disadvantages suffered by developing countries are reflected in the selection of a forum, the choice of arbitrators, and the heavy costs of retaining counsel and meeting the fees of the arbitrators.[4]

DEFINITION AND SOURCES

A good definition of arbitration is that it is 'a consensual system of judicature directed to the resolution of commercial disputes in private'.[5]

An arbitrator, therefore, is described as 'a disinterested person, to whose judgment and decision matters in dispute are referred'.

Some basic ingredients and essential features of arbitration are as follows:

---

2   Shelton, SM, 'Arbitration as an Alternative Means of Dispute Resolution: An Introductory Road Map' (2001) 26(1) and (2) WILJ 84.

3   Clarke, F, 'Solucion de conflicts en CARICOM', paper delivered to the XVI Conference on Inter-American Commercial Arbitration in Belo Horizonte, Brazil, 1997 (unpublished).

4   Fiadjoe, A, *Commonwealth Caribbean Public Law*, 2nd edn, 1999, Cavendish Publishing, p 203.

5   Rowland, PMB, *Arbitration Law and Practice*, 1988, ICAEW, p 1.

(a) The arbitral process is consensual, based on an agreement between the parties.

(b) The parties have procedural freedom. This means that the parties may organise their proceedings as they like and may choose an adversarial or inquisitorial procedure as they like, or a mixture of the two.

(c) The arbitrators must be independent and impartial in accordance with codes of ethics and conduct. A breach of that duty may result in the arbitrator being challenged and eventually removed by the court, or by the arbitration institution concerned. It may also lead to the annulment of the award.

(d) The arbitrator is the master of his own procedure.[6]

(e) The arbitrator must act in accordance with the rules of natural justice.

(f) An arbitral award is binding upon the parties.

The sources of the law of arbitration lie in a number of international conventions, international model laws and model rules, and institutional rules such as those of the International Chamber of Commerce (ICC) and the London Court of International Arbitration (LCIA). To these may be added domestic legislation, reports of awards and academic writings.

ARBITRATION DISTINGUISHED FROM MEDIATION/CONCILIATION

There are five main points of distinction between an arbitration and a mediation. These are as follows:

(a) Though both systems are consensual, an agreement to enter into arbitration will be enforced by the courts, whereas an agreement to enter into a mediation will generally not be enforced by the courts. This is because in mediation, the parties are free to leave at any time.

(b) Arbitration has the quality of delivering a final and binding award. The arbitrator has the legal authority to make a binding award, but the mediator has not.

(c) Whereas arbitration is subject to an extensive statutory regime, mediation is generally not so regulated.

(d) Arbitral procedures are said to have the advantage over the courts of informality, but nonetheless they are constrained by the rules of natural justice. Compare with the situation of the mediator, who is not so bound as he must be free to see the parties separately (go into caucus) or together, and has a discretion as to what or how much information he may disclose to one side or the other.

(e) Most international arbitration rules provide power in the arbitrator to act as an 'amiable compositor'. This gives the arbitrator power to act not only in accordance with rules of law, but also with principles of equity.[7]

---

6   See Diplock in *Bremer Vulcan v South India Shipping* [1981] AC 909.
7   It must be pointed out that 'equity' does not mean the same as in its common law usage.

ADVANTAGES OF ARBITRATION OVER LITIGATION

The explosion in commercial arbitration caused by the enormous increase in world trade and the desire of the international business community to have neutral and competent tribunals to decide their commercial disputes has already been alluded to. This is due to the perception that arbitration has manifest advantages over litigation. Some of those advantages are as follows:

(a) The parties have a free choice to select a tribunal that fits the nature of their dispute. So, for highly technical trade disputes, the parties may select an expert in that field as the arbitrator.

(b) Arbitrations are held in private and they are also protected by the laws of privacy. This could be crucially important in a dispute between rival companies in a competitive business field who would like to keep their know-how, business strategy, etc, from the public.

(c) Ease of enforcement of arbitral awards is a huge advantage. As is well known, enforcing a domestic decision against a government is immensely problematic. That is not so with arbitral awards because domestic laws and international conventions permit the registration and enforcement of these awards (see the Geneva Convention of 1927 and the New York Convention of 1958).

An award has no value unless it can be enforced. One of the principal concerns of those who arbitrate international commercial disputes, therefore, is how to secure the enforcement of an award in a foreign jurisdiction. The Convention on the Recognition and Enforcement of Foreign Tribunal Awards (also known as the New York Convention and the United Nations Convention) was adopted by the United Nations Conference on International Commercial Arbitration on 10 June 1958 and came into force officially on 7 June 1959. The revised Treaty of CARICOM provides in Article 223 (2) and (3) that each member state shall provide appropriate procedures in its legislation to ensure observance of agreements to arbitrate and for the recognition and enforcement of arbitral awards in such disputes. A member state which has implemented the 1958 United Nations Convention on the Recognition and Enforcement of Foreign Arbitral Awards or the Arbitration Rules of the United Nations Commission on International Trade Law shall be deemed to be in compliance with the provisions of para 2 of this Article. Antigua and Barbuda (1989), Barbados (1993), Dominica (1988) and Trinidad & Tobago (1966) are some of the 112 countries which have become parties to the Convention through ratification, accession or succession.

The Convention applies to 'arbitral awards not considered as domestic awards in the state where their recognition and enforcement are sought'.

The Convention provides that:

> ... each Contracting State shall recognise an agreement in writing under which parties undertake to submit to arbitration all or any differences which have arisen or which may arise between them in respect of a defined legal relationship, whether contractually or not, concerning a subject matter capable of settlement by arbitration (Article II.I).

Article III provides that:

> Each Contracting State shall recognise arbitral awards as binding and enforce them in accordance with the rules of procedure of the territory where the award is relied upon, under the conditions laid down in the following articles. There shall not be imposed substantially more onerous conditions or higher fees or charges on the recognition or enforcement of arbitral awards to which the Convention applies than are imposed on the recognition or enforcement of domestic arbitral awards.

Thus, Article III simplifies the procedure and assimilates the enforcement of an international award to that of a domestic award.

The importance of this Convention to developing countries (who are usually the weaker party in bargain) is that it enables them to invoke an international guarantee even in the territory of a stronger power.

Barring extremely unusual circumstances, such as fraud or corruption or absence of jurisdiction in the award, the presumption in favour of the validity of the award prevails. The award can therefore be easily confirmed as a court judgment and payment can be enforced as such.

Costs and speed

These may be controversial in these times but, generally speaking, this would be true of special arbitration such as trade, commodity and maritime disputes. The downside is that arbitration fees are very high and the parties have to pay for the hotel accommodation and the physical facilities of the arbitration.

Uncertainties of foreign litigation

Parties are able to avoid the uncertainties of foreign litigation, such as unfamiliarity with foreign law, questions of forum and jurisdiction, translation of documents, interpretation of evidence, fear of incompetent judges and unfamiliar rules of procedure and evidence, and claims of sovereign immunity.

On balance, then, if those arguments are accepted, arbitration would still carry manifest advantages over litigation.

Shelton lists the following as advantages of arbitration over litigation:[8]

(a) Arbitration proceedings are most suitable for certain specific commercial disputes, eg, in the construction industry and the maritime industry where an arbitrator with a special skill in the trade may be more appropriate than a judge who would not have the special training.

(b) Arbitration is more suited for disputes involving technical matters where a technically skilled arbitrator can be appointed than is litigation.

(c) Arbitration is much more flexible than litigation and in certain types of disputes, it is easier to resolve issues if the strict rules of evidence are not followed.

(d) Arbitration is a lot quicker, if properly managed, than a court case.

(e) Arbitration is better for trade specific issues.

(f) Because arbitration is a contractual animal, it is accordingly more consensual than litigation.

---

8   *Op cit*, fn 2, pp 91–92.

(g) In arbitration, the parties are free, if they agree, to adopt virtually any forum and procedure which they consider suitable in the particular circumstances, while in litigation the parties have no choice of forum, judge or procedure.

(h) The decision of the arbitrator is final in this jurisdiction,[9] while judgments in court cases can be appealed up to the Privy Council. There is, therefore, more certainty in arbitration.

(i) Arbitrations are more confidential than litigation and, therefore, more useful for sensitive and large commercial matters.

(j) Arbitrations using international arbitration rules are now often more acceptable to international contractors than litigation.

(k) Because of the contractual nature of an arbitration, the parties are able to choose the tribunal and the identity of the arbitrators making up the tribunal, which the parties cannot do in litigation. As a result, not only are the arbitrators more likely to be more informed and skilled in the area of the dispute than judges, they are available to do all the interlocutory applications as well as the final hearing. This means that by the time the parties get to the final hearing the arbitrator is totally familiar with the matter, thus leading to a more consistent and interactive adjudication process than in court.

(l) In an arbitration, the location of the hearing can move from place to place in order to facilitate the arbitrator or the parties and their witnesses, while in litigation the location is confined to a particular court. Arbitrations are therefore more convenient.

(m) In an arbitration, the arbitrator can give directions at any stage which they consider appropriate for resolving the dispute, while in litigation the summons for directions is at a particular stage of the proceedings.

Craig, Park and Paulson have their take as well. They say that:

> International Commercial Arbitration is often the only adjudicatory process acceptable to both parties to State contracts. They may feel mutual distrust of each other's national courts. A state may seek arbitration to avoid publicity, or to avoid subjection to a foreign State court which may appear as an affront to its sovereignty. The multinational enterprises may fear that the courts of the host country might be unduly influenced by the government, or that without submission to arbitration there may be no certainty of waiver of the State's immunity.[10]

ARBITRATION IN CARICOM[11]

CARICOM countries have statutes on arbitration which are mostly based on English arbitration legislation of 1889 and 1934, later consolidated into the Arbitration Act 1950. The arbitration laws of the Bahamas, Belize, Guyana, and Jamaica are based on the antiquated 1889 English Arbitration Act, whereas those of Antigua and Barbuda, Barbados, Dominica, Grenada, St Kitts and Nevis, St Lucia, St Vincent & the

---

9   There is a lot of case law on what constitutes 'final'. Readers are referred to the standard English titles on arbitration which deal extensively with the question.

10   *International Chamber of Commerce Arbitration*, 3rd edn, 2000, Oceana Publications, p 17.

11   Materials for this section of Chapter 5 are taken from Alfred Clarke's unpublished paper on arbitration delivered to a conference on Inter-American Commercial Arbitration, 1997, *op cit*, fn 3.

Grenadines and Trinidad & Tobago are based on the more modern English Arbitration Act 1950.

A legitimate question to ask is: why has the Caribbean not moved with speed to update its arbitration laws? In 1991, the Caribbean Law Institute (CLI), in association with the Caribbean Law Institute Centre (CLIC),[12] consulted widely and prepared a model law on both domestic and international arbitration.

The proposals made by the CLI Advisory Committee on Arbitration in 1991 included:

(a) that a distinction should be made between domestic and international arbitration and there should be two enactments dealing with domestic and international arbitration respectively;

(b) that the United Nations Commission on International Trade Law (UNCITRAL) Model Law should be adopted by the CARICOM countries for international arbitrations;

(c) that the UNCITRAL Arbitration Rules should be adopted for international arbitrations to supplement the UNCITRAL Model Law;

(d) that legislation should provide for time limits on the commencement of arbitration proceedings;

(e) that the right of appeal from arbitrators to the courts should be limited and, in this respect, the English arbitration legislation of 1979 should provide a useful precedent; and

(f) in the case of international arbitration, that reasoned awards should be compulsory but they should be given in domestic arbitrations only when requested by the parties.[13]

THE DRAFT MODEL LAW ON DOMESTIC ARBITRATION

The main features of the domestic arbitration draft law will now be discussed. A domestic arbitration agreement means an arbitration which is not an international arbitration agreement, while an international arbitration means an agreement pursuant to which an arbitration is, or if commenced would be, international within the meaning of Article 1(3) of the UNCITRAL Model Law. Thus, there is reference to the UNCITRAL Model Law in the case of two important concepts.

The Bill applies to domestic arbitration agreements and to an arbitration pursuant to such an agreement, except where a dispute has arisen and the parties have subsequently agreed in writing that the agreement is, or is to be treated as an international agreement, or as an international agreement to which the International Arbitration Act (if enacted) shall apply.

---

12 The CLI was established in 1988 and the CLIC in 1994. CLI and the CLIC are administered jointly by the Florida State University and the University of the West Indies. The aim of CLI/CLIC is to further promote law reform in the English speaking Caribbean. Accordingly the CLI/CLIC undertook a number of projects, one of which included a review of the arbitration legislation in the CARICOM countries.

13 In 1991, two model bills, one dealing with domestic arbitration and the other with international commercial arbitration, were drafted by Mr Brymor Pollard, a director of CLI and the Legal Consultant of CARICOM. The draft bills were presented to a meeting of the Fellows of the CLI, who include most of the Attorneys General of the CARICOM states. Neither of the draft bills has as yet been enacted by any CARICOM country.

It also applies to Convention awards, that is, awards made in pursuance of an arbitration agreement in a state or territory other than the state which has enacted this particular legislation, and which is a party to the New York Convention. The Bill states that Convention awards shall, subject to Part IV, be enforceable in the same manner as the award of an arbitrator. 'Court' as used in the Bill means the High Court of the respective jurisdictions.

CONCILIATION

Unlike any of the existing legislation, Part II of the Model Law provides for conciliation. In any case where an arbitration agreement provides for the appointment of a conciliator by a person who is not one of the parties and that person refuses to make the appointment or does not make it within the time specified, or within a reasonable time, the court or a judge thereof may, on the application of any party to the agreement, appoint a conciliator. The conciliator shall have the like powers to act in the conciliation proceedings as if he had been appointed in accordance with the terms of the agreement. The arbitration agreement shall be deemed to contain a provision which terminates the conciliation or arbitration, as the case may be, where the conciliation proceedings fail to produce a settlement acceptable to the parties within three months or such longer period as may be agreed by the parties.

The arbitrator is also permitted to act as conciliator, so long as all the parties to a reference consent in writing and for so long as no party withdraws, in writing, their consent. Further, no objection shall be taken to the conduct of the arbitration proceedings by an arbitrator solely on the ground that they had acted previously as a conciliator in accordance with this section. The authority of an arbitrator appointed by or by virtue of an arbitration agreement shall, unless the contrary intention is expressed in the agreement, be irrevocable except by leave of the court or a judge thereof.

The agreement shall not be discharged by the death of any party thereto, but shall be enforceable by or against the personal representative of the deceased. Further, the authority of an arbitrator shall not be revoked by the death of any party by whom the arbitrator was appointed. However, this provision does not affect the operation of any rule of law by virtue of which any right of action is extinguished by the death of a person.

Clause 8 deals with the issue of staying court proceedings where there is a submission to arbitration. This provision is identical to that which exists in the present law of those countries which have based their laws on the 1950 Arbitration Act of England and Wales. The court has the power to consolidate two or more arbitrations in respect of identical parties where it appears to the court that some common question of law or fact arises in both or all of them, or the relief claimed arises out of the same transaction or series of transactions, or that for some other reason it is desirable to make an order under that section. Section 11 contains similar provisions to those found in the existing laws. Unless a contrary intention is expressed therein, every arbitration agreement shall, if no other mode of reference is provided, be deemed to include a provision that the reference shall be to a single arbitrator. In the case of a reference in the agreement to two arbitrators, it shall be deemed to include a provision that the two arbitrators may appoint a third arbitrator at any time after they are themselves appointed. One wonders, however, why they were not required to appoint the third arbitrator within a specified time, or immediately upon their appointment, as in the English legislation.

Clause 12 deals with the power of parties to fill vacancies left by the refusal to act, incapacity or death of an arbitrator. In such a case, the party who appointed the arbitrator may appoint a new arbitrator. This is certainly an improvement on the existing law, under which it is necessary to go to the courts for such an appointment. This may result in much faster appointments than under the existing law. Further, if one party fails to appoint an arbitrator, whether originally or by way of substitution, for 14 clear days after the other party, having appointed an arbitrator, has served the party making default with notice to make an appointment, then the party who has appointed an arbitrator may appoint that arbitrator to act as sole arbitrator, and that arbitrator's award shall be binding on both parties as if the arbitrator had been appointed by consent. Nevertheless, the court is given the power to set aside any appointment made in pursuance of this section. However, there are no grounds set out for such setting aside, and this may result in the court having an unnecessarily wide discretion.

Majority awards are binding.

The circumstances in the court which may appoint an arbitrator are:

(a) where an arbitration agreement provides that the case reference shall be to a single arbitrator and all the parties do not concur in the appointment of an arbitrator; or

(b) if an appointed arbitrator or third arbitrator refuses to act or is incapable of acting, or dies, and the arbitration agreement does not show that it was intended that the vacancy should not be filled and the parties do not fill the vacancy; or

(c) where a party or an arbitrator is required, or is at liberty, to appoint or concur in the appointment of an arbitrator and does not do so.

In any of these cases, any other party to the arbitration or the arbitrators may serve a written notice on the defaulting party, and if the appointment is not made within seven days, the court or a judge may appoint an arbitrator or a third arbitrator, who shall have the like powers as if they were appointed by consent of all parties. This section also covers the case where an arbitration agreement provides for the appointment of an arbitrator by a person who is neither a party nor an existing arbitrator, and that person refuses to make the appointment within the specified or a reasonable time, in which case a similar procedure is followed for the appointment of the arbitrator.

CONDUCT OF PROCEEDINGS

The Bill deals with the very important question of the substantive law and the procedural law to be applied in arbitration proceedings. Thus, clause 15 provides that an agreement, out of which the dispute or arbitration arises, shall be governed by the domestic municipal law of the place in which it is held unless:

(a) the agreement expresses a contrary intention;

(b) a subsequent agreement, entered into by all the parties to the dispute or arbitration concerned, expresses a contrary intention; or

(c) the parties agree to leave the arbitrator to determine the proper law.

With respect to the procedural law, s 16 provides that, unless a contrary intention is expressed in an arbitration agreement, the agreement shall be governed by the procedural law of that place where the arbitration is held.

A number of matters relating to the conduct of the proceedings are set out in clause 17. This provides that unless a contrary intention is expressed therein, every arbitration agreement shall be deemed to contain the following provisions:

(a) that the parties to the reference and all persons claiming through them shall, subject to any legal objection, submit to be examined by the arbitrator on oath or affirmation and produce all documents within their possession which may be required or called for;

(b) that the witnesses on the references shall, if the arbitrator thinks fit, be examined on oath or affirmation;

(c) that the arbitrator shall, unless a contrary intention is expressed in the agreement, have power to administer oaths to, or take affirmations of, the parties and witnesses on a reference under the agreement;

(d) that an arbitrator may receive any evidence that they consider relevant and shall not be bound by the rules of evidence;

(e) that a party may file a writ of *subpoena ad testificandum* or *subpoena duces tecum*, issued by the court or a judge thereof, but that a person shall not be compelled to produce any document that they could not be compelled to produce in the trial of an action.

The High Court is given a number of supervisory powers in respect of the conduct of arbitration proceedings. The court may make orders for security for costs; disclosure of documents and interrogatories; the giving of evidence by affidavit; examination on oath of any witness before an officer of the court or any other person; the preservation, interim custody or sale of any goods which are the subject matter of the reference; securing the amount in dispute; the detention, preservation or inspection of any property or thing which is the subject of the reference; and interim injunctions or the appointment of a receiver. Further, the court may, on the application of any party to the reference, remove an arbitrator who fails to use all reasonable dispatch in conducting the proceeding and making an award. An arbitrator who is so removed is not entitled to receive any remuneration in respect of their services.

PROVISIONS RELATING TO AWARDS

Subject to clause 32(2), which states that where an award is remitted, the arbitrator shall, unless the order otherwise directs, make their award within three months of the date of the order, and subject to anything to the contrary in the arbitration agreement, an arbitrator shall have power to make an award at any time. The time for making the award may be extended by order of the court or a judge thereof.

The Bill provides for finality of awards. Clause 21 states that unless a contrary intention appears, every arbitration agreement shall, where applicable, be deemed to contain a provision that the award to be made by the arbitrator shall be final and binding on the parties and the persons claiming under them. The Bill also gives the arbitrator the usual power to correct any clerical mistake or error arising from any accidental slip or omission.

In order to secure the finality of the award, the High Court is denied jurisdiction to set aside or remit an award on an arbitration agreement on the ground of errors of fact or law on the face of the award. However, an appeal shall lie to the court on any question of law arising out of an award made on an arbitration agreement, and on such an appeal the court may confirm, vary or set aside the award, or remit the award for the reconsideration of the arbitrator, together with the court's opinion on the question of law which was the subject of the appeal. Such an appeal must be brought with the consent of all the other parties in the reference or with the leave of the court. However, the court must be satisfied that one condition exists before giving leave, namely that the question of law concerned could substantially affect the rights of one or more of the parties to the arbitration agreement, and the court may make leave conditional upon the applicant complying with certain conditions. The court may also order the arbitrator to state the reasons for their award in sufficient detail to enable the court, on an appeal brought under s 27, to consider any question of law arising out of the award.

The court's supervisory powers extend to determining preliminary points of law. Under clause 28, on an application made to it by any of the parties, or with the consent of all the other parties, the court will have jurisdiction to determine any question of law arising in the course of the reference, provided that the determination of the application might produce substantial savings in costs to the parties, and the question of law is one in respect of which leave to appeal would most likely be given under clause 27(3)(b). Such a decision of the court shall be deemed to be a judgment of the court, but no appeal shall lie from such a decision unless the High Court or the Court of Appeal gives leave, and the question of law raised is one of general importance which should be considered by the Court of Appeal.

It is important to note that the right of the parties to determine the law which is to operate in the proceedings is respected by the Bill. Clause 29 provides that the court shall not grant leave to appeal or to submit a question of law to the court without the consent of the parties, if the parties have entered into an agreement in writing which excludes the right of appeal or the right to submit questions of law to the court. Such an exclusion agreement does not apply to a statutory arbitration as provided for under clause 44(1).

The court has the power to remit the matters referred to it for the reconsideration of the arbitrator, and the power to set aside the award if the arbitrator has misconducted themselves or the proceedings, or an arbitration or award has been improperly procured. The court has power under s 33 to revoke the authority of the arbitrator on the ground that the arbitrator may not be impartial, and to order that the agreement shall cease to have effect and the authority of the arbitrator be revoked if the issue of fraud on the part of one of the parties arises. In the case of an arbitrator or arbitrators being removed, the court also has the power to appoint a person or persons to act in the place of the person or persons so removed.

ENFORCEMENT OF AWARD

An award on an arbitration may, by leave of the court or a judge thereof, be enforced in the same manner as a judgment or order to the same effect. The circumstances in which enforcement of a Convention award may be refused are broadly those set out in the Convention itself. These are referred to in clause 49, as follows, namely that the person against whom it is invoked proves that:

(a) a party to the arbitration agreement was under some incapacity; or

(b) the arbitration agreement was not valid under the law to which the parties subjected it, or in the absence of such indication, under the law of the country where the award was made; or

(c) they were not given proper notice of the appointment of the arbitrator or of the arbitration proceedings, or were otherwise unable to present their case; or

(d) the award deals with a difference not contemplated by, or not falling within or beyond, the scope of the submission to arbitration; or

(e) the composition of the arbitral authority or the arbitral procedure was not in accordance with the agreement of the parties or the law of the country where the arbitration took place;

(f) the award has not yet become binding on the parties, or has been set aside or suspended by a competent authority of the country in which, or under the law of which, it was made.

Enforcement of a Convention award may also be refused if the award is in respect of a matter which is not capable of settlement by arbitration, or if it would be contrary to public policy to enforce the award. The award shall, however, be treated as severable in cases where it is possible to enforce decisions on matters submitted to arbitration which can be separated from those matters not so submitted.

A recommendation was made to enact the New York Convention into the domestic law.

INTERNATIONAL COMMERCIAL ARBITRATION BILL (1991)

Clause 3 enacts the UNCITRAL Model Law into the law of the CARICOM country which adopts it, by providing that the Model Law shall have the force of law in that country. Clause 2 provides that, in interpreting the Model Law, recourse may be had to the UNCITRAL report on the work of its Eighteenth Session, and the analytical commentary contained in the report of the Secretary General of the United Nations to the UNCITRAL Eighteenth Session.

The jurisdiction of the domestic courts is very limited. Indeed, Article 5 of the Model Law states that in matters governed by the law, no court shall intervene except where so provided in that law. Article 6 goes on to provide that the functions referred to in Articles 11(3), 11(4), 13(3), 14, 16(3) and 34(2) shall be performed by the court.

The Articles referred to in Article 6 cover a number of areas. Article 11(3) deals with the failure of a party to appoint an arbitrator, the failure of the two arbitrators appointed by the parties to appoint a third arbitrator and the failure of the parties to agree on an arbitrator. In such an event, the court or other authority specified in Article 6 shall make the appointment.

Article 11(4) covers the failure of the parties to act as required under the agreed appointment procedure, or where the parties or two arbitrators are unable to reach an agreement under that procedure, or a third party fails to perform any function entrusted to it under the procedure. In these cases, the court or other authority specified in Article 6 shall act upon the request of any of the parties.

Article 13 deals with the challenge procedure, which the parties are free to agree upon, for challenging an arbitrator. Under para (3), if the challenge under the agreed upon procedure is not successful, the challenging party may, within 30 days of receipt of notice of the decision, request the court to decide on the challenge, which decision shall be subject to no appeal.

Article 14 deals with the failure of the arbitrator to act. If the arbitrator becomes *de facto* or *de jure* unable to perform their functions or fails to act without undue delay, the parties may agree on the termination, or the arbitrator may withdraw from their office. If a controversy remains concerning any of these grounds, any party may request the court to decide on the termination of the mandate, which decision shall be subject to no appeal. It is important to note that while such a request is pending, the arbitral tribunal, including the challenged arbitrator, may continue the arbitral proceedings and make an award. This provision was included so as to prevent abuse by a party using this step to delay or obstruct the proceedings.

An application to the court to set aside an arbitral award is the only recourse in the case of dissatisfaction with the award. This is governed by Article 34, para (2) of which states that an arbitral award may be set aside by the court only if there is proof that:

(a) one of the parties was under some incapacity, or the agreement was not valid under the law to which the parties have subjected it or, failing any indication thereon, under the law of the state which seeks to set aside the arbitral award; or

(b) the party making the application was not given proper notice of the appointment of an arbitrator or of the arbitral proceedings, or was otherwise unable to present his case; or

(c) the award deals with a dispute falling outside the terms of reference of the arbitrators, provided that if the unauthorised decision is severable, only that part of the award that contains decisions on matters not submitted to arbitration may be set aside; or

(d) the composition of the tribunal was not in accordance with the agreement of the parties.

The court may also set aside the award if it finds that the subject matter of the dispute is not capable of settlement by arbitration under the law of the state, or that the award is in conflict with the public policy of the state. Where appropriate and so requested by a party, the court may suspend the setting aside proceedings in order to give the tribunal an opportunity to resume the arbitration, or take such other action as in the tribunal's opinion will eliminate the grounds for setting aside. The application for setting aside may not be made after three months have elapsed from the date on which the judgment was received, or if a request for an interpretation was made under Article 33, from the date on which the arbitral tribunal has disposed of the request.

The court also has a role to play in the recognition and enforcement of awards. Under Article 36, recognition or enforcement of an arbitral award, irrespective of the country in which it was made, may be refused only at the request of the party against whom it is invoked, if that party furnishes to the competent court proof that:

(a) a party to the arbitration agreement was under some incapacity, or the said agreement is not valid under the law to which the parties have subjected it or, failing any indication thereon, under the law of the country where the award was made; or

(b) the party against whom the award is invoked was not given proper notice of the appointment of an arbitrator or of the arbitral proceedings or was otherwise unable to present his case; or

(c) the award deals with a dispute not contemplated by or not falling within the terms of the submission to arbitration, or it contains decisions on matters beyond the scope of the submission to arbitration, provided that, if the decisions on matters submitted to arbitration can be separated from those not so submitted, that part of the award which contains decisions on matters submitted to arbitration may be recognised and enforced.

In addition, if the court finds that the subject matter of the dispute is not capable of settlement by arbitration under the law of the state, or the recognition or enforcement of the award would be contrary to the public policy of the state, it may refuse to recognise or enforce the award.

It is proposed that the provisions of the International Commercial Arbitration Bill be binding upon the Crown (state).

It is also proposed that the following documents appear as schedules to the proposed International Commercial Arbitration Bill:

(a) the report of the United Nations Commission on International Trade Law on the work of its Eighteenth Session held from 2 to 21 June 1985 (United Nations document A/40/17), the text of which is set out in the Second Schedule as an aid to interpretation;

(b) the analytical commentary contained in the report, dated 25 March 1985, of the Secretary General of the United Nations to the Eighteenth Session of the United Nations Commission on International Trade Law (United Nations document A/CN 9/264), the text of which is set out in the Third Schedule; and

(c) the arbitration rules made under the auspices of the United Nations Commission on International Trade Law, commonly known as the UNCITRAL arbitration rules. These rules shall have effect in relation to arbitrations conducted pursuant to the Bill save in cases where rules have been made by the minister under the rule making power in the Bill.

RECOMMENDATIONS OF THE CLI/CLIC

The following recommendations follow the draft model Bills on arbitration:

(a) That the CARICOM countries that have not yet ratified the United Nations Convention on the Recognition and Enforcement of Foreign Arbitral Awards (1958) (the New York Convention) and the Inter-American Convention on International Commercial Arbitration (the Panama Convention) take steps to ratify these conventions in order to establish a viable framework of law for the settlement of international disputes.

(b) That the CARICOM countries modernise and harmonise their respective country's laws to ensure that they reflect current standards and practices employed in the settlement of domestic and international disputes.

(c) That the CARICOM countries adopt the model domestic and international arbitration statutes prepared by the Caribbean Law Institute.

(d) That steps should be taken to study and harmonise dispute resolution practices of multilateral treaty organisations with ADR practices of private sector organisations, such as the American Arbitration Association, the International Chamber of Commerce and the Inter-American Commercial Arbitration Commission.

(e) That the law schools in the CARICOM region expand or modify their curricula to include the study and teaching of arbitration, negotiation and ADR.

(f) That a broad-based programme of education and training be mounted in the CARICOM region to make businessmen and professionals aware of the benefits which may be derived from attempting to settle commercial disputes by arbitration, mediation and/or conciliation.

(g) That steps be taken to disseminate to the general public, within each CARICOM country and internationally, information and advice concerning the arbitration and other alternative dispute resolution options available in the member countries of CARICOM as an adjunct to the promotion of trade and investment in CARICOM.

(h) That an arbitration and dispute resolution centre be established in a CARICOM country, which will provide a means of administering arbitrations and the resolution of disputes, as well as organising programmes of information and education.

(i) That the CARICOM countries associate for the purpose of becoming an Inter-American Commercial Arbitration Commission national section.

(j) Engage in international liaison with the Inter-American Commercial Arbitration Commission in the western hemisphere and globally.

With respect to recommendations (b), (c), (d), (g) and (h), none of them appears to have been implemented thus far. As regards recommendations (b) and (f), it is pleasing to note that CARICOM has adopted Protocol 9[14] on disputes resolution and that the University of the West Indies now teaches a course in ADR. Prior to Protocol 9, the situation was succinctly stated by Professor AR Carnegie[15] as follows:

---

14 Parts of the revised CARICOM Treaty have already been discussed in Chapter 3 on negotiation.

15 Executive Director of the Caribbean Law Institute, in a paper entitled 'Commonwealth Caribbean Regionalism: Legal Aspects' (1979) 33 Year Book of World Affairs 180.

Settlement of disputes

The Commonwealth Caribbean regional movement has no permanent tribunal exercising an international law jurisdiction, notwithstanding the existence of a regional court with jurisdiction in municipal law questions, nor is there any incorporation of United Nations mechanisms for the settlement of disputes, such as the International Court of Justice.

Many of the treaties contain provisions for compulsory settlement of disputes by reference to *ad hoc* arbitration machinery. In the Common Market Annex to the Caribbean Community Treaty, the *ad hoc* machinery is used only at the option of the Council.

Fortunately, that observation has now been overtaken by events.

INTERNATIONAL CONVENTIONS

With the event of mega-blocks and mega-markets generating increased trade between nations and commercial entities, it is reasonable to expect that we shall definitely be witnessing an unprecedented explosion of gigantic proportions in commercial arbitration.

The sources of the law of international arbitration lie in a number of international conventions, such as the New York Convention of 1958, the European Convention of 1961, the Panama Convention of 1975, the Convention Establishing the Multilateral Investment Guarantee Agency of 1985, the Convention on the Settlement of Investment Disputes of 1965, international model laws, model rules and institutional rules, such as those of the International Chamber of Commerce (ICC) and the London Court of International Arbitration (LCIA).

The following CARICOM countries have adopted the New York Convention: Antigua & Barbuda, Barbados, Dominica, St Lucia and Trinidad & Tobago. No CARICOM country has as yet adopted the Panama Convention.

St Kitts & Nevis has signed, but has not ratified, the Convention Establishing the Multilateral Investment Guarantee Agency of 1985 (MIGA).

The Bahamas, Barbados, Belize, Dominica, Grenada, Guyana, Jamaica, St Lucia, St Vincent & the Grenadines and Trinidad & Tobago have ratified the Convention Establishing the Multilateral Investment Guarantee Agency of 1985 (MIGA).

The Bahamas, Barbados, Belize, Dominica, Grenada, Guyana, Jamaica, St Kitts & Nevis, St Lucia, St Vincent & the Grenadines and Trinidad & Tobago have ratified agreements supporting programmes of the US Overseas Private Investment Corporation (OPIC).

Belize has signed, but not ratified, the Convention on the Settlement of Investment Disputes 1965 (ICSID).

Barbados, Grenada, Guyana, Jamaica, St Kitts & Nevis, St Lucia and Trinidad & Tobago have ratified the Convention on the Settlement of Investment Disputes 1965 (ICSID).

Jamaica and Trinidad & Tobago have signed, but have not ratified, the US Bilateral Investment Treaties (USBIT).

Negotiations between Barbados and the USA with respect to the USBIT are still pending.

Grenada has ratified USBIT.

The main arbitration treaties of interests to the region are as follows.

The New York Convention on the Recognition And Enforcement of Foreign Arbitral Awards (1958)

In brief, the Convention provides for the recognition and enforcement of a clause to arbitrate a present or future dispute and, also, the enforcement in another country of the ensuing arbitral award. It recognises the power of a court to stay legal proceedings between the parties to such a clause and order them to arbitrate their dispute. It simplifies and standardises the procedure for enforcing the award in the foreign country and it specifies the grounds on which the enforcement may be refused. Governments ratifying the Convention can do so reserving the right to require reciprocity and also limiting the Convention's applicability to commercial or other specified situations.

The New York Convention has been ratified by the following governments: Antigua & Barbuda, Argentina, Barbados, Bolivia, Canada, Chile, Colombia, Costa Rica, Dominica, Ecuador, Guatemala, Haiti, Mexico, Netherlands, Antilles, Panama, Peru, Trinidad & Tobago, the USA, Uruguay and Venezuela. El Salvador has signed but not ratified the Convention.

The Inter-American Convention on International Commercial Arbitration (1975) (the Panama Convention)

This Convention came into effect on 16 June 1976 and was carefully drawn to be fully compatible with the New York Convention.

The Panama Convention has been ratified by the following countries: Argentina, Brazil, Chile, Colombia, Costa Rica, Ecuador, El Salvador, Guatemala, Honduras, Mexico, Panama, Paraguay, the USA, Uruguay and Venezuela. The Convention is regulated by a Commission.

The role of the Commission

The Commission was established in 1934 as a result of Resolution XLI of the Seventh International Conference of American States at its meeting in Montevideo, Uruguay in December 1933. It maintains and administers, throughout the western hemisphere, a system for settlement of international commercial disputes by arbitration, mediation, conciliation and other alternate means of dispute resolution. The system functions through national sections in Argentina, Bolivia, Brazil, Colombia, Chile, Costa Rica, Dominican Republic, Ecuador, Guatemala, Mexico, Panama, Paraguay, Peru, Spain, Uruguay and the USA. In other southern hemisphere countries, the Commission performs all activities that would otherwise be performed by a national section. The Commission may also accept affiliates.

Working in co-operation with the national sections, the Commission provides services to parties who request conciliation or arbitration in accordance with the rules of the Commission. Arbitrations are conducted by arbitrators, who are specially selected by the parties or by the Commission, in accordance with its rules, utilising existing panels of highly qualified individuals who render awards on the merits of the disputes. Among its other purposes are: to assist in the modification of arbitration laws to facilitate the conduct of arbitrations and the enforcement of foreign arbitral awards; to carry on extensive programs of information and education; and to obtain ratification of the New York Convention (1958) and the Panama Convention (1975).

The Commission has a well-developed liaison relationship with the network of arbitration systems throughout the world, including the International Chamber of Commerce, the Japan Arbitration Association, the Indian Arbitration Council and the Foreign Trade Arbitration Commission in Moscow. A special relationship exists with the American Arbitration Association, which was one of the founders of the Commission in 1934 and which administers IACAC arbitrations in the USA.

There is also a special relationship between the Commission and the Organization of American States (OAS), whose resolution brought the IACAC into existence in 1934. The Inter-American Juridical Committee drafted the document which became the Panama Convention in 1975. The OAS has enacted resolutions over the years urging strengthening of the system and in 1997–99 co-sponsored, with the Commission, a programme of seminars in each of the 16 countries where a national section functions.

International Centre for the Settlement of Investment Disputes (ICSID)

Most of the countries in the western hemisphere have now signed the Convention on the Settlement of Investment Disputes between States and Nationals of other States (18 March 1965, 575 UNTS 159). Those countries are: Argentina, Bahamas, Barbados, Bolivia, Belize, Chile, Colombia, Costa Rica, Ecuador, El Salvador, Grenada, Guatemala, Guyana, Haiti, Honduras, Jamaica, Nicaragua, Panama, Paraguay, Peru, St Kitts & Nevis, St Lucia, Trinidad & Tobago, the USA, Uruguay and Venezuela. All except five (Belize, Colombia, Guatemala, Haiti and Uruguay) of the above countries have also ratified the Convention to become ratifying states.

According to Dr Ibrahim FI Shihata, General Counsel of the World Bank, the main features of the ICSID system are that: it is based on a treaty; it is specialised in that it is limited to investment disputes between a Contracting State and a national of another Contracting State; it gives to a party autonomy and a wide scope in the determination of applicable law and procedure to be followed during the arbitration; it is effective; it is comparatively inexpensive; and, most importantly, it is insulated from the control of national courts.

Clauses providing for the settlement of disputes under ICSID auspices have become a standard feature of investment agreements involving Contracting States and investors from other Contracting States. There are also general references to ICSID arbitration in at least 200 bilateral treaties for the encouragement and protection of investment (bilateral investment treaties) and in the investment legislation of some 20 countries. As at January 2003, 84 cases had been registered and concluded with ICSID.

Multilateral Investment Guarantee Agency (MIGA)

The Multilateral Investment Guarantee Agency (MIGA) was established on 12 April 1988 as a member of the World Bank Group. Its purpose is to encourage foreign direct investment in developing countries by providing guarantees to foreign private investors (that is, political risk insurance) against the risks of transfer restriction, expropriation, and war and civil disturbance in the host country, and to offer investment marketing services to host governments on means to improve their ability to attract foreign direct investment.

Annex II of the Convention establishing MIGA provides for settlement of disputes between a member and the Agency under Article 57. Under Article 58, for the settlement of disputes involving holders of a guarantee or reinsurance, it is provided that:

> Any dispute arising under a contract of guarantee or reinsurance between the parties thereto shall be submitted to arbitration for final determination in accordance with such rules as shall be provided for or referred to in the contract of guarantee or reinsurance.

Article 4(a)(e) states: '... the Tribunal shall determine its procedure and shall be guided in this regard by the arbitration rules adopted pursuant to the Convention on the Settlement of Investment Disputes between States and Nationals of Other States.'

The MIGA Convention has been ratified by 19 industrialised countries including Canada and the USA. The 122 ratifying developing countries include Argentina, Bahamas, Barbados, Belize, Bolivia, Brazil, Chile, Colombia, Costa Rica, Dominica, Dominican Republic, Ecuador, El Salvador, Grenada, Guatemala, Guyana, Haiti, Honduras, Jamaica, Nicaragua, Panama, Paraguay, Peru, St Lucia, St Vincent & the Grenadines, Trinidad & Tobago, Uruguay and Venezuela.

Annex II requires that the parties first attempt to negotiate a settlement before resorting to arbitration. In fact, it is anticipated that all such disputes would be settled amicably through negotiations. Failing negotiation, the parties have the option of attempting a settlement through conciliation or proceeding to arbitration.

RULES OF INTERNATIONAL ARBITRATION

In the quest for an adequate and fair machinery for international commercial arbitration and in order to eliminate uncertainty and procrastination in arbitration proceedings, a number of international arbitral bodies have drawn up their own rules for the conduct of these proceedings. Among such rules are the following:

(a) the rules for the International Chamber of Commerce (ICC) Court of Arbitration (known as the ICC Rules);

(b) the United Nations Commission on International Trade Law (UNCITRAL) Arbitration Rules (known as the UNCITRAL Arbitration Rules);

(c) the International Centre for Settlement of Investment Disputes (ICSID) Rules for Procedure for Arbitration Proceedings (known as the ICSID Arbitration Rules);

(d) the American Arbitration Association (AAA) Arbitration Rules and Supplementary Procedures (known as the AAA Arbitration Rules);

(e) the Permanent Court of Arbitration (PCA) Rules of Arbitration and Conciliation (known as the PCA Rules of Arbitration);

(f) the Association of Chartered Institute of Arbitrators (ACI) Arbitration Rules (known as the ACI Arbitration Rules);

(g) the London Court of International Arbitration Rules (known as the LCIA Rules); and

(h) the rules of the Arbitration Institute of the Stockholm Chamber of Commerce.

There are other rules which are more trade-specific, such as the Grain and Feed Trade Association Arbitration Rules (GAFTA Arbitration Rules) and Maritime Arbitrator's Association Rules.[16]

Of these model rules, perhaps those which appear to attempt some incorporation of the developing world's concerns are those of UNCITRAL and ICSID of the World Bank. Because of the increasing use of the ICSID model rules by the region, a word on the ICSID Convention may be in order.

The International Centre for Settlement of Investment Disputes (ICSID or 'the Centre') is a public international organisation established by a multilateral treaty, the 1965 Convention on the Settlement of Investment Disputes between States and Nationals of Other States ('the Convention').[17] The purpose of ICSID, as set forth in Article 1(2) of the Convention, is to provide facilities for the conciliation and arbitration of investment disputes between Contracting States and nationals of other Contracting States. The jurisdiction of the Centre, or in other terms the scope of the Convention, is elaborated upon in Article 25(1) of the Convention. It defines ICSID's jurisdiction as extending to 'any legal dispute arising directly out of an investment, between a Contracting State (or any constituent subdivision or agency of a Contracting State designated to the Centre by that State) and a national of another Contracting State, which the parties to the dispute consent in writing to submit to the Centre'.

The consent of the parties has been described as the 'cornerstone' of the jurisdiction of the Centre as thus defined.[18] There are also clauses for use in conjunction with the Rules Governing the Additional Facility for the Administration of Proceedings by the Secretariat of ICSID ('the Additional Facility Rules')[19] which are available for certain types of proceedings between states and foreign nationals falling outside the scope of the Convention. A concluding section of the brochure contains an example of an *ad hoc* arbitration clause designating the Secretary General of the Centre as the appointing authority of arbitrators.

As at 3 November 2003, 154 states had signed the Convention, while 139 states had ratified the ICSID Convention. These included the Bahamas, Barbados, Belize,

---

16 Shelton, SM, 'Arbitration as an Alternative Means of Dispute Resolution: An Introductory Road Map' (2001) 26(1) and (2) WILJ 86.

17 The Convention, 575 UNTS 159, is reprinted, together with the Report of the World Bank Executive Directors on the Convention, in Doc ICSID/2. Pursuant to Article 6(1) of the Convention, the Administrative Council of the Centre has adopted Administrative and Financial Regulations, Rules of Procedure for the Institution of Conciliation and Arbitration Proceedings Institution Rules), Rules of Procedure for Conciliation Proceedings (Conciliation Rules) and Rules of Procedure for Arbitration Proceedings (Arbitration Rules). References in this brochure to such Regulations and Rules are to those adopted with effect from 26 September 1984 and reprinted in ICSID Basic Documents, Doc ICSID/15 (Jan 1985).

18 Report of the World Bank Executive Directors on the Convention, *ibid*, para 23.

19 The Additional Facility Rules are reprinted in Doc ICSID/ 11 (June 1979).

Grenada, Guyana, Jamaica, St Vincent & the Grenadines, St Kitts & Nevis, St Lucia and Trinidad & Tobago.

Now, a few comments. First, the ICSID Convention provides a forum for conflict resolution in a framework designed to balance the interests and requirements of all the parties involved, with particular emphasis on a depoliticisation of investment disputes.[20] Secondly, ICSID's facilities are provided to disputants on a voluntary basis. Accordingly, the decision of a state not to subscribe to the ICSID Convention technically has no bearing on its relationship with the World Bank.

Thirdly, under Article 25(4) of the Convention, any contracting state may limit the class of disputes that it may place before ICSID's auspices. Under this authority, Jamaica has excluded from the jurisdiction of ICSID disputes relating to 'minerals or other natural resources'. Guyana also made a similar reservation as Jamaica but subsequently withdrew its declaration.

The Jamaican declaration led to a series of arbitrations when Jamaica sought to withdraw from ICSID jurisdiction retroactively. In 1974, in spite of a provision regarding the 'stabilisation' of the relevant tax system, Jamaica decided to increase significantly the taxes payable by investors. One month before that decision was published, Jamaica notified ICSID that disputes arising out of an 'investment relating to minerals or other natural resources' would not be subject to ICSID jurisdiction and sought to give to that notification retrospective effect. Immediately after the commencement of the new tax legislation, the investors affected by it instituted ICSID arbitration proceedings. A preliminary issue to determine was whether the notification by Jamaica deprived ICSID of jurisdiction. The arbitral tribunal held that the consent to ICSID arbitration, given in the investment agreements, could not be unilaterally withdrawn through such a notification or otherwise.[21]

While the Convention requires that the dispute arise 'directly out of an investment', it deliberately does not define the latter term. The Report of the World Bank Executive Directors on the Convention explains that such definition was not attempted 'given the essential requirement of consent by the parties'.[22] Parties, thus, have much, though not unlimited, discretion to determine whether their transaction constitutes an investment. The fact that the parties consent to submit a dispute to the Centre, of course, implies that they consider it to arise out of an investment. If the parties wish to strengthen the presumption, they may include an explicit statement to that effect in the consent agreement. Thus, the parties have considerably greater freedom to determine whether their dispute is one that is suitable for ICSID's intervention. It is said that 'this lack of definition, which was deliberate has enabled the ICSID Convention to accommodate both traditional types of investment in the form of capital contributions and new types of investment including service contracts and transfers of technology'.

Fourthly, the ICSID Rules are flexible enough to allow the parties to derogate from them in order to accommodate their particular needs. So, for example, the rules governing the number of arbitrators and the manner of their appointment are

---

20   Shihata, IF, *Towards a Greater Depoliticization of Investment Disputes: The Roles of ICSID and MIGA*, 1992, ICSID publication, pp 1–32.
21   See *ICSID Case No ARB/74/2* and others; also (1976) 17 Harv Int LJ 98.
22   *Op cit*, fn 17.

permissive. Those Rules only apply as default clauses where the parties do not stipulate otherwise.

Fifthly, the Rules ensure the efficacy of an award, when made. The procedure laid down in Article 54(2) of the Convention provides that a party may obtain recognition and enforcement of the award by furnishing a certified copy thereof to the competent court or other authority designated for the purpose in each contracting state. Here, too, it is said that 'this simple procedure eliminates the problems of the recognition and enforcement of foreign arbitral awards, which subsist in domestic laws and *under other international conventions*'.[23]

Finally, Article 42(1) of the Convention provides that a tribunal shall decide a dispute in accordance with such rules of law as may be agreed by the parties. The parties are free to agree on rules of law, defined as they choose. They may refer to a national law, international law, a combination of national and international law, or a law frozen in time or subject to certain modifications.[24]

Article 42(3) of the Convention provides that a tribunal may decide a dispute *ex aequo et bono* if the parties so agree. This is somewhat of a departure from the basic rule that an arbitrator must decide a case according to law. It permits an arbitrator to factor into the decision the principles of equity and good conscience without ignoring the fundamental rules of arbitration.

PLACE OF ARBITRATION

Because the choice and location of arbitration considerably affects the costs, developing countries in the Caribbean need to pay some attention to the creation of a regional centre for arbitration. In settling on a choice of venue, considerations of economic, social, political and legal implication must be taken into account. Currently, the venue is chosen purely on grounds of convenience and, invariably, all are exotic and extremely expensive locations such as London, Geneva, Paris, Hong Kong, Washington and New York.

The question of a venue for arbitration ties in with the larger responsibility of how to draft an arbitration clause to take care of specific concerns. As pointed out by Stephen Bond:[25]

---

23 *Op cit*, fn 17, emphasis added.

24 If the parties do not reach agreement on the matter, then Article 42(1) of the Convention specifies that the Tribunal shall apply 'the law of the Contracting State party to the dispute (including its rules on the conflict of laws) and such rules of international law as may be applicable'.

25 Bond, SR, Former Secretary General of the ICC International Court of Arbitration, 'How to Draft an Arbitration Clause' (1989) J Int Arb 66.
Other essential elements of a well-drafted arbitration clause referred to in the article are:
(a) *ad hoc* or institutional arbitration;
(b) the dangers in the standard arbitration clause;
(c) the applicable law;
(d) the composition of the arbitral tribunal;
(e) the language of the arbitration;
(f) waiver of appeal/exclusion agreement; and
(g) entry of judgment stipulation.

The importance of the place of arbitration cannot be overestimated. Its legislation determines the likelihood and extent of involvement of national courts in the conduct of the arbitration (either for judicial 'assistance' or 'interference'), the likelihood of enforceability of the arbitral award (depending on what international conventions the situs State is a party to), and the extent and nature of any mandatory procedural rules that you will have to adhere to in the conduct of the arbitration. (For example, in Saudi Arabia, the arbitrators must be Muslim and male.) Such factors are of far greater importance than the touristic attractions of any particular place that sometimes appear to be the decisive factor in making this decision.

Referring to some dramatic illustrations, Bond says:

> The choice of the place of arbitration may literally determine the outcome of the case. In one ICC arbitration[26] between a Finnish corporation and an Australian corporation, London was selected as the place of arbitration in the arbitration clause. The case involved royalty payments allegedly not made and the purported cancellation of the relevant agreement in 1976. In 1982 the licensor initiated arbitration. The arbitrator found that because the arbitration was taking place in England, the statute of limitations contained in the English Limitation Act had to be applied. So, even assuming that Finnish law was applicable and Finnish law had no comparable statute of limitations, the arbitrator applied the relevant English 6-year statute of limitations and barred all claims arising prior to 1976, which effectively meant all claims. (A subsequent amendment to the law exempts from the scope of the Limitation Act international arbitrations in England where neither party is English.)
>
> Yet a final example, to show that even this apparently simple choice cannot be made lightly. A case in a United States Federal Court involved an arbitration in a contract between American and Iranian parties drafted before the Iranian Revolution which had fixed Iran as the site of the arbitration. The US Court refused to accept a request by one of the parties to the contracts to shift the *situs* of the arbitration to the United States. The Court stated that it had:
>
> > No statutory or equitable mandate that allows us to redraft the agreement premised on the convenience of the parties *ex post*. ... There is neither doctrine nor policy that supplies (the Iranian party) a polestar with which to circumnavigate the plain language of its forum selection clause and thereby avoid its initial, unequivocal and contractually chosen course.

THE TREND TOWARDS HARMONISATION AND THE FUTURE

The growth in international commercial arbitration has provoked rapid development towards the harmonisation of the law and, particularly, the practice of international arbitration. The prime examples are the New York Convention of 1958 and the UNCITRAL Model Law and the UNCITRAL Rules.

The trend in harmonisation also accounts for the many new arbitration statutes in a number of countries, for example, the UK Arbitration Act 1979, similar acts in Hong Kong, Australia, France, Belgium, the Netherlands and Switzerland and the CLI Model Laws for the Caribbean. Mention must be made of the well-known international arbitral institutions such as International Chamber of Commerce, the

---

26 *Licensor Oy (Finland) v Licensee Pty (Australia)* (1985) 2(1) J Int Arb 75.

American Arbitration Association, the London Court of International Arbitration and the International Centre for Settlement of Investment Disputes.

Another area of significant expansion, as a result of globalisation, has been intellectual property and its impact on arbitration. This trinity of globalisation, intellectual property and arbitration has led to the use of arbitration for the settlement of domain name disputes in cyberspace.

Global trade, treaties and markets provide a necessary impetus to sustained economic activity and trade. Where there is trade, there are trade disputes. Clearly, the volume and intensity of trade, as a result of free enterprise and open markets, means that no one country would have the capacity to handle and deal with commercial disputes intra-nationally. This growth in trade will undoubtedly stimulate interest in commercial arbitration. So, despite all criticisms, arbitration is likely to grow by leaps and bounds. One commentator has observed that 'the lifeblood of globalization is foreign direct investment, which usually consists of equity investment by a firm in a foreign country'.[27]

With the tremendous increase in international trade and investments, there has evolved a pattern of bilateral investment treaties (BITS), each with its own dispute settlement terminology. Many of these have similarities and, in recognition of the common denominators as well as the possibilities of overlap and confrontation, the trade ministers of the Organization of American States member countries established, on 16 May 1997 in Belo Horizonte, Brazil, a new working group to collect and catalogue information and recommend measures to harmonise the disparities.

That working group was mandated to pursue a common policy on dispute settlement within the overall goal of reaching a Free Trade Area of the Americas as envisioned by the summit meeting of heads of state and governments in Miami in 1994.

Mention may also be made of the FTAA Working Group on Dispute Settlement of the OAS which, at the Second Ministerial Trade Meeting in Cartagena, Colombia, 21 March 1996, was requested to compile information on the dispute settlement mechanisms being used in bilateral and subregional trade agreements in the USA, Canada, Latin America and the Caribbean. The Trade Unit and the Secretariat of Legal Affairs of the OAS thereafter prepared an initial response comparing the dispute settlement provisions of 18 regional trade agreements with the World Trade Organization Dispute Settlement Understanding.[28]

International commercial arbitration continues to face a number of challenges brought about by the forces of globalisation. Among these are cultural sensitivies, the problem of overlapping jurisdictions and remedies, harmonisation of arbitration rules, accountability of arbitrators, compatibility of arbitration with public policy and national sovereignty. As neatly put by Cremades and Cairns, 'it would be a grave mistake to ignore the challenges of the brave new world of international arbitration'.

---

27 Cremades, BM and Cairns, DJA, 'The Brave New World of Global Arbitration' (2002) 3 Journal of World Investment 1–41.
28 This document, entitled 'Dispute Settlement Mechanisms in Regional and Sub-Regional Trade Integration Arrangements' is to be found in its reference Gi/LATU/WG.DISP/97/DOC.1/rev 1 of 7 July 1997 on Dispute Settlement.

In a paper on inter-American commercial arbitration,[29] Charles Marberg drew attention to the rapidly changing face of international commercial arbitration and made a linkage to the projected accelerated pace of these developments as a result of helpful financial assistance from the Inter-American Development Bank. Through the IDB, funds have been made available in several countries to analyse the existing legal structures and prepare legislation which will bring the national juridical systems into harmony with contemporary practices of arbitration, mediation and conciliation.

In the light of the multiplicity of commercial arbitration systems and rules, the search for the use of the correct arbitration and alternative dispute resolution procedure to resolve an inter-American commercial dispute will require a high degree of skill and care on the part of attorneys.

SOME QUESTIONS TO PONDER

(a) What is arbitration? How does it differ from litigation? From mediation?

(b) Should arbitrators approach cases like judges, like jurors, or in some other way?

(c) Should arbitrators apply the law to the facts or, instead, attempt to reach a decision that is fair or, perhaps, reach a decision that is accepted by the parties?

(d) From a societal standpoint, what are some of the potential advantages and disadvantages of private binding arbitration as compared to litigation?

(e) From a litigant's standpoint, what are some of the potential advantages and disadvantages of private binding arbitration as compared to litigation?

(f) What makes arbitration particularly appealing in the international commercial context?

(g) Why are arbitral awards generally more enforceable than court awards in foreign countries?

(h) What accounts for the relative lack of enthusiasm for arbitration in the Caribbean?

(i) In what circumstances may a court refuse to enforce an arbitral award?

(j) Can an arbitral award be reversed because it violates public policy?

---

29 Delivered on 19 September 1997 in Belo Horizonte, Brazil (unpublished).

CHAPTER 6

DISPUTE RESOLUTION MECHANISMS IN THE WORLD TRADE ORGANIZATION

INTRODUCTION

So important is the dispute resolution mechanism introduced into the WTO that it merits special attention. Indeed, it is accepted by many that the adoption of the WTO dispute settlement mechanism was one of the signal achievements of the Uruguay Round, indeed, the centerpiece of the WTO. This is because, unlike many international organisations, the 'WTO has a dispute settlement system, to which its members must submit, with the authority to issue binding legal judgments on issues of great political and economic significance'.[1] With some euphoria, the first WTO Director General has described dispute resolution as 'the WTO's most individual contribution to the stability of the global economy because it helps the global community's ability to resolve highly-charged disputes on the trade area'.[2] To appreciate the import of this introduction, it may be useful to trace, albeit very briefly, the history behind the WTO.

The WTO Agreement, which came into force in 1995, is inextricably linked to the umbilical cord of the GATT. Indeed, the GATT principles, which the WTO Agreement has adopted, remain at the core of this global arrangement for international trade. GATT was influenced principally by economic and political benefits for settling agreed rules between nations for regulating trade. Among the *economic* arguments for common rules of free trade were:

(a) the law of comparative advantage;

(b) economies of scale;

(c) consumer benefit from greater competition;

(d) domestic industries spurred to greater efficiency by import competition; and

(e) promotion of foreign investment and introduction of technology.

Among the *political* arguments were the belief that free trade led to:

(a) openness of the economy;

(b) reduction of the likelihood of war; and

(c) greater political stability.

The origins of GATT can be traced to the Great Depression of the 1930s, which led countries to take unilateral action by way of imposing high tariffs, import quotas and export subsidies in order to protect balance of payments. Governments realised that this was self-defeating, leading to uneven and discriminatory bilateral trade

---

1   Lichtenbaum, P, 'Procedural Issues in WTO Dispute Resolution' (1998) 19(4) Michigan Journal of International Law 1195–274; Petersmann, E, 'International Trade Law and the GATT/WTO Dispute Settlement System, 1948–1996: An Introduction' (1997) 11 Studies in Transnational Economic Law.

2   Ruggiero, R, 'The Future Path of the Multilateral Trading System', address to the Korean Business Association on 17 April 1997, available at www.wto.org/english/news_e/sprr_e/seoul_e.htm.

arrangements.[3] The inefficiencies inherent in bilateral, as opposed to multilateral, arrangements led to the need for permanent institutions to regulate the world economy. This was the milieu in which global institutions such as the World Bank (then called the International Bank for Reconstruction and Development), the IMF and the International Trade Organization were born. The International Trade Organization (ITO) did not receive the support of the US. It died a natural death but that death led to the birth of GATT.

CORNERSTONE PRINCIPLES

While GATT had a number of structural problems,[4] it contained a number of cornerstone principles which have been continued in the WTO Agreement. That explains why a fleeting reference to GATT has been necessary. Among the cornerstone principles preserved by the WTO Agreement are:

(a) most favoured nation clause;

(b) binding tariff regimes;

(c) equal treatment of nations;

(d) right to freedom of transit;

(e) right of members to impose anti-dumping and countervailing duties;

(f) uniform rules for the valuation of imports for custom purposes;

(g) labelling for the sake of consumer protection;

(h) transparency of laws and regulations governing international trade; and

(i) prohibition of use of import or export quotas.

As of today, the WTO has over 144 members and covers about 90% of world trade. Its functions include:

(a) administering WTO agreements;

(b) acting as a forum for trade regulations;

(c) handling trade disputes;

(d) monitoring national trade policies;

(e) technical assistance and training for developing countries; and

(f) co-operation with other international organisations.

---

3   The best known of these reciprocal agreements are the US Reciprocal Trade Agreements Act of 1934, inspired by US Secretary of State, Cordell Hull. Cordell Hull is credited with negotiating 32 US bilateral agreements over a period of 11 years.

4   Among the weaknesses of GATT were the following: GATT covered only trade in goods but not in services; trade in textiles was covered by separate agreements that provided managed rather than free trade; there were major exceptions for trade in agricultural products and waivers from the general rules were granted to powerful members; the dispute resolution system was weak. Any member could block the adoption of a panel report. Also, there were no time limits and there was a lack of consistency among reports. Finally, there was no appellate review.

There are a number of annexes to the WTO Agreement which ought to be of interest to the student of ADR.[5]

Important aspects of the WTO Agreement include the following principles or philosophies:

(a) a single undertaking whereby nations may either take it or leave it;[6]

(b) inclusion of trade in agricultural goods and textiles;

(c) inclusion of trade in services;

(d) inclusion of intellectual property rights;

(e) strengthening of the dispute resolution system.

It is the last philosophy that leads directly to consideration of the dispute resolution mechanism scheme set up by the WTO Agreement.[7] But, before such consideration, it may be sensible to set out the ostensible advantages of WTO membership. These can be summarised as follows:

(a) market access;

(b) rules-based systems;

(c) access to dispute resolution processes;

(d) stability of trade relationships;

(e) lock-in economic reforms;

(f) attraction of foreign investment; and

(g) benefits of an open market.

---

5   Annexes to the WTO Agreement include the following:
     Agreements on Trade in Goods
     GATT 1974
         Specific Agreements:
         Agriculture
         Sanitary and Phytosanitary Measures (SPS)
         Textiles and Clothing
         Technical Barriers in Trade (TBT)
         Trade-Related Investment Measures (TRIMS)
         Implementation of Article VI (Anti-dumping)
         Implementation of Article VII (Customs Valuation)
         Preshipment Inspection
         Rules of Origin
         Improper Licensing
         Subsidies and Countervailing Measures (SCM)
         Safeguards
     General Agreement on Trade in Services (GATS)
     Agreement on Trade-Related Aspects of Intellectual Property Rights (TRIPS)
     Dispute Settlement Understanding (DSU)
     Trade Policy Review Mechanism (TPRM), and
     Plurilateral Trade Agreements.
6   This observation has to be adjusted to take into account the plurilateral agreements allowed by the WTO.
7   For the inspired student, one of the best books on the WTO is Hoekman, B, Mattoo, A and English, P (eds), *Development, Trade and the WTO (A Handbook)*, 2000, The World Bank, especially Chapters 9 and 10. See also *The Legal Texts: The Results of the Uruguay Round of Multilateral Trade Negotiations*, 1999, WTO/Cambridge University Press.

These are, of course, controversial from the viewpoint of developing countries who feel that they have not received a fair share of the expansion of trade. Indeed, it is acknowledged that developed countries have, since 1995, imposed abnormally high tariffs on items of particular interest to developing countries, such as clothing and textiles, footwear, leather, travel goods, fish, processed foods and agricultural products.[8] The Chief Economist to the World Bank made the following telling observation:

> As developing countries do take steps to open their economies and expand their exports, in too many sectors they find themselves confronting significant trade barriers – leaving them, in effect, with neither aid nor trade. They quickly run up against dumping duties, when no economist would say they are really engaged in dumping, or they face protected or restricted markets in their areas of natural comparative advantage, like agriculture or textiles ...

> Thus, to many in the developing world, trade policy in the more advanced countries seems to be more a matter of self-interest than of general principle. When good economic analysis works in favour of self-interest, it is invoked; but when it does not, so much the worse for economic principles. 'Yes', the advanced countries seem to be ruling the economies in transition (and the emerging economies), 'produce what you can – but if you gain a competitive advantage over our firms, beware!' Too often, there is a not-so-subtle subtext: 'Clearly, if there were a level playing field, we could outperform you. Since you seem to be underselling us, it could only be because you are engaging in unfair trade practices!'[9]

DISPUTE RESOLUTION

Interesting as these wider issues are, attention must be turned to the dispute settlement procedure which, many would argue, is perhaps the single most important change to the system brought about by the Uruguay Round. Dispute settlement is governed by Articles XXII and XXIII of the GATT, supplemented by the Dispute Settlement Understanding (DSU), which was adopted as part of the Uruguay Round. Before 1955, the GATT dispute resolution system had the following shortcomings:

(a) there were no effective time limits to a dispute;

(b) the cases dragged on for a long time;

(c) there was a lack of consistency in decisions handed down;

(d) there were no permanent, only *ad hoc*, panels;

(e) there was no right of appeal;

(f) a losing party could block the adoption and implementation of a panel report; and

(g) enforcement was inadequate.

Now, under the WTO Agreement, a panel report must be adopted unless all members agree that it should not. Also, strict time limits have been introduced – roughly 15 months for the decision (including the appeal, if any), and another 15 months for

---

8   Macrory, P, 'Developing Countries and the WTO', a paper prepared for the Nefas/Nepal-American Chamber of Commerce Seminar on WTO and Globalisation, 21–22 November 2000.

9   Stiglitz, JE, 'Two Principles for the Next Round, Or How to Bring Developing Countries in from the Cold', speech delivered on 21 September 1999, available at www.worldbank.org/knowledge/chiefecon/articles/geneva.htm.

implementation. An appellate body is now a permanent feature of the new regime, with the responsibility to review panel decisions upon the request of a party. It has been said that this has introduced greater consistency in the process. According to Claude Berfield,[10] the new dispute resolution scheme makes the WTO a unique international organisation, because 'no other international body presides over rules that extend so deeply into the economic life and fabric of domestic economies, and no other body possesses a strictly binding dispute settlement system, complete with legal retaliation'.

That statement may well be a slight exaggeration. For example, decisions of the International Court of Justice (ICJ) are always binding, once the court gets jurisdiction to hear the case. What is accurate is that parties to a dispute before the ICJ must *first* grant consent to jurisdiction, so that UN members do not have to access the ICJ's jurisdiction unless they are bound by an expressed or *forum prorogatum* consent. It must be pointed out that the Law of the Sea Convention also has a compulsory dispute settlement mechanism.

Annex 2 to the Marrakesh Agreement, establishing the WTO Agreement, sets out the rules and procedures governing the settlement of disputes, otherwise known as The Dispute Settlement Understanding (DSU). Persons desirous of learning details as to how the dispute resolution mechanism works are advised to study Annex 2. However, some pertinent observations may be made now. The principles which underpin the WTO Agreement are transparency and procedural fairness in trade regimes, access to the market and fair competition within the market.

WTO law is enforced in two ways:

(a) outside the WTO, through informal bilateral negotiations or challenges in a domestic forum in which WTO law replicates domestic law; and

(b) inside the WTO, from inquiries through WTO bodies and the initiation of formal proceedings under the DSU.

It must be pointed out at the outset that the DSU represents quite a small part of the enforcement procedures within the WTO. Not surprisingly, most enforcement procedures in the WTO are informal, through bilateral negotiation conducted by diplomatic representatives, but within WTO rules. Against that backdrop of informality, WTO rules are enforced through diplomatic discourse.

In the civil law tradition, and especially in Latin America, domestic law almost equates with international law and vice versa.[11] This provides an additional advantage to a complaining country that could, literally, file a WTO complaint in its domestic court. Such a party may then be able to obtain remedies, such as an injunction and damages, which are not available under the WTO arrangements. This unique situation shows an example where WTO rules may be enforced *but wholly outside the WTO regime*.

---

10 Berfield, C, 'WTO Dispute Resolution', unpublished manuscript, 1999.
11 It must be pointed out that Chile actually used such an argument in the *Price Band* case, but the argument was ignored and the Chilean law was held to violate WTO law. See also the clash between Brazil law and WTO law discussed in Carnegie, AR, 'Conflict of International Law Regimes' (2000) XXVII Comité Jorídico Interamericano: Curso de Derecho Internacional 517.

Within the WTO, many informal avenues for the settlement of disputes are available to nations through referrals to various WTO bodies and committees.[12] By raising issues in a 'public' forum within the WTO, committee or council system, nations get to resolve disputes informally, purely through group pressure. That should please ADR practitioners.

MAIN FEATURES OF WTO DISPUTE SETTLEMENT

An underlying feature of the dispute settlement process is the recognition that the WTO is a club of sovereign nations which do not like being dictated to. In such a milieu, it makes good sense to promote mutually agreeable solutions and long-term relationships based on national interests.

Another feature is a reiteration of the basic point that dispute resolution in the WTO is only a means of negotiation. That is why 'winning' a case is only the first stage in a long battle of further negotiations. This is because the WTO has no direct enforcement mechanism. A verdict provides an opportunity for the offending state to bring itself into compliance with WTO obligations.

A number of other peculiar features need to be noted.

It is permissible for the members not in direct dispute to participate in a disputed case by lending their support. This is no more than a recognition of the principle that there is strength in numbers. Also, it provides group protection in a case where a developing country seeks to take on a big player. Alternatively, a party may intervene in a case as a full, but independent, complainant, as a third party.

Yet another feature is the single forum or 'single undertaking'. What this means is that in one single complaint, it is permissible to ventilate as many issues as possible – services, quotas, trips, etc.

While private parties do not have a right of audience – the WTO only binds nations – they have a big stake in the outcomes of complaints. Currently, the evidence shows that only nations may raise complaints before the WTO.

Unlike the case with the old GATT process, a defending party cannot block the process of dispute resolution. The decisions of the panel and the appellate body stand, unless *all* the members, including the winning party, decide to reject the overcome. That is the insurance which ensures that the decision of the arbitral panel remains intact.

The principal remedy available is a decision which invites the offending nation to bring itself within WTO compliance. At the highest, the panel may make suggestions as to how to do so. This means that, normally, no past grievance can be remedied through the WTO. WTO remedies are prospective and not retroactive, though WTO cases have decided that a past law can be struck down for its present and continuing incompatibility. Again, this is part of the deferential system among sovereign states. So, compensation, if awarded, can only refer to future loss in trading opportunities.

---

12 Examples are the committees on market access, agriculture, sanitary and phytosanitary measures, technical barriers to trade, customs valuation, rules of origin, etc. Also, the WTO works through councils such as the Council for Trade in Goods, the Council for Trade-Related Aspects of Intellectual Property Rights and the Council for Trade-in-Services.

Such compensation is negotiable where compliance is not forthcoming. The offending state can put forward trade-offs by way of satisfying the compensation order. Where no negotiated position is reached on compensation, it is permissible for the winning party to retaliate. While this may be legally logical, it is a bad economic outcome for the trading system. The rules allow for an arbitrated solution to a stalemate, with the concurrence of the dispute resolution body.

FOUR STAGES OF WTO DISPUTE SETTLEMENT

The formal process of initiating a dispute resolution process before the WTO involves four clear stages.

First, a complaining nation must go through a stage of informal consultations. This stage takes between three and four months. Should the consultations fail, then the second stage is activated. The second stage, which involves panel proceedings, takes roughly between nine and 12 months. The decision of the panel can be appealed to the appellate review body, whose proceedings take between three and four months. That constitutes the third stage.

The final stage is the implementation period, which usually takes up to 15 months.

The totality of the process falls within a period of 30 to 35 months. For most high-tech industries, for example, the turnaround cycle is about six months. How, then, does a WTO process, which takes up to three years, help the dispute resolution regime? The answer must lie in a few critical observations. First, no other international organisation has an enforcement regime such as the WTO has.[13]

Secondly, cases brought by nations are not of the type that seek short-term resolutions. They necessarily involve long-term solutions that promote long-term relationships. At times, these cases are brought with the express purpose of setting precedents and standards for future conduct. The advice to the ADR practitioner is that the WTO regime is not geared to the short-term or immediate commercial, trade benefit but, rather, to the long-term promotion of trading relationships among nations.

WTO dispute settlement: consultation (DSU Article 4)

This stage of the process provides a forum for a last attempt to resolve a dispute before resorting to panel procedure. Since this stage is very much informal, other WTO member countries can participate if they have a 'substantial trade interest'. According to the rules of procedure, this stage must span a period of at least 60 days before a request for a panel can be made. In case of urgent applications, as, for example, in the case of perishable goods, the time limit may be abridged to 20 days.

---

13 ICJ cases take years just to settle jurisdiction and, at the end, compliance is entirely at the whim of the losing nation. Of course, under the UN Charter, there is recourse to the Security Council for non-compliance with its judgments in Article 94, but this provision is mired in the politics of the Security Council. In the WTO, jurisdiction is conceded by all nations.

WTO dispute settlement: panel proceedings (Articles 6–12)

A panel is established by the Dispute Settlement Body (DSB), normally at the second request of a member. Unlike the case with other arbitral tribunals, three neutral panellists are proposed by the WTO Secretariat for the consideration of the parties. If the parties cannot agree, the Director General is authorised to compose a panel for the parties. Parties may then file briefs and present arguments at two subsequent hearings. Unlike regular arbitrations, third party WTO members can also file briefs and appear at hearings.

WTO dispute settlement: appellate review (Article 17)

There is one curious feature of the hearing process. Three of seven sitting appellate body members (not selected by the parties) hear each appeal; however, all seven deliberate on the case. This may be anathema to the trial lawyer but is permissible in the WTO on grounds of politics and consensus generation.

Appeals are limited to issues of law and legal interpretation. No appeal is allowed on findings of fact. A notable feature of the process is that the hearing is extremely quick. A hearing lasts no more than 30 days and a decision is handed down within 60 to 90 days.

WTO dispute settlement: implementation (Articles 21–22)

In the area of implementation, the WTO process differs significantly from other processes. A defending party is given a 'reasonable period of time' within which to implement a decision. If implementation is difficult or impossible within a reasonable time limit, it is permissible for the parties to negotiate a mutually acceptable time limit. Should that fail, recourse may be had to the services of an arbitrator who may sit and report within a period of 15 months.

Alternatives under DSU

Parties may also have recourse to alternative procedures such as 'good offices' or 'conciliation' or 'mediation'.[14] These processes are not exclusive of the panel process. When Article 5 is invoked, implementation provisions[15] do *not* apply. As noted above, parties may have recourse to arbitration[16] as an alternative to the panel process. When arbitration provisions are invoked, the implementation provisions do apply.

DEVELOPING COUNTRIES AND DISPUTE SETTLEMENT

The DSU contains a number of special rules relating to developing countries.[17] These are as follows:

---

14 Article 5.
15 Articles 21 and 22.
16 Article 25.
17 Of course, these rules apply to LDCs as well. There are additional rules, described in the next section, that apply to LDCs alone.

(a) The minimum time for consultations can be extended beyond the normal 60 days where a developing country is involved (DSU Article 12.10).

(b) During consultations, 'special consideration' must be given to the interests of developing countries (Article 4.10).

(c) In a case involving developed and developing country members, the developing country can ask that at least one panel member be drawn from a developing country (Article 8.10).

(d) The panel must give the developing country sufficient time to prepare and present its arguments (Article 12.10).

(e) The panel report must indicate how special and differential treatment was considered (Article 12.11).

(f) The panel must pay particular attention to the impact of its decision on developing countries (Article 21.2).

(g) In an action brought by a developing country, the DSB must consider what further action might be appropriate, taking account not only of the trade coverage of the measures complained of, but also of their impact on the developing country (Article 21.7–8).

(h) The WTO Secretariat is to make qualified legal experts available to provide advice with respect to dispute settlement (Article 27.2).

(i) The WTO Secretariat is to conduct training courses for interested members (Article 27.3).

EVALUATION AND ASSESSMENT

As at March 2004, 305 cases had been filed with the WTO. Roughly half of these cases were resolved at the consultations stage, thus demonstrating the importance of consultations as an essential tool in negotiations. According to a study by Macrory,[18] as at 2000, 38 cases had been completed, that is, had resulted in a panel report that was not appealed and was adopted by the DSB, or an appellate body. The complainant was successful in 34 of these cases. This high success rate suggests that the consultation stage is successful in weeding out weak cases. The respondent either dropped the offending measure or indicated its intention to comply in 22 out of 34 cases, and mutually acceptable solutions were reached in an additional seven cases.[19] In two cases, the complainants have challenged the respondent's efforts to implement the WTO ruling as inadequate.[20] In only three cases has retaliation been authorised. Two of these involved cases brought by the USA against the EU: *Bananas*, in which the USA has imposed 100% duties on more than USA$300 million of imports from the EU, and *Beef Hormones*, in which the USA has retaliated against more than USA$100 million of imports from the EU. In 2003, the EU threatened retaliation against the USA over the latter's protectionist policies over steel; the USA has since agreed to lift its additional steel duties.

---

18 See also *op cit*, Macrory, fn 8.

19 These statistics are taken from 'Overview of the State-of-play of WTO Disputes', a periodically updated table that appears on the WTO's website, www.wto.org.

20 The most controversial of these is *United States – Tax Treatment for 'Foreign Sales Corporations'*, WT/DS/101/1 – in which the EU has complained that the law passed by the United States amending the tax law in a way that is intended to comply with the WTO ruling, in fact, fails to do so.

The appellate body has been quite activist. Although it has reversed few panel decisions, it has quite frequently modified panel opinions and has often criticised the panel's reasoning, sometimes in surprisingly harsh terms. It applies the Vienna Convention on the Interpretation of Treaties when attempting to discern the meaning of the provisions of the agreement in question, and it generally performs a heavily textual analysis of the relevant language.[21]

The statistics suggest that the system has worked well in removing trade barriers. In 29 out of the 34 completed cases in which violations were found, the offending measure has been or, apparently, will be removed, or the matter has been resolved between the parties in some other mutually satisfactory way.

While most cases have been between developed countries, it is also true that there have been quite a few between developing countries. What is comforting is that the WTO system has provided a singular opportunity for otherwise small developing countries to take on the EU and the USA and win. In all those cases, the losing party modified its behaviour in compliance with the ruling of the WTO. This is extremely significant. Over textiles, Costa Rica and India took on the USA and won.[22] Over the import of shrimps, India, Malaysia, Pakistan and Thailand took on the USA, which attempted to ban imports, and won.[23] So did Venezuela and Brazil against the USA over restrictions on imports of gasoline.[24] Brazil won against the EU in a case involving restrictions on imports of poultry.[25] And in 2004, Antigua & Barbuda has won against the USA over Internet gambling.

These examples do not only represent victories against developed countries, they also show that developed countries have been forced into a culture of compliance. For example, in the Costa Rican and Indian textiles cases and the Venezuelan and Brazilian gasoline case, the USA simply dropped the offending measures. On the shrimp case and the textile case, the USA is discussing compliance with the complaining countries.

However, the WTO has no independent power to enforce its judgments. Its power is limited to authorising a complaining country to retaliate by raising its tariffs against imports from the offending country. Of course, retaliation has teeth and can bite where the dispute is between two major trading nations. Recently, the USA has imposed 100% tariffs on hundreds of millions of dollars of imports from the EU as a result of the EU's failure to comply with the WTO's rulings in the *Bananas* and *Beef Hormones* cases.[26]

---

21 In *United States – Antidumping Duties on Dynamic Random Access Memory Semiconductors (DRAMS) of One Megabit or Above From Korea*, WT/DS/99/1, for example, the Appellate Body engaged in a lengthy discussion as to whether the term 'not unlikely' meant the same as 'likely'.

22 *United States – Restrictions on Cotton and Man-Made Fiber Underwear*, WT/DS 24; *United States – Measures Affecting Imports of Woven Shirts and Blouses*, WT/DS 33.

23 *United States – Import Prohibition of Certain Shrimp and Shrimp Products*, WT/DS 54, 55, 59 and 64.

24 *United States – Standards for Reformulated and Conventional Gasoline*, WT/DS 2 and 4.

25 *European Community – Measures Affecting Importation of Certain Poultry Products*, WT/DS 69.

26 *European Community – Regime for the Importation, Sale and Distribution of Bananas*, WT/DS 27; *European Community – Measures Affecting Beef and Meat Products (Hormones)*, WT/DS 26 and 48.

Lack of transparency

In the WTO, briefs in a dispute are confidential and the meetings are closed. While this may be consistent with the basic tenets of ADR, it is felt by some commentators that this goes against one of the very principles of the WTO system – transparency. A case could well be made for public hearings in which confidential information may be expunged from the public record, while permitting the panel to hold *in camera* hearings if warranted.

Power to remit a case

At present, the appellate body only has power to review legal issues, based on the facts as found by the panel. In domestic law, where the appellate body believes that the panel has made an error in law, or has not made the necessary factual findings to which the correct legal principles can be applied, it has the power to remit the case to the lower body.[27] Some have argued for an amendment to the DSU to confer specifically on the appellate body the power to remand cases.[28]

The innocent bystander problem

The absence of a remedy, by way of compensation, could lead to a situation where innocent third parties were punished if an offending country did not eliminate or modify the offending measure within a 'reasonable time', usually 15 months. In a situation where the offending country offers compensation, tariffs will be lowered on other products, whose domestic manufacturers will be unexpectedly exposed to greater competition from imports. Where the winning party retaliates, industries in the offending country, with no direct stake in the dispute, could face high trade barriers, and consumers in the complaining countries will pay higher prices for imports.

CONCLUSION

From the viewpoint of developing countries, the biggest downside to the dispute resolution system has to be the cost of invoking the process. Although the operating costs are shared by countries according to the UN formula, a WTO dispute is complex and costly. The USA and the EU have well-trained staff, based in Geneva, with sole responsibility to handle trade disputes. For developing nations, reliance is usually placed on the retention of private lawyers whose fees are not known to be on the modest side. Two initial steps have been taken to alleviate the problems relating to costs. First, there is a United Nations Conference on Trade and Development (UNCTAD) initiative whereby lawyers are encouraged to take on WTO cases for developing countries, free of charge. Secondly, and more positively, is the initiative to set up the Advisory Center on WTO Law in Geneva, with the express purpose that the

---

27 See, for example, the Administrative Justice Act 1980 of Barbados.
28 On occasions, the appellate body has filled the gap by making its own findings of fact based on the record, but this is not acceptable to all countries. See Application, 'Shrimp-Turtle – Unscrambling the Facts' (1999) J Int Economic Law, pp 477, 478–79.

centre represent developing countries in dispute settlement proceedings. It is not designed to be free. Rather, it would charge hourly rates that would vary depending on a country's level of foreign trade. This points to the urgent necessity for developing countries to build essential knowledge and insights about the rules, rights and operations of the WTO. It must also be borne in mind that developing countries are not powerless. The lesson of Seattle's failure and Doha's success is that developing countries have real strength in the WTO because of the organisation's requirement for consensus.

Writing on 'Developing countries and the WTO dispute settlement system',[29] Valentina Delich arrives at conclusions which closely replicate the points made by way of an evaluation. She writes:

> The Dispute Settlement Understanding brought about a positive and beneficial change for developing countries. Weaker states have a better chance to defend their interests in a rule-oriented than in a power-oriented system. However, since the DSU provisions relating to enforcement of S&D language in WTO agreements are ineffective, developing countries do not enjoy a 'neutral' playing field. Although the DSU is not biased against any party in a dispute, developing countries are less well equipped to participate in the process: they have fewer people with the appropriate training, they are less experienced, and they can bring fewer financial resources to bear. Therefore, although the DSU is an asset, developing countries must work to obtain international financing for training and capacity building and for the establishment of a joint mechanism among developing countries to screen industrial country trade policies of interest to them – not only to reduce the costs of the screening but also to coordinate the submission of joint cases. In addition, developing countries could use cases in which they are involved as a way to identify gaps in WTO agreements that need to be addressed through negotiations.

> Reform of the dispute settlement system does not appear to be a priority on the negotiating agenda of developing countries. Their efforts are mainly directed toward defending their interests as best they can in current cases, bridging the gap with industrial countries in terms of legal expertise, and establishing more effective enforcement and retaliatory devices.

The question that may well be asked is what is the justification for addressing, in an ADR book, a subject which is so rooted in the vortex of contentious litigation. The answer is twofold. First, the impact of the WTO on the lives and fortunes of the world demands it. Secondly, as has been noted earlier in this book, ADR is no longer antithetical to litigation. They complement each other.

---

29 In Hoekman, B, Mattoo, A and English, P (eds), *Development, Trade and the WTO (A Handbook)*, 2000, The World Bank, p 79.

CHAPTER 7

ADR AND THE CRIMINAL JUSTICE SYSTEM

INTRODUCTION

Throughout this book, and especially in Chapter 1, some of the basic shortcomings and ills of the civil litigation process, as well as the alienation of litigants associated with them, have been considered. Indeed, the same shortcomings afflict the criminal justice system and, perhaps, do so in an even more damaging fashion. The general feeling of the litigant in the criminal justice system is one of alienation, disenchantment and disenfranchisement. This is precisely so because crime has hitherto been regarded as an offence against the state. For example, the victim is detached from the process except when required to testify in court. Offenders hardly have the opportunity to be confronted with the consequences of their actions. Neither the family of the victim nor the community is brought into the process in any direct way. Not many recognise such a system as being capable of achieving 'justice' for all. Besides, the rapid escalation of crime suggests that the current system is unable to cope effectively with the challenges to society.

It is no wonder, then, that major law reform efforts in the wider Commonwealth have sought to focus on 'access to justice' issues. These reform efforts speak to a paradigm shift in how a modern and just society may seek to manage conflict. Furthermore, these efforts reflect the need for an ADR change of culture and a radical re-appraisal of the traditional approach to dispute settlement. More and more, there is the increasing recognition that the ills of the litigation process pose a crisis not only for governments but also for the judiciary, the legal process itself and the populace at large. If, as Lord Diplock put it in *Bremar v South India Shipping Corporation Ltd*,[1] 'every civilized system of government requires that the state should make available to all its citizens a means for the just and peaceful settlement of disputes between them as to their respective rights', then the present system, which caters to less than 10% of litigants' claims, fails the test because it denies access to justice to so many.

The processes which are to be discussed below represent some of the possible answers by the state to the challenges posed.

Lord Woolf has set out the general principles which should inform a credible justice system. These are that:

(a) it should be fair, and be seen to be so;

(b) procedures and cost should be proportionate to the nature of the issues involved;

(c) it should deal with cases with reasonable speed;

(d) it should be understandable to those who use it;

(e) it should be responsive to the needs of those who use it;

(f) it should provide as much certainty as the nature of particular cases allows; and

(g) it should be effective, adequately resourced and organised so as to give effect to the principles above.

---

1   [1981] AC 909, p 917. See also Devlin J, 'Is It Right to Cling to a System that Offers Perfections for the Few and Nothing At All for the Many?' in Zander, M (ed), *What's Wrong With the Law?*, 1970, British Broadcasting Corporation, pp 75–77.

In pursuing these principles, the overall objective should be to:

(a) improve access to justice and reduce the cost of litigation;

(b) reduce the complacency of the rules and modernise terminology; and

(c) remove unnecessary distinctions of practice and procedure.

In a foreword to *The ADR Practice Guide*,[2] Lord Bingham of Cornhill welcomed the transformation of the procedure of the courts with these telling words: 'Conventional litigation processes and ADR are not enemies, but partners. Neither can ignore the development in the other.' These principles, though enunciated with civil justice in mind, are equally applicable to the criminal justice system.

Below are discussed some of the major ADR initiatives in the criminal justice systems of the Caribbean region, in the areas of legislation, community policing, and restorative justice.

LEGISLATIVE INITIATIVES IN MEDIATION

Without a conscious decision to introduce court annexed ADR into the jurisprudence of the Caribbean, some initiatives in Barbados, Jamaica and Trinidad & Tobago seem to have commenced a creeping process in that direction. The general principle in all three countries' legislation is the introduction into the law of a mediation process whereby the court appoints a mediator who considers alternatives to imprisonment.[3]

The Penal System Reform Act 1998 of Barbados

Part III of this Act, which deals with mediation, is only part of a larger penal reform package designed to direct young offenders away from prison.[4] Section 20(2) is instructive. It says that:

(2) For the purposes of this Part, mediation means, subject to subsection (3), the settlement, by a third person called a 'mediator', of a dispute or difference between one party and another by the employment of methods which consist of or include the discharge by one party of one or more of the following obligations:

(a) doing unpaid work for the benefit of the other;

(b) paying compensation to the other;

(c) participating in an education or rehabilitation programme.

Section 20(4) envisages the appointment of mediators from a list 'approved' by the Minister Responsible for Legal Affairs, and based on 'adequate knowledge of mediation'.

---

2   Mackie, K *et al*, 2000, Butterworths.

3   In Trinidad & Tobago's Community Mediation Act, No 13 of 1998, this approach extends to some civil matters as well.

4   The Long Title to the Act says: 'An Act to enlarge the powers of the criminal courts to pass in proper cases sentences other than sentences of imprisonment; to enable certain offences to be dealt with by civil mediation instead of criminal prosecution; to lay down certain principles to be followed by courts when exercising their powers of sentencing; by an amendment to the Juvenile Offenders Act to raise the age of criminal responsibility; and for connected and incidental purposes.'

It must be noted that mediation is available only to a person who is 'charged for the first time with a scheduled offence'[5] and 'if that person is 21 years of age or under and had not before been charged with, or convicted of, any offence'.[6] Even where eligible, the accused must apply for mediation. Such application shall be made in duplicate in a form acceptable to the court.[7] A court may not make a mediation order unless it is satisfied that:

(a) the charge is one that may appropriately be dealt with by mediation;

(b) the complainant has agreed that the charge should be dealt with in that way; and

(c) both the complainant and the accused have agreed on a common mediator.

The Director of Public Prosecutions (DPP) is entitled to be heard by the court, before the court determines to make a mediation order. Some may question the wisdom of interposing the DPP in what is essentially a consensual process. But an argument in defence of the provision could well be found in the constitutional responsibility of the DPP to have a final say in all criminal prosecutions.

The Act enjoins the court to make a mediation order, of 12 months' duration at a time, suspending the trial of the offence and referring the subject matter of the charge to the appointed mediator.[8] During the period of the mediation, the court may require the defendant to submit to the supervision of a probation order. Section 27 requires the court to explain the consequences of a mediation order to the accused person, before it is issued. A failure to comply with the terms of a mediation order may result in a revocation of the order and the resumption of the trial. Consistent with the principles of mediation, an incriminating statement made during the mediation is not admissible in a court of law.

Once a mediation has been concluded successfully, the court shall dismiss the charge in respect of which the order was made.[9]

The Act is an important first step in the introduction of ADR principles into the criminal justice system. It is to be welcomed on that ground. However, the Act could

---

5   The summary of offences are listed in the Third Schedule are:
     (1) Malicious Injury to Property Act, Cap 140, s 23: destroying fence, stile or gate
     (2) Offences Against the Person Act, Cap 141
         s 25: common assault
         s 26: assault occasioning harm
         s 27: other assaults
     (3) Praedial Larceny Prevention Act, Cap 142A
         s 4: conveying produce or livestock of more than one person
         s 11: purchasing (selling) produce or livestock outside market without obtaining (issuing)
             receipt
     (4) Trespass to Property (Reform) Act, Cap 155B
         s 5(1)(a)–(d): petty trespass
     (5) Highways Act, Cap 289
         s 44(1): using obscene language on highway
     (6) Minor Offences Act, 1998-1
         s 2(1)(c)–(g): disorderly behaviour
         s 3(g): being in a dwelling-house, etc, for purpose of committing arrestable offence.
6   Section 21.
7   Sections 22–24.
8   Section 26(1)–(4).
9   Section 31.

be improved in some basic areas. A strong case could be made for eliminating the age limit of 21 years or under, as well as the requirement of being a first time offender. These requirements impact negatively on the fundamental principle that ADR is a consensual process. Furthermore, there is no need to provide such a restrictive list of outcomes.[10] So long as the parties can come up with creative solutions, which are within the law, there is no reason why the law should shun them. After all, one of the principal advantages of pursuing ADR is for the parties to come up with creative solutions, through problem solving techniques, to provide a win-win outcome for the parties. Anyway, why should the right to apply for mediation rest only with the defendant? Should the complainant also not be allowed that flexibility and choice?

The Community Mediation Act 1988 of Trinidad & Tobago

This piece of legislation is very similar to that of Barbados, though the Trinidad legislation goes much further. The latter provides for mediation in both criminal and civil matters. In that sense, it breaks new ground.

Like the Barbadian Act, this one, too, limits mediation in criminal matters to a person who is charged for the first time with a scheduled offence[11] and who has not been convicted of any other offence.[12] The same objection raised against the restrictive nature of the Barbados legislation could be raised here as well. In a clear improvement on the Barbados legislation, s 4 extends the right to apply for a mediation to both 'the defendant and the *de facto* complainant'.[13] Such an application may only be granted when the offence falls within the list of offences in Sched 1, the application receives the favourable endorsement of a probation officer and the parties agree to the process. Here also, the DPP or his representatives 'shall be entitled to be heard by the court' on the application.[14] A mediation order suspends the trial and commits the case to a mediator. But before the mediation order is made, the court shall explain to the defendant, clearly and precisely, the purpose and effect of the order, the consequences which may follow if the offender disobeys that order and the power of the court to review its order.[15]

Like the Barbadian legislation, the mediation order lasts for 12 months at a time and it requires the defendant to submit to the supervision of a probation officer.[16] During the mediation, the parties may be accompanied by their lawyers. The expected outcomes of the mediation – which again are very limited – are:

---

10   Section 20(2)(a)–(c).
11   The Scheduled Offences are (list from the statute):
    (a) assault and battery contrary to section 4;
    (b) assault contrary to section 5(1);
    (c) aggravated assault contrary to section 5(2);
    (d) damaging property contrary to section 25;
    (e) being found on, entering or leaving cultivated lands without lawful cause or excuse contrary to section 41(1);
    (f) being in an enclosed place for an unlawful purpose contrary to section 46(d);
    (g) using violent or obscene language or disturbing the peace contrary to section 49.
12   Section 3.
13   Why the complainant is described as a *de facto* complainant is not too clear.
14   Section 7(2).
15   Section 8(2).
16   Section 9.

(a) community service;

(b) work for the *de facto* complainant;

(c) participation in an educational or rehabilitative programme; and

(d) compensation, of a sum not exceeding $5,000.

Any incriminating statement made in the course of the mediation, as well as the mediator's report, are inadmissible in a court of law. This is consistent with the principles of mediation.

As noted earlier, the Trinidadian legislation extends to mediation in civil matters as well. The following civil matters are eligible for mediation by virtue of s 14(1):

(a) matters falling for determination by a court under s 8 of the Petty Civil Courts Act 1980;

(b) applications for ancillary relief following the grant of a *decree nisi* of divorce or a decree of judicial separation;

(c) applications falling for determination by a court under the Matrimonial Proceedings and Property Act 1973 (1980 Rev) for the custody, education, supervision and maintenance of children;

(d) applications for the maintenance of, and access to, children and maintenance of a spouse or dependant under the Family Law (Guardianship of Minors, Domicile and Maintenance) Act 1981.

It is open to either party to apply to have the matter mediated directly by a mediator agreed to by both parties. The court shall then adjourn for the parties to agree on a mediator. On the adjourned date, the court then makes an order formally appointing the mediator and suspending the court hearing, until a report is received from the mediator.[17]

Unlike the Barbados legislation, the Trinidad legislation attempts to extend the application of mediation to certain summary offences and civil matters. The Minister Responsible for Legal Affairs is empowered to designate centres for community mediation in criminal and civil matters. The mediator is given power to:

(a) co-opt, with the agreement of the parties, persons from the community in which the mediation centre is located, who may have expertise or the type of influence required for the particular mediation process; and

(b) request the support of any social groups, community organisations or non-governmental organisations where such support is required for the success of the mediation process.[18]

The Act then restates some of the fundamental principles of mediation by providing for immunity from suit for the mediator and confers confidentiality on the mediator and every person concerned with the administration of the mediation centres or the mediation process.[19]

By way of comment, it would be fair to say that the Trinidad legislation is far more extensive than the Barbadian legislation. It also has some very commendable features in it, such as the establishment of mediation centres, extension into civil matters and the reinforcement of the principles of confidentiality and immunity of the mediator

---

17 Sections 14(2) and (3), and 15.
18 Section 16(2)(a) and (b).
19 Sections 18 and 19.

from legal proceedings. Despite these welcoming features, however, the law also has some shortcomings. With respect to mediation in criminal matters, the law is limited in scope and covers only very minor and petty offences. One can understand that, for public policy reasons, serious crimes ought not to be mediated. But that is no reason to swing the pendulum to the other extreme whereby only petty crimes are now covered by the law. Also, the expected outcomes of a mediation of a crime are very limited indeed. They also strike at the heart of the philosophy which boasts that mediation is a consensual process.

With respect to mediation in civil matters, perhaps the only legitimate criticism that one could make is that the Act attempts to marry the simplest types of cases for mediation (such as petty civil matters) with the most complicated ones (of family mediation, such as custody and maintenance). Family mediation is, indeed, so very specialised that not every accredited mediator is competent to practise it.[20]

The Resident Magistrates Court (Amendment) Rules 1999 and the Criminal Justice (Reform) Rules 2001 of Jamaica

The introduction of mediation in to the court system of Jamaica appears to be a logical development from the fact that Jamaica boasts a functioning Dispute Resolution Foundation. The Dispute Resolution Foundation, formerly the Mediation Council of Jamaica, was incorporated under the Companies Act on 11 July 1994. Core funding for the Foundation's operations was provided by the United States Agency for

---

20   For a discussion of some of the intricacies of family mediation, see, for example, Umbreit, MS, *Mediating Interpersonal Conflicts*, 1995, CPI Publishing, Chapter 5. Other useful references that may be consulted are:

Bruyere, R, 'The Compassion Factor' in Carlson, R, and Shield, B (eds), *Healers on Healing*, 1989, Tarcher.

Capra, F, *Uncommon Wisdom: Conversations with Remarkable People*, 1988, Simon & Schuster.

Carlson, R and Shield, B (eds), *Healers on Healing*, 1989, Tarcher.

Fisher, R and Brown, S, *Getting Together: Building Relationships That Get to Yes*, 1988, Houghton Mifflin.

Gold, L, 'Lawyer Therapist Team Mediation', in Folberg, J and Milne, A (eds), *Divorce Mediation*, 1988, Guilford.

Gold, L, *Between Love and Hate: A Guide to Civilized Divorce*, 1992, Plenum.

Jampolsky, G, *Teach Only Love*, 1983, Bantam Books.

Lankton, S, 'A States of Consciousness Model of Ericksonian Hypnosis', in Lankton, S (ed), *Ericksonian Monographs No 1: Elements and Dimensions of an Ericksonian Approach*, 1985, Brunner/Mazel.

Lankton, S and Lankton, C, *The Answer Within: A Clinical Framework of Ericksonian Hynotherapy*, 1983, Brunner/Mazel.

May, R, 'The Emphathetic Relationship', in Carlson, R and Shield, B (eds), *Healers on Healing*, 1989, Tarcher.

Prather, H, 'Love is Healing', in Carlson, R and Shield, B (eds), *Healers on Healing*, 1989, Tarcher.

Remen, RN, 'The Search for Healing', in Carlson, R and Shield, B (eds), *Healers on Healing*, 1989, Tarcher.

Saposnek, DT, *Mediating Child Custody Disputes: A Systematic Guide for Family Therapists, Court Counselors, Attorneys, and Judges*, 1983, Jossey-Bass.

Satir, V, *Making Contact*, 1976, Celestial Arts.

Schwartz, J, 'Healing, Love, and Empowerment', in Carlson, R and Shield, B (eds), *Healers and Healing*, 1989, Tarcher.

Sinitar, M, *Healing Choices, Elegant Choices*, 1988, Paulist Press.

van der Hart, O, *Rituals in Psychotherapy: Transition and Continuity*, 1983, Irvington.

Walsh, R, *The Spirit of Shamanism*, 1990, Tarcher.

International Development (USAID) under the latter's Sustainable Justice Improvement Programme. The Foundation seeks to implement a very successful model of dispute resolution, which is widely used by businesses and courts in the USA, Hong Kong, Canada, Australia and the UK.

The principal objectives of the Foundation are to:

(a) establish methods of resolving disputes in Jamaica which are supplementary, complementary or alternative to litigation, called ADR techniques;

(b) encourage and educate the public about using ADR techniques to handle conflicts and differences without resorting to violence;

(c) establish several dispute resolution facilities in communities throughout Jamaica;

(d) explore and establish such ADR techniques as methods of resolving domestic, commercial, industrial, political and social disputes among members of the Jamaican community; and

(e) increase the use of mediation services by the legal profession as a dispute resolution option.

The work of the Foundation is given legal recognition in the court rules, to be discussed below.

Section 26 of the 1999 amended rules places the responsibility to offer mediation in a trial, on the judge. Where the judge is of the opinion that mediation may be of assistance to the parties, the judge may:

(a) advise the parties to attend upon an approved mediator; and

(b) adjourn the proceedings to enable that attendance.

Section 27(2) provides confidentiality to the parties in a mediation.

Section 28 is instructive. It provides that:

(a) The Chief Justice may, on the recommendation of the Dispute Resolution Foundation, appoint persons to be approved mediators for the purposes of these Rules.

(b) The names of all persons appointed under paragraph (1) shall be published in the *Gazette*.

(c) The Chief Justice may, after consultation with the Dispute Resolution Foundation, by notice in the *Gazette*, revoke the appointment of any mediator under paragraph (1) where the Chief Justice is satisfied that the mediator is not adequately carrying out the functions required under rule 26.

This section thus gives validity to the essential mediation role of the Dispute Resolution Foundation.

The Criminal Justice (Reform) Rules of 2001 provide the detailed regulatory mechanism for the actual conduct of the mediation. Section 10(1), (7), (8) and (9) states:

(1) A mediation order made under section 16 of the Act shall be in accordance with Form 6 of the Schedule, and the provisions of this rule shall apply to mediation proceedings pursuant to mediation orders. ...

(7) The mediator may determine the manner in which the mediation proceedings are conducted and shall ensure that such proceedings are conducted in a manner that facilitates the sharing of relevant information by the parties.

(8) Where there is a delay in conducting mediation proceedings such that the mediator is of the view that the proceedings are unlikely to be completed within

the time specified in the mediation order as the time within which the mediation shall be concluded, the mediator may apply in writing to the Court for an extension of that time, and the Court may grant the application if it thinks it reasonable to do so.

(9) It shall be the responsibility of the mediator, where an agreement is reached between the parties in the mediation proceedings, to prepare a mediation agreement incorporating the material terms of the agreement, and for that purpose the mediator may obtain such legal, technical or other assistance as the mediator may require in the preparation of the agreement.

Consistent with the principles of mediation, sub-ss (10) and (11) stipulate that:

(10) A mediation agreement prepared pursuant to paragraph (9) shall be–

   (a) signed by all the parties thereto; and

   (b) submitted to the Court along with the mediation report, and a copy of the agreement shall be–

      (i) given to each party to the mediation upon the signing thereof;

      (ii) retained by the mediation centre.

(11) A party shall not be bound by any statement made or agreement arrived at in mediation proceedings unless the statement or agreement is contained in a mediation agreement prepared pursuant to paragraph (9) and signed by that party.

MEDIATION AND COMMUNITY POLICING

Community policing involves a fundamental rethinking of the role of law enforcement in our times. It is generally acknowledged that this shift of focus from the police officer to the citizen has enormous benefits for society. These range from reduced calls by citizens on police manpower to improved police-community relations. Of course, to achieve these benefits a great deal of work is required to restore the confidence of the populace in the police force, on the one hand, and skills training of the police, on the other. Indeed, the philosophy behind the skills training of the police is to shift their focus from a police *force* to a police *service*.

Writing in the context of policing in New York, Christopher Cooper, a specialist in community policing, had this to say:[21]

Consider that community policing champions citizen empowerment. It attempts to do away with notions that the police are an occupying army and that citizens have little say in the policing of their communities. New York City's troubles, as well as other jurisdictions, are in many ways rooted in the police department's unwillingness to tap communities as resources in maintaining order.

If patrol police officers interact with citizens using mediation skills and address interpersonal disputes (which are amenable to mediation) using mediation, many of the objectives of community policing are realized. Mediation skills, because of their politeness characteristics promote professional and positive social interaction. In handling interpersonal dispute scenes with mediation, police officers/mediators provide a problem solving process in which they empower citizens. Through the transference of decision making power, the officer is conveying deference and offering

---

21   (1999) 17(1) Conflict Resolution Notes 7.

the self-responsibility and freedom that citizens rightfully expect to exercise in their lives.

This translates to police deference for members of a community participating in watching over their own community. For this reason, use of mediation by patrol officers should be seen as a requisite component of community policing initiatives. This makes sense since both seek to foster positive police-community relations, empower citizens, show deference to citizens, and reduce confrontations between police officers and citizens.

He concludes as follows:

Whether it is New York City or Kansas City, I believe that as we enter into a new millennium, police training needs to be taken to the next level. This means training police officers not just in mediation skills but certifying them as mediators. If a police department decides against having its officers trained as mediators, it should at least allow its officers to receive mediation skills training. Either way, the adaptation into patrol police work of the conflict resolution methodology known as mediation can contribute to improved police-citizen interaction.

With the help of the Dispute Resolution Foundation, the Jamaica constabulary has been undergoing basic training in mediation skills. This is to be welcomed. Indeed, this model should be the standard for emulation by other CARICOM countries. While acknowledging that the Jamaica initiative is a beginning, a lot more needs to be done. The following are some basic suggestions:

(a) enhance the intellectual and knowledge base of public officers through structured skills training;

(b) modernise the police handbook and procedures to recognise the importance of community policing and outlining the circumstances in which mediation should be employed;

(c) allocate sufficient time to police who are involved in community policing to be away from their desk;

(d) establish mediation units/centres in police stations across the island; and

(e) offer incentives and rewards for diffusing explosive situations.[22]

---

22 The importance of this topic is reflected in the enormous amount of literature which has built up in recent years. What follows is a minuscule selection:

Bard, M, *The Function of the Police in Crisis Intervention and Conflict Management*, 1975, US Department of Justice.

Bard, M, *Family Crisis Intervention: From Concept to Implementation*, 1973, US Department of Justice.

Bard, M, *Training Police as Specialists in Family Crisis Intervention*, 1970, US Department of Justice.

Cooper, C, *Mediation & Arbitration by Patrol Police Officers*, 1999, University Press of America.

Goldstein, H, *Problem-Oriented Policing*, 1990, McGraw-Hill.

Louie, R, 'Crisis Intervention: A Police Model for Dispute Settlement' (1981) 15(2) Journal of California Enforce, pp 70–77.

Pruit, DG and Rubin, JZ, *Social Conflict: Escalation, Stalemate, and Settlement*, 1986, Random House.

Slaikeu, K, *When Push Comes to Shove: A Practical Guide to Mediating Disputes*, 1996, Jossey-Bass.

Volpe, M and Christian, T 'Mediation: New Addition to Cop's Toolbox' (1989) *Law Enforcement News*, 15 June, pp 8, 13.

Volpe, M, 'The Police Role', in Wright, M, and Galaway, B (eds), *Mediation and Criminal Justice: Victims, Offenders and Community*, 1989, Sage, pp 229–38.

Williams, P, 'Police and Mediation: Win-Win Partnership' (1997) *Oregon Chiefs of Police Magazine*, November, 24–26.

Advantages

Several advantages accrue to society from community policing. Chief among them are the following:

(a) enhancement of public confidence in law enforcement;

(b) increased social stability;

(c) reduction in danger to law officers;

(d) avoidance or reduction in societal violence;

(e) promotion of a positive image for the police as friends of the community, rather than simply tools of law enforcement;

(f) peaceful co-existence in neighbourhoods;

(g) enhancement of relationships;

(h) savings in police time from unnecessary arrests and trials;

(i) fewer repeat calls on police time;

(j) avoidance of, or reduction in, litigation;

(k) quick resolution of disputes; and

(l) diminishing the need for use of physical force by the police.

Community policing, then, is geared to attacking the view that the police are an occupying force and that citizens have no say in how their communities are policed. In short, it seems to tap the communities as a major resource in maintaining law and order.[23] Improved police-citizen relations can only augur well for good community relations, a violence-free environment and self-empowerment to citizens. To advance community policing, there is the need for some units of the police force to be trained in the basics of mediation. The implementation of such new policies will also call for a review of existing police manuals and handbooks, mandating the use of mediation methodology, coupled with a reward scheme for successful diffusion of community tension. Introducing mediation into policing is to introduce unconventional policing practices. This innovation also calls for the establishment of mediation centres to

---

23   There is a considerable volume of literature on community policing. The motivated reader may consult the following, among many:

Bard, M, *The Function of the Police in Crisis Intervention and Conflict Management*, 1975, US Department of Justice.

Bard, M, *Family Crisis Intervention: From Concept to Implementation*, 1973, US Department of Justice.

Bard, M, *Training Police as Specialists in Family Crisis Intervention*, 1970, US Department of Justice.

Black, D, *The Manners and Customs of the Police*, 1980, Academic Press.

Cooper, C, *Mediation & Arbitration by Patrol Police Officers*, 1999, University Press of America.

Folberg, J and Taylor, A, *Mediation: A Comprehensive Guide to Resolving Conflict Without Litigation*, 1984, Jossey-Bass.

Goldstein, H, *Problem-Oriented Policing*, 1990, McGraw-Hill.

Louie, R, 'Crisis Intervention: A Police Model for Dispute Settlement' (1981) 15(2) Journal of California Enforcement 70–77.

Pruit, DG and Rubin, JZ, *Social Conflict: Escalation, Stalemate, and Settlement*, 1986, Random House.

Slaikeu, K, *When Push Comes to Shove: A Practical Guide to Mediating Disputes*, 1996, Jossey-Bass.

Volpe, M, 'The Police Role', in Wright, M and Galaway, B (eds), *Mediation and Criminal Justice: Victims, Offenders and Community*, 1989, Sage, pp 229–38.

Williams, P, 'Police and Mediation: Win-Win Partnership' (1997) *Oregon Chiefs of Police Magazine*, November, 24–26.

which police mediators can refer those cases which reflect deep-seated underlying issues, and which are not easily resolved as those disputes which are episodic.

Stressing the importance of mediation training, Christopher Cooper writes:[24]

> Though preferable, officers do not necessarily need to become certified mediators. Mediation training can improve officers' interpersonal skills and show them how their attitudes and behaviour influence the actions of others. As a result, they can better handle disputes and prevent incidents from escalating. In doing so, they avoid injury to themselves and others while increasing citizen satisfaction with the police response. Understandably, satisfied citizens remain less likely to file complaints against the department.
>
> Perhaps mediation achieves its best results in bolstering existing community policing philosophy, programs, and missions. For example, community policing champions citizen empowerment. When patrol officers make mediation available to citizens, they empower them to handle many of their own disputes. In addition, officers who offer mediation services show appropriate deference to the responsibility and freedom that most citizens expect to exercise in their lives. Moreover, when officers become third-party intermediaries, they appear less as outsiders and more as a part of the communities they serve. Thus agencies should view mediation as a requisite component of community policing initiatives because both seek to foster positive police-community relations, empower and show deference to citizens, and reduce confrontations between police officers and citizens.

He concludes:

> Every time they answer a call for service, patrol officers use interpersonal skills. Some incidents, however, require more time and skill than officers have. Training officers to mediate disputes takes time and a commitment to trying unconventional policing practices. But when departments use mediation to resolve conflicts in their communities, they empower residents to take responsibility for their actions and to resolve their own problems, not just in arguments with their neighbors but in other areas of their lives, as well. Thus, when officers take the time to mediate disputes, they help citizens exercise their constitutional rights while freeing themselves to solve other problems instead of answering repeat calls for service. In the end, a little extra attention goes a long way.

Some challenges

The introduction of community policing requires the need for attitudinal change, not only on the part of the police but on the part of the community at large. Some would even argue that in any society in which crime is endemic, it is a luxury to talk of community policing without first immobilising the warlords and destroying their gangs and criminal cells. Be that as it may, several steps can be taken towards meeting some of the challenges inherent in the introduction of community policing. Among such steps are:

(a) attitudinal change in the police force, from force, coercion and arrest to mediated solutions;

(b) releasing pressure on the police force by allowing extra time for community policing;

---

24 (2000) 69(2) FBI Law Enforcement Bulletin 7–8.

(c) infrastructural support in terms of equipment, mobility and technology;

(d) revision of outdated police manuals and work practices;

(e) acquisition of mediation skills; and

(f) highlighting confidentiality issues in mediation.

The high incidence of crime in the region makes a compelling case to try other lawful, but unconventional, methods of policing to stem the tide. Community policing offers such an approach. Studies conducted in the USA and elsewhere would tend to show that many beneficial results have accrued to communities that have applied the remedies of community policing.

The Jamaican model

An exciting experiment is under way in Jamaica with respect to community policing. It is general knowledge that crime in Jamaica is unusually high. The use of tough police tactics to contain this high incidence of crime has been tried, but with unsuccessful results. Just as societies are rethinking disputes, may it also be the case that Jamaica needs to rethink its policing strategy? Jamaica may be in the limelight because of the unusually high crime statistics but the problems and the lessons to be learnt are applicable to the region as a whole. It is the contention of this book that there ought to be a complete re-think of the role of law enforcement in this area and the application of new strategies through the application of ADR in criminal cases. Already, there is in widespread use neighbourhood watch committees throughout the region, working in tandem with the police. That experience can now be deepened by introducing the tenets of community policing.

On 28 September 2001, the United States Agency for International Development (USAID) executed a five-year, Strategic Objective Grant Agreement with the government of Jamaica for 'improved citizen security and participation in democratic processes'. One key component of the programme is the improvement of community policing. The project document states that 'this police assistance program is the only one of its kind in the world and presents a unique opportunity for the relevant parties to its implementation to work together in partnership to produce a model worthy of worldwide emulation'. Perhaps this may be overly optimistic, especially in the absence of any prior empirical evidence or data. Nevertheless, the aim of improving the operational environment of the criminal justice system is laudable.

Some of the laudable benchmarks of the project are:

(a) The establishment of a computerised case tracking system for 23 Resident Magistrates Courts (RMS), which will allow these courts to store, access and disseminate information on their caseloads in a more efficient fashion.

(b) The electronic recording of RMS court proceedings is to be assisted through the provision of automated court reporting equipment, which will be used by trained court reporters provided to the courts by the Ministry of Justice.

(c) The modernisation of the Coroners Court in Kingston, as part of the resident magistrates' courts modernisation effort.

(d) The strengthening of police community relations in at least two inner city communities beginning with the pilot community of Grants Pen. A 3-year co-operative agreement was signed by USAID/Jamaica and the Police Executive Research Forum (PERF) of the United States on 3 October 2002.

The project document indicates that the community policing component of the USAID/Jamaica democracy and governance programme, implemented by the Police Executive Research Forum, is a $6 million Jamaican initiative that seeks to address successfully the fundamental constraints to improving police and community relationships in Jamaica. The pilot to the programme will take place in Grants Pen community. There are three major components under the programme: the development of a model police station/post in targeted communities; improving community relations; and public education.

The development of a model police station/post

(a) Under this segment of the programme, technical assistance will be provided to develop operational policies, procedures and training plans for the Jamaica constabulary force.

(b) Technical assistance will also be provided to ensure that the police station/posts constructed by the private sector will have a design and space configuration which allows for the unrestricted use by members of the community who wish to conduct community-related activities.

(c) A community policing advisor will be responsible for providing technical assistance to the police personnel assigned to Grants Pen, to assist them in developing a comprehensive strategy and implementation plan to reduce violence, increase safety and build confidence in the police, based on an integrated community development approach.

(d) A comprehensive training plan will be developed and implemented that will embody specialised intervention in areas such as conflict resolution, domestic violence reduction and prevention strategies and general crime prevention strategies, using less confrontational approaches.

Community relations

(a) The development and implementation of training programmes for community citizenry, including community leaders, are designed to address how the community should interact with the police.

(b) An outreach programme to 'rival' communities with a view to involving them in training related to conflict resolution.

(c) To expose residents to mock trials in which they could participate, to become familiarised with how the formal legal system operates and remedies which can be obtained thereunder.

(d) The support of by the American Chamber of Commerce (AMCHAM) to mobilise private sector support.

(e) The development of a mentoring programme.

(f) The establishment of a community council.

The design and dissemination of relevant public outreach information

A strategic and essential part of this programme is to design and disseminate information to the public on a sustained basis, highlighting the positive benefits of community policing.

The Jamaican Model is a bold and imaginative experiment, which will be keenly followed by all those who are interested in the reduction of crime in their communities.

RESTORATIVE JUSTICE

Basic principles

The basic thrust of the movement for restorative justice is one of accountability and fairness in the criminal justice system as between offenders, victims, families and society at large. It seeks to bring together those parties most directly affected by a crime to attempt a collective mediation in a manner that squares with their sense of justice. The criminal justice system is not free from the strictures, which were made earlier, against the civil justice system.

Principal among these are the unresponsiveness to the needs of victims of crime, the inadequacy of the remedies (usually a fine or imprisonment) without addressing the interests of those harmed by the offence, the slow and time-consuming nature of the trial, and the disproportionate cost to the state.[25]

Proponents of restorative justice would argue that it places emphasis on healing relationships that have been broken by conflict and crime. The basic principle of restorative justice is that crime is a violation of people and relationships, and a disruption of community peace. It challenges the conventional view that crime is only an offence against the state. Accordingly, restorative justice involves a tripartite participation of victims, offenders and the community directly affected by the crime, in exploring creative solutions that target reconciliation and the restoration of peace in the community. Clearly, this new thrust is, once again, a revolutionary shift from the traditional adversarial justice system, which is found wanting when appropriate, creative and effective solutions are required to deal with crime and its effects on the victim, the offender and the community.

Restorative justice programmes have grown by leaps and bounds in the USA, Canada, the UK, Germany, Scandinavia, Eastern Europe, Australia and New Zealand, among others. The Caribbean, sadly, is not on this list.

The following are some of the basic principles which drive restorative justice:[26]

(a) The offence is primarily against the victim and secondarily against the state.

(b) Restitution is important in restoring the relationship between victim and offender.

(c) Restitution may be achieved by way of reparation, usually in the form of compensation or some form of community service.

(d) Reconciliation between victim and offender is also seen as an important objective of restorative justice, but not universally so. Some people feel that victims should not be pressed to forgive and become reconciled with their offender until they are ready to do so. (This is one of the main reasons why victim-offender reconciliation programs in the USA changed their name to victim-offender mediation programs.)

---

25 Restorative justice may also apply to civil conflicts as, for example, in cases such as environmental law, corporate law, labour relations, bankruptcy and family relationships. For the purposes of this book, the discussion will be limited to criminal law.

26 Quoted from Brown, H and Marriott, A, *ADR Principles and Practice*, 1999, Sweet & Maxwell, p 295.

(e) Communication and negotiation between the victim and offender is possible and often desirable to consider how to redress the wrong.

(f) Offenders are required to take responsibility for their actions and are given the opportunity to make amends.

These broad principles of restorative justice are promoted as an alternative to the present criminal justice system based on punishment and deterrence.

The question that may be asked is what accounts for this phenomenal growth despite the scepticism of many? Umbreitt seems to have the answer:

> The concept of a crime victim sitting face-to-face with the perpetrator is difficult for many public officials and citizens to grasp. People who are unfamiliar with the actual process of victim-offender mediation frequently ask questions. Why would any victim want to meet the criminal? What's in it for the victim? Why would an offender be willing to meet his or her victim? What is there to mediate or negotiate anyway?
>
> Despite these concerns, in a growing number of communities throughout North America and Europe, many hundreds of crime victims are meeting their offenders in the presence of trained mediators to tell them how the crimes affected the victims personally. They can get answers to lingering questions, such as Why me? and Were you watching my movements? Those who have committed certain types of criminal offenses are able to tell their stories, portray a more human dimension of their characters, own up to their behavior, and make amends. Together, both parties have the opportunity to negotiate a mutually agreeable restitution plan.[27]

His rationale for victim-offender mediation is highly persuasive. He says:

> The criminal justice system focuses almost entirely upon the offender. It is dominated by a 'train 'em, nail 'em, and jail 'em' philosophy that often does little to meet the emotional and material needs of the actual victim. Crime victims are nearly always placed in a totally passive position by the criminal justice system, and have minimal direct participation in or influence upon the process of holding the offenders accountable. Oftentimes they don't receive even basic assistance or information about the cases.
>
> Most victims feel powerless and vulnerable; some feel twice victimized, first by the offender and then by an uncaring criminal justice system that does not have time for them. Offenders rarely comprehend, much less confront the human dimension of their criminal behavior. They often fail to recognize that victims are real people, not just objects to be abused. Also, offenders have many rationalizations for their behaviors, It is not unusual for anger, frustration, and conflict to increase as the victim and offender move through the justice process.
>
> Instead of continuing the frequent depersonalization of victims and offenders in the criminal and juvenile justice systems, the victim-offender mediation process draws upon restorative justice principles that recognize that crime is fundamentally against people, and not just against the state. Victim-offender mediation facilitates a very active and personal process to work at conflict resolution by emphasizing the importance of restoring emotional and material losses. The people most affected by the crime are allowed the opportunity to become actively involved in resolving the conflict, in the belief that holding offenders personally accountable for their behavior and achieving some closure for the victim is far more important than focusing on past

---

27   Umbreit, MS, *Mediating Interpersonal Conflicts*, 1995, CPI Publishing, pp 135–36.

criminal behavior through ever-increasing levels of costly punishment. In contrast, the court system marginalizes the victim by relegating him or her to a passive role and requires of the offender little or no direct accountability to the person wronged. Further, the system reinforces an adversarial dynamic, and offers little emotional closure for the victim or offender.[28]

Methodology or process

Three approaches are generally used in the practice of restorative justice. These are:

(a) family group conferencing;

(b) victim-offender mediation; and

(c) sentencing and healing circles.

Victim-offender mediation involves a two party process, with the assistance of a trained mediator. Family group conferencing involves a wider group of participants, including representatives of the community. Sentencing involves the inclusion of principles in the criminal law to provide reparations for harm done to victims or the community, promoting a sense of responsibility in offenders while getting those offenders to acknowledge the harm which they would have done to the victims and the community. The use of circles stems from traditional methods of settling disputes, usually involving community elders. It is not unknown for circles to have been used, at the sentencing stage or following imprisonment, to assist a criminal to settle back in the community.

A few words about victim-offender reconciliation would be in order. Victim-offender mediation programmes (VOMP) or victim-offender reconciliation programmes (VORP), as they are sometimes called, bring offenders and victims together in a face-to-face encounter, with the assistance of a trained mediator. The process attempts to personalise the crime by getting the offenders to learn the effect of their crimes on the victims, while the victims get the opportunity to bare their feelings to the offender. In the criminal trial process, victims are usually sidelined and rarely ever have the opportunity to express their feelings. The process provides the opportunity for the offender to take responsibility for their actions and to help shape the outcome of a restitution agreement with the victim. Such restitution may take several forms, not excluding the following:

(a) restoring the victim's losses;

(b) payment of money;

(c) doing works for the victim;

(d) community service;

(e) any other form of restitution acceptable to the victim; and

(f) reintegration of the victim or the offender into society.

It should be recalled that the Community Mediation Acts of Barbados and Trinidad & Tobago reflect these principles of restitution.

Below is a comparative chart of the respective assumptions behind retributive and restorative justice.

---

28 *Ibid*, pp 138–39.

Retributive and restorative assumptions

[Source: Adapted from Zehr, 1990][29]

Retributive justice	Restorative justice
Crime is an act against the state, a violation of a law an abstract idea.	Crime is an act against another person or the community.
The criminal justice system controls crime.	Crime control lies primarily in the community.
Offender accountability defined as taking punishment.	Accountability defined as assuming responsibility and taking action to repair harm.
Punishment is effective; threat of punishment deters crime; punishment changes behaviour.	Punishment alone is not effective in changing behaviour and is disruptive in community harmony and good relationships.
Victims are peripheral to the process.	Victims are central to the process of resolving a crime.
The offender is defined by deficits.	The offender is defined by capacity to make reparation.
Focus on establishing blame, on guilt, on past (did he/she do it?).	Focus on problem solving, on liabilities or obligations, on future (what should be done).
Emphasis on adversarial relationship.	Emphasis on dialogue and negotiation.
Imposition of pain to punish/deter.	Restitution as a means of restoring both parties' goal of reconciliation/restoration.
Community on sideline, represented abstractly by state.	Community as facilitator in restorative process.
Response focused on offender's past behaviour.	Response focused on harmful consequences of offender's behaviour, emphasis on the future.
Dependence upon proxy professionals.	Direct involvement by participants.

---

29 Zehr, H, 'Retributive Justice, Restorative Justice', Mennonite Central Committee.

Effective compliance

Research has shown that restorative justice has proved to be more effective than the criminal justice systems in improving satisfaction for both victims and offenders, securing offender compliance with restitution orders and decreasing recidivism. If that is the case, then for the purposes of the Caribbean region, perhaps victim-offender mediation programmes could also be used as a powerful tool for the societal control of crime.

Research results from a cross-section of the North American programmes:

> ... show that about two-thirds of the cases referred resulted in a face-to-face mediation meeting; over 95% of the cases mediated resulted in a written restitution agreement; over 90% of those restitution agreements are completed within one year. On the other hand, the actual rate of payment of court-ordered restitution (nationally) is typically only from 20–30%.[30]

The Victim-Offender Reconciliation Program Information and Resource Center of Canada provides a credible justification for these reasonable results, as follows:

> Why is there such a huge difference in restitution compliance? Offenders seldom experience court-ordered restitution as a moral obligation. It seems like just one more fine being levied against them by an impersonal court system. When the restitution obligation is reached voluntarily and face-to-face, offenders experience it in a very different way. Perhaps most important, after facing the victims of their crimes, offenders commit fewer and less serious offenses than similar offenders who are processed by the traditional juvenile or criminal justice system.[31]

Its mission statement, reproduced below, clearly reinforces the case for using restorative justice processes for the social control of crime:

> To bring restorative justice reform to our criminal and juvenile justice systems, to empower victims, offenders and communities to heal the effects of crime, to curb recidivism and to offer our society a more effective and humanistic alternative to the growing outcry for more prisons and more punishment.

Crime statistics

There is no gainsaying the fact that crime is on the increase throughout the Caribbean region. In an end of year review of the crime situation in Barbados, the island's Commissioner of Police noted that Barbados has:

> ... been having a 'frenetic and challenging' year with increases in violent crimes up to the end of November. These crimes included serious bodily harm, robbery, assaults and minor woundings. Apart from this, '... the number of cases in which firearms were used to perpetrate offences also showed an increase'.

> The statistics show that from January to November there were 206 cases of violent crimes which ... was 'a significant rise over the 149 cases recorded for the corresponding period in 2001'. The Commissioner noted that such crimes do not bode well for the stability of our former idyllic society ...

---

30   Umbreit, M, *Mediating Interpersonal Conflicts*, 1995, CPI Publishing, p 155.
31   'Can Mediation Produce Restorative Justice for Victims and Offenders?', available at www.vorp.com/articles/crime.html.

In our homes there has also been increased violence, with some 1374 cases reported so far this year. The overview certainly is not idyllic.[32]

In an editorial commentary on the above statement, the *Daily Nation* stated as follows:

This trend of increasingly violent crimes is one that is already creating an environment of unease in neighbouring Guyana, Trinidad and Tobago and Jamaica. In Guyana, more than 60 people have been murdered this year, including at least ten policemen. Trinidad and Tobago saw more than 160 murders; in Jamaica, the figure has rushed past 1020, and in Barbados it has reached 24.

In Trinidad and Guyana, there have also been kidnappings and a number of daring daylight robberies, which signal that the criminal elements are prepared to create even more fear in these countries.

In Barbados, we have responded to gun crimes by introducing tough sentencing for the possession of illegal firearms, but handguns still seem to hold some fascination for a number of our citizens even when they are not harbouring any criminal intent.

Be that as it may, [the Commissioner of Police] has directed our attention to what can become an even more frenetic situation if we do not take steps to curb the violence. For a start, private citizens must be prepared to continue their assistance to the police in dealing with the criminal element in our country.

What we are seeing as a crime spiral in neighbouring countries did not occur overnight. Citizens who could have alerted the police often failed to do so and the criminal-minded now threaten to have the upperhand.[33]

Clearly, the seeming ease with which people resort to violence to resolve conflicts indicates an apparent deficit among the populace in the social skills necessary for peaceful co-existence. According to Barbados' Commissioner of Police, this lack of self-control stretched to all age groups in society. 'What is notable,' he said, 'is that it is not only youthful men and women who manifest such violence, but older persons as well.'[34]

Strategies to control crime

The question that may be asked is how may restorative justice processes be used to help with the societal control of crime? The answer lies in strategies designed to help society devise collective approaches to conflict in every sphere of society. So, an integrated approach to crime control ought to include the following strategies, among others:

(a) Community initiatives which engage the public in constructive alternatives to the present model of criminal justice, the development of restorative justice initiatives, training and evaluation schemes.

---

32 (2002) *Daily Nation*, 30 December, Barbados. See also Rickey Singh, Regional Security Challenge, in (2003) *Daily Nation*, 7 January. That article refers to gun-related murder and criminal violence including kidnappings and armed robberies in the region as a plague. He also produces the following chilling statistics of the murder rate in 2002 as 11 in the eastern Caribbean, 60 in Guyana, 171 in Trinidad & Tobago and 1,045 in Jamaica.

33 *Ibid.*

34 (2002) *Midweek Nation*, 25 and 26 December, p 1.

(b) Schools and youth initiatives which must involve children in early learning and practice in conflict resolution, support for teachers and schools which teach and practise the creation of a peaceful learning environment, and improve problem solving opportunities in schools.

(c) Environment and public policy initiatives which engage citizens in consensus building processes on important public issues.

(d) Organisational and workplace initiatives which encourage approaches to conflict in the workplace that support healthy, respectful relationships.

(e) Media and conflict portrayal initiatives which help media personnel develop analytical skills in conflict resolution designed to educate the public rather than sensationalise crime.

(f) Teaching and training support initiatives which promote education and skills training in conflict resolution, especially for facilitators who must have 'good understanding of local cultures and communities' and excellent interpersonal skills.

(g) Legislative framework to embrace those initiatives through the Ministry of Legal Affairs and crime prevention units, and the correctional services. Guidelines and standards which should have the backing of law may involve the following:

- the conditions for the referral of cases to restorative justice programmes;
- the handling of cases following a restorative process;
- the qualifications, training and assessment of facilitators;
- the administration of restorative justice programmes;
- standards of competence and ethical rules governing operation of restorative justice porgrammes; and
- procedural safeguards for all the parties.

(h) Application of problem solving approaches to crime by the police force. This involves the elements of problem identification, problem solving and maintenance and monitoring. The various components of the community, the nature of its people and its problems need to be identified and worked on co-operatively.

International initiatives

Since 1997, the United Nations Commission on Crime Prevention and Criminal Justice has been working on a draft declaration of basic principles on the use of restorative justice programs in criminal matters. The UN draft exhorts member states to review their practices in support of crime victims, including mechanisms for mediation and restorative justice. By the first quarter of 2004, this has not happened as suggested by the UN.[35] Its adoption, when completed, by regional governments will provide another strong impetus to move towards the uniform application of restorative justice guidelines.

A concluding observation is that restorative justice is now an emerging field of alternative dispute resolution, and one that has great potential for the orderly management of social behaviour and, therefore, the control of crime.

---

35 See Daniel Van Ness on the Restorative Justice website, www.restorativejustice.org.

CONCLUSION

This chapter has examined a number of initiatives which could impact significantly on how societies may expand the field of non-adversarial dispute resolution. Also, these initiatives could have beneficial effect on society's efforts to control crime and minimise the consequences of crime. In a region which is afflicted with increasing levels of crime, it is hoped that lawmakers, leaders of thought and designers of public policy may be persuaded that the potential gains in trying out these initiatives far outweigh the potential risks of doing nothing.

CHAPTER 8

CASELOAD MANAGEMENT

CASELOAD MANAGEMENT

Caseload management, which is also known as caseflow management, is an off-shoot of the ADR explosion. It is a compendium phrase used to describe the set of actions that a court may take to monitor and control the progress of a case before it, from initiation to post-disposition court work.

If caseload management is successfully applied, then the following may be the successful outcome:

(a) litigation would be avoided wherever possible;

(b) parties of limited financial means would be able to conduct litigation on a more equal footing;

(c) litigation would be less adversarial and more co-operative;

(d) litigation would be less complex; and

(e) the timescale of litigation would be shorter and more certain.

Through the methodology of a judge-driven engine, it seeks to introduce justice and speed to dispute settlement, with the following objectives:

(a) to put the parties before the court on an even footing;

(b) to save or cut down on expense and increase accessibility;

(c) to allocate court resources in proportion to the subject matter of the dispute;

(d) to be expeditious and effective;

(e) to ensure fairness;

(f) to be responsive to the needs of the parties;

(g) to ensure a more timely disposition of cases; and

(h) to improve the quality of dispute resolution and dispute resolution processes.

In order to achieve these aims, three things ought to happen: the present lawyer-driven litigation management process needs to change to a system of judge-driven case management; the court management process needs to be improved; and the standards of the Bench and Bar need to be raised.

Among the nations of the Organisation of Eastern Caribbean States (OECS), and in Jamaica and Trinidad & Tobago, there is a quiet ongoing revolution taking place on these very lines. The systematic change which is being advocated requires a complete transformation in the culture of litigation, as it is known today. Under this system, it is the court, and not the lawyer, that assumes responsibility for litigation before it. This change is also designed to water down the concept of adversarial litigation and trial by ambush. This imposes on litigants a duty of disclosure to one another as well as to the court. This change also requires a paradigm shift in the ethical values of the Bar, from simply a duty to the client to a duty to both the client and justice.

The case management system is also used to filter cases, identifying those that are susceptible to mediation and ADR processes. At the case management conference, the case is prepared for trial and time standards are fixed, all within 90 days of the filing of a writ in the three jurisdictions. Naturally, this system works best in the context of some form of automation and the use of technology in contemporary systems. Studies have shown that merely by improving management systems through the use of technology, there have been improvements in the quality of justice of between 50% and 75%. If the cases that must go to trial are to be dealt with by the judges, then the primary concern, in relation to those cases, must be the preparation of, the quality of and the accountability of that Bench. The judge has to manage the court professionally, must be courteous to litigants, must enforce time management deadlines and must adopt a hostile attitude to adjournments. In this new regime, the court must also be sensitive to the cultures of society, the prevailing ethics of society and hot button issues, such as gender. In other words, the judge must be sensitive to the social context in which justice is to be dispensed. This requires, of the judge, very high ethical standards, a very high level of professionalism and, of course, exposure to continuing judicial training.

Other key elements include clear direction and leadership by the judiciary, the deployment of efficient strategies, a cadre of well-trained personnel, adequate resources and effective technological support systems. Especially in jurisdictions to which caseflow management is new, there must be ongoing and continuous monitoring with a view to improving the system.

In an address to the Faculty of Law in Barbados on 28 February 2000, Sir David Simmons, now Chief Justice of Barbados, predicted that:

> In this region you can expect that within the next ten (10) years there will be radical changes in the culture and traditions of legal practice.
>
> First, ongoing negotiations ... [will lead to a modernisation of] the administration of justice by the use of technology and contemporary systems.
>
> Secondly, throughout the Commonwealth, there is a continuous movement to change the traditions of practice from being party-driven to a more-judge-driven culture. Case flow management and similar practices will require that all of us learn again the new Rules of Civil Procedure which will have as their central objective, the speedier access to justice.
>
> Thirdly, the adversarial approach to practice will gradually be diminished and the healthy techniques of settlement and ADR will come to the fore.[1]

Well, those challenges have already arrived. Some progress has been achieved with respect to the use of technology and the introduction of caseflow management. The OECS, Jamaica and Trinidad & Tobago have altered their court Rules in order to permit the application of caseload management techniques within the context of litigation.[2] Those of the OECS will be used as a reference point because, apart from the Rules themselves, there has been a practical application of them through a court-connected mediation pilot project. This pilot project was introduced by a Practice Direction which provided for the referral of case-managed civil actions filed in the

---

1   'Challenges for the Legal Profession in the 21st Century – Some Thoughts', unpublished paper.
2   As Attorney General, Sir David Simmons, now CJ, piloted a project to have new rules written for the Supreme Court to introduce caseload management. These rules are being subjected to wide consultation.

High Court, or possibly the Court of Appeal, and necessarily linked to a mediation program. The overriding objective of the Rules is to empower the courts to dispose of cases in a just manner. In order to be able to do so, Part 25.1(h) of the Rules requires that the court must actively manage cases by 'encouraging parties to use any appropriate form of dispute resolution including, in particular, mediation, if the court considers it appropriate and facilitating the use of such procedures'. This then provides the regulatory framework for the application of court-connected mediation.

A referral to mediation may be made by a master or judge at a case management conference. Once the order has been made, the parties cannot opt out of the referral order except by leave of the master or judge. By way of a policy decision, the following matters may not be made the subject of a referral order:[3]

(a) family proceedings;

(b) insolvency (including winding up of companies);

(c) non-contentious probate proceedings;

(d) proceedings when the High Court is acting as a prize court; and

(e) any other proceedings in the Supreme Court instituted under any enactment, in so far as Rules made under that enactment regulate those proceedings.

A referral order, when filed in the court office, shall be dispatched to the mediation co-ordinator by the registrar of the High Court. Referral criteria are set out in Rule 2 of the Practice Rules. A master or a judge shall take into account all relevant circumstances, including the following, when considering whether to refer a case to mediation or not. These are whether:

(a) there is an ongoing relationship between the parties;

(b) parties want a collaborative process to resolve their dispute;

(c) parties seek a flexible process that will enable creative solutions;

(d) parties do not want to risk the unpredictable outcome of a trial;

(e) opportunities for joint gains are not available through the court; or

(f) any other criteria considered appropriate by the master or judge.

Under Rule 3, a party may apply to the court to vacate a referral order within 15 days of the making of such order, upon showing good and substantial reason to the master or judge.

The first mediation session shall be conducted within 30 days of the referral order with the possibility of an extension if a party so requests with good reason.[4] In considering whether to extend the time within which the mediation is to be conducted the master or judge shall take into account all circumstances, including:

(a) the number of parties and the complexity of the issues in the action; and

(b) whether the mediation will be more likely to succeed if it is postponed to allow the parties to acquire more information.[5]

---

3   Supreme Court Civil Procedure Rules 2000, First Schedule, Rule 1.1.
4   Rule 4.
5   Rule 5.

Rule 7 deals with the selection of a mediator by the parties. It states:

> **7.1** All court-connected mediation shall be conducted by:
>
> (a) a mediator mutually agreed to by the parties; or
>
> (b) a mediator assigned by the master or judge if the parties fail to agree on the selection of a mediator.
>
> **7.2** The parties may select the mediator either:
>
> (a) at the case management conference; or
>
> (b) within 10 days of the Referral Order.
>
> **7.3** The claimant shall file a Notice of Selection of Mediator within 10 days of the Referral Order advising the Mediation Co-ordinator of the mediator selected.
>
> **7.4** If the Mediation Co-ordinator does not receive the notice as required in 7.3 above, he shall refer the matter to the Registrar of the High Court.
>
> **7.5** The Registrar shall refer the matter to the master or judge who shall assign a mediator from the Roster of Mediators and issue a Notice of Selection of Mediator by the master or judge to the parties advising them of the mediator selected.

Once a mediator has been selected and the notice of selection appropriately filed, it is then up to the mediation co-ordinator:

(a) in consultation with the parties and the mediator, to fix a date for the mediation session; and

(b) to serve on every party a notice of scheduled mediation stating the place, date and time of the mediation.

Regulation 9 sets out the procedure before the mediation session. At least seven days before the mediation session, each party shall forward to the mediator a copy of the statement of case in the matter. If the parties have agreed to settle, or have settled, the matter prior to the scheduled mediation session, they must cancel the mediation appointment and advise the mediation co-ordinator of the terms of the agreement or settlement.

Once mediation has been ordered, attendance is compulsory for the parties.[6] The parties are required to attend a three hour mediation session. After the first three hours, the mediation may be continued if the parties and the mediator agree to do so and the parties agree to pay the scheduled additional hourly rate.

A party who requires another person's approval before agreeing to a settlement shall, before the mediation session, arrange to have ready access to the other person throughout the session.

With the consent of all parties and the mediator, a mediation session may be adjourned at any time. In the event of an adjournment, the parties must reschedule the mediation session within the time limits set out in the practice direction.

Where a party fails to attend a mediation within half an hour of the appointed time the mediator shall cancel the session, and immediately lodge with the mediation co-ordinator a certificate of non-compliance for filing at the court office.[7] When a certificate of non-compliance is filed with the court office, the registrar shall refer the

---

6   Rule 10.
7   Rule 11.

matter to the master or judge who may make an appropriate order to refer the case back to a case management conference or impose costs on the defaulting party.[8]

As is the case with mediation, the parties are required to enter into a confidentiality agreement whereby:

(a) statements and documents produced in a mediation session, and not otherwise disclosable, are not subject to disclosure through discovery or any other process and are not admissible into evidence for any purpose, including impeaching credibility;

(b) the notes, records and recollections of the mediator conducting the session are confidential and protected from disclosure for all purposes; and

(c) at no time shall any party summon, subpoena or call the mediator as a witness to testify as to the fact of the mediation or as to any oral or written communication made at any stage of the mediation.

A mediator's report must be lodged with the mediation co-ordinator for filing at the court office at the end of the mediation session.[9]

If there is an agreement resolving some or all of the issues in the dispute:

(a) it shall be signed by the parties and the mediator and lodged with the mediation co-ordinator for filing at the court office; and

(b) within seven days after the agreement is signed, the parties shall apply to the court for an order in terms of the agreement and the master or judge shall make such order as he deems fit.

If, however, the parties fail to make an application to the court for an order in terms of the signed agreement within seven days after the agreement is signed, the master or judge shall make an order under part 26.2 of the Rules.[10]

If no agreement is reached that resolves all the issues in dispute, the matter shall be returned to case management.[11]

EVALUATION AND ASSESSMENT

The Rules which gave rise to the practice direction came into effect on 19 July 2002 and were to terminate on 17 April 2003, unless otherwise extended. They have now been extended indefinitely. The evaluation conducted of the pilot project shows 'a high level of satisfaction' with all aspects of the mediation programme, and matters mediated ranged from employment disputes dealing with severance payments, land disputes, vacant possession of property, debt collection to running down actions. This bodes well for the expansion of the pilot to the region as a whole. The mediation fee of EC$500 for a three hour session is considered to be reasonable, especially as that fee is shared by both parties equally.

---

8 Rule 12.
9 Rule 14.
10 Rule 15.
11 Rule 16.

This project is to be highly commended for the care and prudence with which the scheme was introduced. Critical issues such as quality control, budgetary control and management, training and public relations were fully addressed. One of the issues that was raised earlier about the introduction of ADR into the legal system had to do with the fear that jurisprudence, reliant as it is on judicial precedent, would suffer from ADR. The St Lucian pilot project has provided credible evidence to dispel that fear. Historically, only about 10% of cases filed actually end up in trial. The introduction of ADR has not disturbed that ratio at all. This means that, happily, the jurisprudence will not suffer and the development of precedent will not be handicapped in any significant way.

THE JAMAICAN EXPERIENCE

No discussion of the Jamaican experience would be complete without first making reference to the Dispute Resolution Foundation (DRF), which was established in 1994, as a successor organisation to the Mediation Council of Jamaica. Its mandate is the promotion of ADR in Jamaica, especially through the use of mediation and the promotion of good governance through conflict resolution and other strategies. The Foundation has been involved in training mediators in Jamaica with a 40 hour basic course, a 20 hour advanced course and a practicum of five cases of audited and mediated sessions.

Prior to the promulgation of the Judicature (Resident) Magistrates (Amendment) Act 1999, there was a consistent drive to engage the judiciary and magistracy in:

(a) advocating the use of available dispute resolution processes;

(b) referring matters coming before them for mediation, where appropriate;

(c) supporting an effective Mediation Referral Agency in the form of the DRF and a roster of mediators;

(d) building a working knowledge of mediation and other dispute resolution processes, as well as access, fees, enforcement and related matters; and

(e) advising disputants, court staff and attorneys about the integrated or court-connected processes and the relevance of neutrality, confidentiality and privilege.

On 30 December 1999, the Resident Magistrates Court (Amendment) Rules came into effect. They were to be read as one with the Resident Magistrates Court Rules 1933. The intention of the new Rules was, clearly, to reinforce the use of mediation in the court process. Section 26(1) provides that:

Where, in the course of the proceedings in an action, the Judge is of the opinion that mediation may be of assistance to the parties the Judge may–

(a) advise the parties to attend upon an approved mediator; and

(b) adjourn the proceedings to enable that attendance.

'Approved mediator' is dealt with in s 28:

(1) The Chief Justice may, on the recommendation of the Dispute Resolution Foundation, appoint persons to be approved mediators for the purposes of these Rules.

(2) The names of all persons appointed under paragraph (1) shall be published in the Gazette.

(3) The Chief Justice may, after consultation with the Dispute Resolution Foundation, by notice in the Gazette, revoke the appointment of any mediator under paragraph (1) where the Chief Justice is satisfied that the mediator is not adequately carrying out the functions required under rule 26.

That is a clear legislative endorsement of the work of the Dispute Resolution Foundation, a well deserved recognition of its track record of solid achievement.

Post mediation procedure is set out in s 27:

(1) If after attending upon an approved mediator, the parties–

  (a) declare that they have arrived at a settlement, the terms of that settlement shall be endorsed upon the records and shall be binding upon the parties;

  (b) fail to arrive at a settlement, the matter shall be heard and determined by the Resident Magistrate.

(2) In proceedings under paragraph (1)(b), no party shall adduce in evidence anything said or done by any party during the course of mediation.

Beyond these Rules, there is a Supreme Court civil mediation pilot project, which commenced in January 2003, simultaneously with new civil procedure Rules. The pilot project has also been extended indefinitely. The new Rules, it is said, will have 'many of the provisions of the OECS Civil Procedure Rules but will have a more detailed procedure for mediation, through a Practice Direction now under consideration by the Chief Justice'.[12] Indications are that:

The court is anticipated to outsource the management and delivery of the mediation service under the court's direction and supervision to the mediation referral agency.

All matters in the Supreme Court and new Civil Procedure Rules will be eligible for the mediation pilot except for:

- administrative law proceedings (under part 56);

- writs of habeas corpus (under part 57);

- bail applications (under part 58);

- admiralty proceedings (under part 70); and

- fixed date claims (under rule 8.1).

---

12 Bernard Madden, C, 5–6 December 2002, presentation to Caribbean Law Institute Workshop, St Lucia.

It is anticipated that access to the pilot will be by referral in circumstances such as:

- Upon filing of first defence where the Attorneys-at-Law in the matter have agreed to participate in the pilot project and on notification by the Registrar; or

- By referral from a case management conference by a designated Judge, Registrar or Master; or

- By notice to the Registrar within 14 days of filing defence; or

- On application on consent by the parties at a case management conference; or

- By the referral through random selection 7 days after filing of first defence based on criteria approved by the Mediation Project Steering Committee; or

- By settlement week and other backlog-reduction strategies agreed by the Rules Committee of the Supreme Court.

The challenges include delivery of a quality, timely, confidential, service which is credible because of its ability to engage litigants, attorneys, the court, and the public more effectively in resolving large and costly disputes.[13]

These Rules have since been superceded by a court-connected mediation Practice Direction,[14] issued by the Chief Justice, which took effect from 1 January 2003. Its essential principles are modelled on the pilot project in St Lucia and, like that of St Lucia, the pilot was renewed and made permanent. This bodes well for the harmonisation of laws and a unified regional approach to the solution of common problems.

A unique Barbadian initiative

In Barbados, an interesting initiative has been formalised in legislation, which could help reduce the caseload of the courts. This is contained in the Consumer Guarantees Act no 21 of 2002, which deals with:

(a) the guarantees available to consumers upon the supply of goods and services; and

(b) the rights of redress against suppliers and manufacturers in respect of a failure of goods or services to comply with any such guarantees.

Part VII of the Act sets out the mechanisms for the resolution of disputes. A consumer claims tribunal is established to deal with the right of redress of persons who have complaints against guarantees made in respect of goods by suppliers and manufacturers.

An aggrieved person may refer a complaint to a public counsel who may:

(a) endeavour to assist the aggrieved person by mediating on their behalf with the person against whom they seek to enforce the right; and

(b) where a settlement is not achieved, represent the aggrieved person in proceedings before the tribunal.

---

13   *Ibid.*
14   Number SC 2002-2.

The function of the tribunal is to enforce the rights conferred upon consumers and others by this Act.

The jurisdiction of the tribunal is to determine complaints made to it where the value of the subject matter of the complaint does not exceed the sum of $10,000 and, subject to s 48:[15]

(2) ... to make awards and other decisions in accordance with its powers under this Act.

(3) Subject to section 48, an award or other decision made by the Tribunal in exercise of its powers under this Act is final and is not subject to any appeal.

The Tribunal shall not proceed to determine a complaint unless it is satisfied that the complainant has made all reasonable efforts to obtain redress for his complaint and has failed to obtain such redress.

The Tribunal may make such enquiries, and hold such hearings, as it thinks fit for the purpose of discharging its duty.

The tribunal is given ancillary power to grant relief:[16]

Where a consumer cancels under this Act a contract for the supply of a service, a court or the Tribunal in any proceedings or on application made for the purpose may from time to time, if it is just and practicable to do so, make an order or orders granting relief under this section.

An order under this section may–

(a) vest in any party to the proceedings the whole or any part of any real or personal property that was the subject of the contract or was the whole or part of the consideration for it;

(b) direct any party to the proceedings to transfer or assign to any other such party or to give him the possession of the whole or any part of any real or personal property that was the subject of the contract or was the whole or part of the consideration for it;

(c) without prejudice to any right to recover damages, direct any party to the proceedings to pay to any other such party such sum as the court or Tribunal thinks just;

(d) direct any party to the proceedings to do or refrain from doing in relation to any other party any act or thing as the court or Tribunal thinks just;

(e) permit a supplier to retain the whole or part of any money paid or other consideration provided in respect of the service under the contract.

Any such order, or any provision of it, may be made upon such terms and subject to such conditions as the court or Tribunal thinks fit, not being in any case a term or condition that would have the effect of preventing a claim for damages by any party.

In considering whether to make an order under this section, and in considering the terms of any order it proposes to make, the court or Tribunal shall have regard to–

---

15 Section 48 provides that an appeal lies to the Court of Appeal in accordance with rules of court on a question of law from any decision of, or arising in any proceedings before the Tribunal under, or by virtue of, this Act.

16 Section 46.

(a) any benefit or advantage obtained by the consumer by reason of anything done by the supplier in or for the purpose of supplying the service;

(b) the value, in the opinion of the court or Tribunal, of any work or service performed by the supplier in or for the purpose of supplying the service;

(c) any expenditure incurred by the consumer or the supplier in or for the purpose of the performance of the service;

(d) the extent to which the supplier or the consumer was or would have been able to perform the contract in whole or in part; and

(e) such other matters as the court or Tribunal thinks fit.

No order shall be made under subsection (2)(a) that would have the effect of depriving a person, not being a party to the contract, of the possession of or an estate in any property acquired by him in good faith and for valuable consideration.

No order shall be made under this section in respect of any property if any party to the contract has so altered his position in relation to the property, whether before or after the cancellation of the contract, that, having regard to all relevant circumstances, it would in the opinion of the court of Tribunal be inequitable to any party to make such an order.

An application for an order under this section may be made by–

(a) the consumer;

(b) the supplier;

(c) any person claiming through or under the consumer or the supplier; or

(d) any other person if it is material for him to know whether relief under this section will be granted.

Where–

(a) an order or award is made by the Tribunal under this Act; and

(b) the Registrar of the Tribunal certifies that the order or award has been so made, and specifies the terms of the order or award in the certificate,

the order or award is enforceable as if it were an order made by a magistrate's court in civil proceedings.

A certificate of the Registrar under subsection (1) is conclusive evidence of the matters specified in the certificate.

The results from this uniquely ingenious piece of legislation will require study and students of ADR will be watching with bated breath to see the proven results from this piece of social engineering. It would be interesting to conduct an evaluation of this pilot project and to draw on lessons learned for the future.

CHAPTER 9

CONCLUSION

In this concluding chapter, some critical policy issues are examined, the nexus between ADR and public law is reviewed and some projections for the future are made.

Some critical policy issues

If the notion is accepted that in many respects litigation is to the client what surgery is to the patient, then a number of public policy issues need to be addressed. This section attempts to raise some of these issues.

Is there to be a duty on a lawyer to advise their client about ADR?

A number of leading commentators[1] have argued for the adoption of a rule that imposes a duty on a lawyer to present ADR options to their client. They argue from that premise that a failure to so inform a client is a legal wrong against the client for which the lawyer may be sued for malpractice or negligence. As with all public policy issues, views are divided on the right approach to reach a desirable end. Opponents of this proposal argue that it is indeed objectionable to use litigation to compel lawyers to present ADR options to their clients. They say that malpractice suits against lawyers will add to the number of cases before the courts, thus adding to the caseload unnecessarily.

Perhaps the answer lies somewhere in the middle, the search for an approach that would lead to the desirable goal of offering choices to litigants, other than the hitherto popular one of litigation. Of course, the need to offer ADR to litigants has some clear benefits since this exploration could lead to alternative and creative means of resolving the disputes that are more likely to preserve relationships and save financial and emotional expense.

In the absence of a specific rule in the Code of Professional Conduct of the Bar in the Caribbean region, it is to be hoped that, through creative interpretations of existing rules on professional competence, the Bar in the region will become interested enough to alter the present rules to enable such a rule to be adopted. In any case, with the increasing adoption of ADR processes in the court system, the region has to face this issue frontally, and sooner rather than later.

---

1   One such commentator is Professor Robert F Cochran, Jr in 'Must Lawyers Tell Clients About ADR?' (1993) Arbitration Journal 8. See also Sander, F, 'At Issue; Professional Responsibility: Should There be a Duty to Advise of ADR Options? Yes: An Aid to Clients' (1990) ABA Journal 50; Cochran Jr, RF, 'Legal Representation and the Next Steps Toward Client Control: Attorney Malpractice for the Failure to Allow the Client to Control Negotiation and Pursue Alternatives to Litigation' (1990) 47 Washington & Lee Law Review 819–77.

A re-examination of the code of ethics?

The legal profession throughout the region is guided by a code of ethics. That of Barbados is as representative as any. Section 18(1) of the Legal Profession Act of Barbados[2] establishes a disciplinary committee charged with the duty of upholding standards of professional conduct.

Sub-sections (4)(a) and (b) mandate the disciplinary committee to make rules:

(a) prescribing standards of professional etiquette and professional conduct of attorneys-at-law, and may by such rules direct that any specified breach of the rules shall constitute grave professional misconduct;

(b) prescribing anything which may be or is required to be prescribed for the purposes of this Part.

The Legal Profession Code of Ethics 1988[3] is the end product of the above section. Professional misconduct is defined in relation to the profession and the attorney themself, the state and the public, clients, the courts and the administration of justice, and to an attorney's fellow attorneys.

In relation to clients specifically, ss 24 and 25 are germane to the discussion at hand. These sections say:

24

(1) An attorney-at-law shall always act in the best interests of his client, represent him honestly, competently and zealously and endeavour by all fair and honourable means to obtain for him the benefit of any and every remedy and defence which is authorised by law, steadfastly bearing in mind that the duties and responsibilities of the attorney-at-law are to be carried out within and not without the bounds of the law.

(2) *The interests of his client* and the exigencies of the administration of justice *should always be the first concern* of an attorney-at-law and rank before his right to compensation for his services.

25

(1) Before advising on a client's cause an attorney-at-law should obtain *full knowledge thereof* and give a candid opinion of the *merits or demerits* and *probable results of pending or contemplated litigation.*

(2) An attorney-at-law should beware of proffering bold and confident assurances to his client (especially where employment may depend on such assurances) always bearing in mind that seldom are all the law and facts on the side of his client.

(3) Whenever the controversy admits of fair adjustment, an attorney-at-law should inform his client accordingly and advise *to avoid or settle litigation.*[4]

It is probable that these regulations could be stretched to cover the lawyer's role in ADR. However, there is increased recognition that a lawyer's intervention in ADR calls for more than the traditional rules covered by the Code of Ethics. For example, family mediation is considered to be a specialised and highly skilled area of law

---

2   Cap 370A.
3   SI 1988 No 113.
4   Emphasis added.

practice, requiring a great deal of circumspection and exceptional tact. So, in the UK, for example, there is a special code in the Family Mediation Code of Practice to govern that area of practice and to deal with situations of power imbalance.[5] Similarly, a case can be made for recognising additional responsibilities for lawyers involved in civil and commercial mediation.

Surely this calls for the establishment of uniform standards of competence, based on some form of training? It is also a recognition of the fact that a lawyer practising ADR has different duties and obligations from one who is acting for a client in a representative capacity as opposed to acting as a neutral third party. The role of a neutral third party is, itself, not free from further ethical dilemmas for, in that capacity, the lawyer mediator has tremendous opportunity to influence the course of the settlement one way or the other. One such opportunity could arise when the mediation goes into a caucus. Also, in order to maintain an objectively fair process, the mediator must be proactive in creating those conditions which promote even-handedness and reduce threats of power imbalances.

Confidentiality in a mediator also raises critical issues for the ADR process, especially when that duty is pitched against the public interest. Should a mediator learn of a case of sexual assault on a minor during a family mediation, coupled with a threat of further repetition of such assault, which duty ought to prevail: confidentiality or the public interest? These acute dilemmas ought to be resolved by the collective will of the legal profession in the form of guidelines emanating from the Bar associations.

The call, then, is for the Bar associations of the region to address the need for the inclusion of specific provisions in their existing codes to take account of the specialised requirements of the practice of ADR. Questions such as what constitutes an absolute bar or a qualified bar to mediation can be taken up in the necessary revisions.

In the recent case of *Re Errol Niles*,[6] the Court of Appeal of Barbados made a call for a radical review of the Legal Profession Act of Barbados. This is what the court said:

> Before parting with this case we feel obliged to make some general comments about the Legal Profession Act and the functioning of the Disciplinary Committee.
>
> During this year, this Court has had to deal with four cases involving recommendations from the Disciplinary Committee for the discipline of attorneys-at-law. These cases have highlighted the need for the enactment of new legislation to replace the existing Legal Profession Act. We were told that there is a Committee appointed to make recommendations for new legislation. We would therefore urge the Committee to accelerate its work in this regard.
>
> It seems to us that the procedure for discipline requires the development of a more detailed code than presently exists under the Fifth Schedule. And the manner in which the Committee has proceeded over the last 30 years must be changed.

---

5   For example, the UK College of Family Mediators Code deals specifically with the scope of mediation, some general principles, neutrality, impartiality, independence and conflicts of interest, confidentiality, privilege and legal proceedings, the welfare of children and violence within the family.

6   Court of Appeal, Barbados, decided October 2003 (unreported).

Disciplinary proceedings against an attorney-at-law are primarily aimed at the protection of the public. But a court or other tribunal dealing with the discipline of legal practitioners must observe the requirements of procedural fairness before making decisions about professional misconduct.

It is unsatisfactory that, after 30 years, there is no provision in the Act for the assignment of legal counsel to unrepresented complainants. In the absence of legal counsel, the Committee seeks to elicit the evidence by a series of questions from persons who are invariably unfamiliar with and unskilled in legal matters. It is, of course, proper for a judge or decision maker to ask questions of parties and witnesses for the purpose of clarification and it is indeed necessary for judicial assistance to be offered to persons who are unrepresented in criminal trials. But, it is always a question of degree to what extent an adjuducator should intervene 'depriving himself of the advantage of calm and dispassionate observation' – *per* Lord Greene MR in *Yuill v Yuill* [1945] 1 All ER 183 at 189. Lest the Committee be accused (as they were in this case) of being prosecutor and judge offending the principle of natural justice that *nemo iudex in sua causa debet*, it would be a more acceptable practice to appoint one of the seven attorneys-at-law on the Committee to lead the evidence and conduct cross-examination. That member of the Committee should thereafter take no part in the deliberations of the Committee.

This call for a re-write of the legislation, which is fully supported, ought to provide the impetus for a consideration of the ethical dilemmas which currently afflict the ADR process.

As the writer has commented in a case note on *Re Errol Niles*:

This is a wide-ranging decision of great public importance in Public Law. It is hoped that the points canvassed here and the principles so lucidly espoused by the Court of Appeal would receive the urgent attention of the Attorney General's Ministry in re-drafting the Legal Profession Act in such a way as to afford adequate protection to the general public while, at the same time, offering full protection to attorneys-at-law in the exercise of their constitutional rights to equal protection before the law.[7]

Enforcement issues

Of course ADR outcomes which are court-connected do not carry problems of enforcement. Once adopted by the court, those outcomes become judgments of the court which may be enforced in the usual manner with the assistance of court marshalls.[8]

Problems arise, however, with those resolutions which are made voluntarily by the disputants outside the court system. A great deal rests on the intentions of the parties. It is not unreasonable to expect that parties who have voluntarily participated in a process will also implement the outcomes reached. The question is whether the failure by one party to honour the terms of a settlement can be attacked on legal grounds. This is where ADR could borrow from the law of contract by enforcing the outcome as a contract. While an approach to the court may defeat the whole purpose of using ADR in the first place, it seems that there is no other way, short of self-help, to realise the agreed outcomes of the ADR process.

---

7   Fiadjoe, A, 'Disciplinary Proceedings Against the Bar – What is the Proper Role of the Court of Appeal?', accepted for publication in December 2004 Caribbean Law Review.

8   See the discussion of the St Lucian court connected mediation in Chapter 8.

The nexus between ADR and public law

This section seeks to make *patent* what has been latent throughout this book, the inexorable nexus between ADR and public law, as a result of the shift from government to governance.

As Professor Cecil Carr observed as far back as 1941, government used to be regarded as the sole provider of services and the only guardian of the public wealth. This is how he put it:

> Whereas the State used to be merely politician, judge and protector, it has now become schoolmaster, doctor, housebuilder, road-master, town-planner, public utility supplier and all the rest of it ... De Tocqueville observed in 1866 that the state 'everywhere interferes more than it did, it regulates more undertakings, and undertakings of a lesser kind; and it gains a firmer footing every day, about, around and above all private persons, to assist, to advise, and to coerce them'.[9]

Modern commentators have stressed the ever-growing power of the state and how the growth has affected the relations between the state and its citizens. Professor Wade set out it in this way:

> If the state is to care for its citizens from the cradle to the grave, to protect their environment, to educate them at all stages, to provide them with employment, training, houses, medical services, pensions, and, in the last resort, food, clothing, and shelter, it needs a huge administrative apparatus. Relatively little can be done merely by passing Acts of Parliament and leaving it to the courts to enforce them. There are far too many problems of detail, and far too many matters which cannot be decided in advance. No one may erect a building without planning permission, but no system of general rules can prescribe every case. There must be discretionary power. If discretionary power is to be tolerable, it must be kept under two kinds of control: political control through Parliament, and legal control through the courts. Equally there must be control over the boundaries of legal power, as to which there is normally no discretion.[10]

In 1981, the Justice All Souls Report described the modern state similarly as follows:

> The state has assumed an ever increasing range of responsibilities. Through nationalisation it controls most of the basic industries and the goods and services they supply. It runs a comprehensive system of social services providing benefits from just before the cradle (by way of pre-natal services and a maternity grant) to the grave (with a death grant) and in between it provides education, a health service, sickness benefits, unemployment benefits and old age pensions.

> The state also seeks to control much of the environment in which we live ...

> This enormous growth in the nature and ambit of state power can be illustrated in a number of ways. First, there has been a vast increase in public expenditure.

> Secondly, there has also been a massive increase in the number of those employed to administer our affairs.

---

9   Quoted in Harlow, C and Rawlings, R, *Law And Administration*, 1984, Weidenfeld & Nicolson, p 5.
10   Wade, W, *Administrative Law*, 1998, OUP, Preface to the 6th edn, p 4.

> Thirdly, there has been a spate of increasingly complex Acts of Parliament and regulations flowing from the government machine.[11]

In that kind of milieu, the principal preoccupation of public law has been to ensure that individual rights and liberties are adequately protected. This challenge has become even more sharpened as the state is now an entrepreneur, controlling industry and providing services and benefits. Public law has been struggling to keep pace with these developments in cases such as *R v Panel on Takeovers and Mergers ex p Datafin plc*,[12] *Williams Construction Ltd v AG of Barbados*,[13] and *Rambachan v Trinidad & Tobago Televison*[14] show.

These challenges have now taken on a new dynamism as a result of the move from government to governance. Douglas Lewis describes the new thrust ably in these words:

> Government speaks of older ways, whereby parliaments, the Executive and the Civil Service deliver in a more or less direct fashion what was promised in election manifestos. Furthermore, there was a clear-ish break between the public and private spheres with government expected to leave the latter substantially untouched. All this has changed. Not only has government at the centre given up trying to deliver many 'public goods', but it sees as its task in a competitive and globalised world the need to act as the strategic fulcrum for the nation as a whole, including much of the private sector.
>
> Government remains the strategic hub around which the nation turns, but what it is engaged in is 'governance' whereby it orchestrates a wide range of actors (to mix a metaphor) not only to provide public goods but to achieve 'added value' for the nation. Government was always a tricky business, but governance is worryingly complex. It engages in partnerships, it encourages and stimulates them, it prods and suggests, it awards and monitors contracts, it regulates for competitive markets and social purposes. In short, it seeks to pursue the nation's interests by whatever means and methodologies available and is inevitably engaged in experimentation to determine which delivery system best fits which public goods. This is a far cry from traditional political science and yet, to a large extent, our public law is still living with that past.[15]

Governance now involves the creation of new relationships among those bodies which have been democratically elected, government ministries and agencies, private bodies of all shades, public interest groups, the media and the citizens.[16] Governance is forcing governments to increasingly off-load its functions through privatisation, contracting out and similar strategies. Clearly, the involvement of so many disparate

---

11 *Op cit*, fn 9, p 6.
12 [1987] 1 All ER 504.
13 (1994) 45 WIR 94.
14 Suit No 4789 of 1982, H Ct T&T.
15 Lewis, ND, *Law And Governance*, 2001, Cavendish Publishing, Preface, pp v and vi.
16 The definition provided by The Commission on Global Governance says:

> ... the sum of the many ways individuals and institutions, public and private, manage their common affairs. It is a continuing process through which conflicting or diverse interests may be accommodated and co-operative action may be taken. It includes formal institutions and regimes empowered to enforce compliance, as well as informal arrangements, that people and institutions have agreed to or perceive to be in their interest.

Commission on Global Governance, 1995, *Our Global Neighbourhood*, UN, quoted in Lewis, ND, *ibid*, p 4.

players – what one may call a motley assortment of various interest groups in governance – must have some direct impact on the enjoyment of fundamental rights by the citizenry. It calls for a rethink of the rights culture which has informed the process of dispute resolution through litigation. The protection of rights has hitherto been limited to standing rules which have sought to protect individualism in a form of economic, proprietary and pecuniary rights, much to the sidelining of other interests. All of this has occurred notwithstanding the unchallenged opinion that the dividing line between public and private has increasingly become unsure indeed.

The new culture of governance would call for the recognition of both traditional and non-traditional rights, individual as well as collective, together with those that we may classify as 'developing rights'.

Managing the various and varied constituencies requires more than simply maintaining legal and constitutional probity between the players. It critically requires the creation of new mechanisms, the adaption of old ones and the recognition of new dispute resolution processes. It is incumbent on states to devise these processes to help resolve conflicts early, especially at the policy level.

The combined activities of the numerous players in governance, such as large corporations, trade unions and quasi-governmental entities, may result in public concerns which the traditional dispute resolution process may not be willing to handle, especially if one has regard to the strict requirements of *locus standi*. Yet citizens may well have serious concerns about environmental policy, or land use or the execution of government policy, without producing a plaintiff whose grievance will be entertained by the courts.

At present, under the fundamental rights protection clause in Caribbean constitutions, a person whose rights or freedoms have been infringed, or are likely to be infringed, may have recourse to some remedy from the Supreme Court. The alternative route is to allege some invalidity against the constitution without a direct invasion of the claimant's rights. If successful, a party may only be limited to a declaration. The limitation of remedies to declarations only is in itself hard to justify.

A liberalised case for standing always has the potential to contend with the floodgates argument. It is submitted that ADR offers a way out of the difficulty. Many of the non-traditional rights can be the subject of mediation across communities, societies and differing interests. In one of the best articulated cases for the recognition of non-traditional rights and interests, WA Bogart had this telling observation to make:[17]

> The notion of courts as the distant and aloof arbiters of disputes between two equal individuals is deeply ingrained in our legal culture. Part of the reason for this is laudable. We want very much to believe that we have a system not only of law but also of justice in which each of us can seek redress on an even and equitable basis. That is a norm to which we cling with tenacity. We also believe it because many of us want to preserve an area of private ordering. So a system that allows disputants to solve problems for themselves, to work out their own answers, to come to an agreement and to resist an answer imposed upon them has great appeal. We want a system where we can argue about means but means which will allow each one of us to seek ends directed to our own particular desires. To do that, we project the same attributes upon all parties; we cast them all as free, independent and equal actors

---

17   In Sharpe, RJ (ed), *Charter Litigation*, 1987, Butterworths, pp 23 and 24.

capable of making decisions and accepting responsibility for them. We see the judge pronouncing a solution (if called upon to do so by parties who have not otherwise settled), but one meticulously confined so as not disturb or to disrupt only minimally those who are not parties to the litigation.

But the lesson for the law at the close of the twentieth century must surely be that it cannot only concern itself with means and exclude ends if it seeks to lay claim to justice. Ends now are more than just economic quests and the struggle for individual liberty, as important as these are. Significant areas of the law such as occupational health and safety, worker's compensation, products liability, consumer protection and landlord and tenant legislation show how self-determination and altruism are competing ideologies which yield differing substantive legal results depending upon the context. Even more tentative and abstract values such as quiet, health, access to nature and the environment, a sense of individuality and a sense of position in social organization impress themselves upon our individual and collective consciousness and, in turn, upon the law.

This is where the potential to use ADR processes to resolve some of these difficulties could be deftly deployed. It must also be pointed out that in the Caribbean region, people are not accustomed to mounting class actions to vindicate public interest rights. A solution lies along the lines of mediation involving multiple parties. An example of such a solution occurred in Belize when the Dispute Resolution Foundation of Jamaica mediated an environmental dispute involving three groups made up of 35 representatives and at least 14 major issues. That story needs to be told.[18]

The Crooked Tree Wildlife Sanctuary, located some 32 miles north of Belize City, is one of six protected areas of Belize managed by the Belize Audubon Society (BAS). The sanctuary is 16,000 acres in area and is primarily lagoons, marshlands and waterways. Home to over 350 species of wading birds and water fowls, including migratory species and the world famous Jabiru stork, this pristine area is regarded as one of Belize's premier birding regions. Also present are numerous species of wildlife, including the white tailed deer, black howler monkeys, green and spiny-tailed iguanas and morelet crocodiles.

Situated in the middle of the sanctuary is the village of Crooked Tree, a community with a logging history dating back some 250 years. Up until 1981, before the construction of a causeway, the village was accessible only by a small riverboat. The villagers lived in relative seclusion, resulting in the development of a distinct cultural identity. They consider the wildlife area and the surrounding forests and savannahs as an integral part of their every-day life. Throughout the years, these people have hunted, fished, raised cattle, and grown crops there, realising the need for the conservation and protection of the area's natural resources.

As tourism is developing in Belize and more tourists are visiting the Crooked Tree Wildlife Sanctuary, the BAS, having managed the sanctuary since 1984, is constantly implementing ways in which villagers can use tourism as an alternative to logging, boosting the economic status of their village.

Ongoing at this time were educational awareness programs designed to sensitise and educate the inhabitants, who live in the surrounding communities, to the benefits of preserving the sanctuary.

---

18 The author is, indeed, grateful to Donna Parchment of the Dispute Resolution Foundation of Jamaica for allowing the free use of her papers on the mediation.

The conflict which had torn the Crooked Tree village, set in deep rural eastern Belize, dates back to the early 1990s. But the story began years before that, in 1984, when the Belizean government gave the BAS a mandate to manage a number of sites, which were established as protected areas under the National Parks System Act of 1984, to preserve the country's most fragile natural resources. The BAS, according to its executive director, Ted Castillo, had been actively promoting an appreciation and awareness of the country's marine life, its many species of resident and migrant birds, butterflies, plants, wildlife – including the jaguar and its natural preys – and wetland forests. There were workshops, seminars and all the usual facets of a public education programme.

However, when the organisation tried to implement the draft of a management plan that would regulate traditional hunting and fishing practices, the people of Crooked Tree village objected. The objections developed into a five year conflict between the government and the people who had, for 230 years, lived in almost absolute isolation. Their only contact with Belize City was by means of a two day boat ride.

The last 20 years have seen some changes – a causeway now links the village to the city and legislation has been introduced – but, as Castillo explained, it was his organisation's implementation of the management plan that the people found disturbing. Several initiatives were attempted, including the creation of an advisory council, with the assistance of the Belize Tourism Industry Association, to organise a business association, and to implement a management plan. The management plan was rejected and decision making hampered in a climate of discontent and distrust on various issues.

It was within this context that the Dispute Resolution Foundation was invited to conduct a community dialogue to mediate the inevitable difficulties in the situation, and to provide a springboard for a new thrust to educate and sensitise community members about wise use of their resources, increase local support for conservation, promote greater community involvement and improve communication between the sanctuary managers and the local population.

Using the seven stage mediation model,[19] the mediators were able to establish that the participants shared one fundamental concern, namely how to preserve the wetlands for the benefit of current and future populations without unduly disrupting the traditional way of life of the immediate residents of affected areas. The participants also agreed that one of their greatest difficulties was communication at all levels.

In evaluating the lessons learnt from what turned out to be a successful mediation, it could be said that the Belize experience provided an opportunity for community dialogue and mediation. Here was a conflict resolution process involving over 35 parties, comprising four main interest groups. Each had a stake in the outcome of the process, not only from the point of view of the interest group to which they belonged, but also as individuals who were affected in one way or another by what happened in the Crooked Tree Wildlife Sanctuary.

---

19 These stages are introduction, problem determination, summarisation, issue identification, generation and evaluation of alternatives, selection of appropriate alternatives and conclusion.

In a typical mediation, there are two parties, whether or not represented, who are locked in dispute over some personal matter between them. By and large, this is the scenario which appears in the role plays used in training exercises. This has often led persons, being exposed to mediation for the first time, to assert that it is not appropriate to any but that type of dispute. Belize gives the lie to that assertion.

Trainees and new mediators are always reminded that the process, while following a particular structure, must remain flexible. That flexibility was tried and proven when the seven stage mediation model was applied to the Crooked Tree situation. Modifications were required primarily at stages I, II and III – introduction, problem determination and summarisation. With so many people involved, and so much at stake, the introduction stage had to be turned into a training session to ensure that it achieved its purposes. At the problem determination stage, ways had to be found to accommodate the frank and free expression of the feelings and views of the 35 participants, without descending into babel! Apparently, the methods devised worked, as most of the participants afterwards agreed that they had been given a chance to express themselves fully.

Throughout the process, the greatest challenges for the facilitators were organising and controlling the flow of information, maintaining the balance of power and staying within the time constraints. A preliminary response to these challenges was the decision to use two mediators working in tandem, rather than the usual one. It was also thought that flip charts and audio recordings would prove useful to supplement the personal notes of the mediators. The visual impact of the former had the extremely helpful effect of not only keeping the participants focused, but also of enabling the immediate identification of any inaccuracies, inconsistencies or misunderstandings. The audio recordings, on the other hand, were not actually consulted, and this may have been due to difficulties associated with identifying the respective speakers. A video recording may have proven more useful, especially in a training setting, but its absence had no negative effect on the process.

With specific regard to the time constraints, the fact that there was a preset schedule, which had to be adhered to, meant that there were limits to the extent to which some matters arising could be explored. It is a moot point whether preset time limits are advisable. On the one hand, preset time limits may force parties to be creative, open-minded and focused, to ensure that goals are achieved while, on the other hand, they may create tension which produces the opposite effect.

In the main, preset time limits should be avoided, and should only be imposed when it becomes clear that the parties are engaged in time-wasting tactics. It is conceded that in the case of the Crooked Tree Wildlife Sanctuary, it would have been difficult to operate outside of some time limits; but it is thought that, perhaps, three days, rather than two, would have provided more comfortable margins for both the participants and the facilitators.

The participants were asked to do an evaluation at the end of the workshop. Two-thirds of them completed the form provided. The information gleaned offers significant insights into the effectiveness of the mediation process. All, except one person affected by business appointments elsewhere, agreed emphatically that they had been given the chance to participate fully by expressing their concerns and obtaining clarification of various matters. Although a small minority of the participants were a little reserved (answering 'somewhat' to some of these questions), they each admitted to an increased understanding of the concerns of the other players and the ways in which balance can be achieved between use and preservation of the natural ecosystem in the Crooked Tree Wildlife Sanctuary. They felt their issues were dealt with adequately and expressed interest in attending future workshops concerning the sanctuary. Suggested topics for such workshops included management and planning, tourism and economic development, conservation, the relevant laws, power, respect, communication and other issues arising in the relationships between the players, and problem solving techniques. All of this serves to indicate that all the goals of the intervention had been achieved. But by far the most telling demonstration of that accomplishment is the fact that all but one of the respondents expressed their personal commitment to the decisions taken at the workshop and the fact that the vast majority were able and willing to identify specific contributions that they intended to make to the continuing dialogue and search for balance. Note was made of the patience, experience, skill, understanding, control, neutrality, friendliness and professionalism of the facilitators, and the extent to which these qualities contributed to what one participant described as 'the success of this workshop'. These remarks serve as testimony to the fact that the basic principles and techniques of mediation can be used effectively in almost any setting, to assist in the resolution of almost any kind of dispute.

But effective processes and requisite skills notwithstanding, a lasting resolution to any conflict can be achieved only where parties are willing to affirm, and co-operate with, each other, as well as maintain a commitment to the agreements hammered out between them, and the combined interests which those agreements are designed to serve.

The people and government of Belize through the various participants, government agencies, the BAS, the residents of Crooked Tree village and others interested in the Wildlife Sanctuary have demonstrated that peaceful and effective resolution of disputes can be attained even where problems appear insurmountable.

Should this trend continue for the increasing deployment of ADR processes, the need for well-trained and certified mediators would become evident. This speaks to the development of an action plan, which delivers a roster of trained mediators throughout the Caribbean region in a sustained and structured way. In short, the case can be made for mediation to be recognised as a profession. Indeed, the process has already begun with the requirement that a roster of mediators be established, with the approval of the Chief Justice, in the OECS and Jamaica, as part of the court-connected mediation pilot projects in those jurisdictions.

Some issues that need to be addressed are:

(a) regulation of mediators;

(b) accreditation;

(c) complaints mechanisms;

(d) continuing mediation training;

(e) funding for training, private and public; and

(f) indemnity insurance for mediators.

The future of ADR in the Caribbean

This book has sought to make a case for the conscious integration of ADR and ADR processes into the Commonwealth Caribbean legal system. The point has also been made that even without a conscious decision by CARICOM states to embrace ADR, there is already the genesis of ADR processes infusing the legal system.

With greater awareness of the benefits to be gained from applying ADR, both from societal and personal standpoints, it can be predicted that ADR is likely to conquer and annex new territory to its empire in the near future. At any rate, the introduction of caseload management into the court system opens yet another important gateway for ADR. Information technology also makes it impossible for the Caribbean region to be left behind in the midst of such a vast information bank on the benefits of ADR.

The lesson out there is simple and straightforward: the earlier CARICOM governments get on board the ADR train, the better for their societies and legal system.

APPENDIX

ROLE PLAYS[1]

ROLE PLAY ONE

PURPOSE OF THE EXERCISE: To give the mediator experience in managing the process and dealing with emotions. The parent should be very emotional.

NATURE OF THE DISPUTE: The child, a 13-year-old high school student, has been sent home from school because she does not have the required school books. She remains out of school. The parent is very angry, but at the moment is not able to pay for the school books. The parent was at work and no one at home when the child was sent home from school.

THE PARTIES

INITIATOR: The parent of the child is angry because the child was sent home from school. It is the policy of the school that parents purchase books for their child and money had been saved to buy the books. However, the money saved had to be used to pay the electricity bill, as the public utility service was going to disconnect the light for non-payment of the bill. As a result, the child has been sent home. The parent feels there should be some flexibility and allowance made for lower income parents. The parent is angry because there are so few jobs available for unskilled persons that it is difficult to make ends meet.

RESPONDENT: The principal of the school feels it is the parents' responsibility to buy their own children's school books because that is the policy of the school system. He/she is fed up with people who want exceptions to be made for them. He/she feels that this parent is just being difficult as the child has been in the school system for six years and the policy is well-known and has not changed in all that time. The principal is a well-educated person.

GOAL: Your goal as a role player is to present the information provided and to enable a resolution of the dispute.

POSSIBLE SOLUTION

The parent agrees to make payments on the child's school books. A small token payment will be made today in return for which the child will be allowed back into classes immediately with the necessary books. A proper schedule of payments is to be drawn up and agreed on by both parties, who will sign the document as part of the resolution.

---

1   Kind courtesy of Donna Parchment and of the Dispute Resolution Foundation.

ROLE PLAY TWO

PURPOSE OF THE EXERCISE: To give the mediator experience in creative problem solving in interpersonal relationships.

NATURE OF THE DISPUTE: Winston, a popular DJ, wants to charge his girlfriend, Patricia, with larceny because, while he was away from their Kingston home on business, she took some jewellery that was his property, including a bracelet valued at USA$10,000.

THE PARTIES

INITIATOR: Winston is angry and hurt because the woman he trusted stole his expensive jewellery. While Patricia feels that what is his is hers, Winston believes that they each have their own property.

RESPONDENT: Patricia is sorry for taking the jewellery. She took the jewellery and sold it in order to have spending money while Winston was away from home. Patricia thinks that because they live together she is entitled to make use of the jewellery. She is upset with Winston because he does not spend enough time with her and he always acts interested in all the other women who hang around him. In addition, she wants to marry Winston and feels that what is his is hers.

POSSIBLE SOLUTION

Be creative but settle the case. Note: Winston may want an apology and an explanation, while Patricia may want respect and commitment. Create a solution where trust can be re-established between the two parties to enable the parties to continue their relationship in peace.

ROLE PLAY THREE

PURPOSE OF THE EXERCISE: To practice mediating a large scale problem, involving several individuals and parties, who share some interests in common and others not.

NATURE OF THE DISPUTE: Eighty-one trade union workers were dismissed after they went on strike when a fellow worker was arrested for larceny following a search of her person at the workplace. This was only one of many grievances of the workers. The union said that what triggered the strike was an assault by a security guard on one of the workers. Some of the workers on strike have 13 to 18 years of service with the company.

THE PARTIES

INITIATOR: A representative of the union who wants the employees with long service to go back to work, but only after some of the many grievances are addressed. The union and its members feel that their grievances have been continually disregarded. Lots of promises have been made, but there has been no follow-through. The workers are really fed up and the strike has explosive potential. Some workers have little savings and do not want a prolonged strike or closure of the company, whilst others are willing to risk the company. The union has no funds to give to workers in the interim, so fears another union may come in.

RESPONDENT: A representative of the company with authority to mediate. The company does not want to lose 81 workers, but also does not want to give the appearance that they will tolerate workers going on strike. The company has had trouble with the union before and feels that the union is getting too much power. In fact, the management of the company feel that the union is getting a little 'trigger-happy'. The company stands to lose USA$1,000,000 per day over the next 10 days and then USA$500,000 per day thereafter if production does not resume. They would welcome another union.

POSSIBLE SOLUTIONS

(1) The representative of the company will look into the cause of the disruption with the security guard who searched the worker and, although they will not admit fault, the company will offer to dismiss the security guard. The authorities will give each employee a manual and will hold seminars on what is plant procedure and what rights and obligations the workers have when they are on duty at the plant. In return, each dismissed worker will appear before a panel made up of a representative of the union, a member of management and a neutral third party for an evaluation of each person's past history. (Most of the workers with 13 years or more will have a good past history.)

(2) Another solution could be that a representative of the union and the company would sit down with a neutral third party and go over all the grievances and prepare a timetable for resolving them.

(3) Other.

ROLE PLAY FOUR

PURPOSE OF THE EXERCISE: While many issues will arise in this exercise, the educational purpose of the exercise is to give the mediator experience in dealing with parties who ramble, get upset, interrupt and who are strongly committed to their positions. (Gender and age will shape the discussion here.) The mediator may be the minister, a member of the church or an outside agency to which the church has referred the conflict, which has been disrupting church life.

NATURE OF THE DISPUTE: This is a dispute between parishioners of a church. The dispute involves a clash of values. It involves constant disruptions of church services by young children who attend church with their parents.

THE PARTIES

INITIATOR: An older parishioner who has attended this particular church for years. During the years when his children were young, he left them at home with a babysitter. He allowed them to attend church when he felt they were old enough to understand the service and to remain quiet. He feels that young children should not attend church services. He rambles in his presentation, he interrupts the respondent, and he gets upset (not too upset) in the mediation when the respondent does not agree with him.

RESPONDENT: A younger parishioner who regularly attends church with her three young children. She feels that religious training is important and that children should attend church with their parents. She also interrupts, gets upset (not too upset) when her values are challenged, and is firmly committed to her position. She is more reluctant than the initiator to see the other person's point of view.

POSSIBLE SOLUTIONS

(1) Leave the children at home.

(2) Attend a different church service.

(3) Both parties to agree to encourage the church to add a parents' room which is visible from the sanctuary.

ROLE PLAY FIVE

PURPOSE OF THE EXERCISE: To give the mediator experience in facilitating a mediation of a criminal offence and family violence.

NATURE OF THE DISPUTE: Domestic violence between husband and wife. The husband hit his wife when she was urging him to get a job.

THE PARTIES

INITIATOR: Audrey wants to bring charges against her husband for hitting her; however, she does not want him to go to jail. She wants him to get a job, get off the crack/cocaine and be good to her and their three children. She remembers what he was like before he started taking drugs. She wants him to show her and the community his remorse by volunteering at the local Golden Age Home or infirmary.

RESPONDENT: Trevor does not want to go to jail. He feels that there are no jobs to be had that would allow him to have pride if he goes to jail. He is now in a well-paid job where they have not confronted him on the drug problem as he has been hiding it at work.

He loves the children and is willing to go through drug treatment for their sake. However, he needs Audrey to listen to him and stand by him and not treat him like a 'naughty boy'. Her nagging and constant criticisms make it hard for him to have pride. He wants to do something public to show that he is sorry and thinks he can help at the local infirmary.

POSSIBLE SOLUTIONS

(1) Audrey will not file charges if Trevor completes drug treatment.

(2) Trevor is not to come home until he is free of the drugs.

(3) Audrey will see Trevor at counselling sessions and he can visit the children on Sundays when she drops them off at his mother's home.

ROLE PLAY SIX

PURPOSE OF THE EXERCISE: While many issues will arise in this exercise, the educational purpose of the exercise is to demonstrate how to conduct a caucus. Caucusing with the parties permits the mediator to:

(1) determine each party's bottom line;

(2) explore confidential information;

(3) suggest to one party, outside the other's hearing, that their position seems extreme; and

(4) examine and discuss the strengths and weaknesses of a party's solution.

NATURE OF THE DISPUTE: A personal injury claim resulting from a slip and fall in the supermarket.

THE PARTIES

INITIATOR: Eighteen months ago, the initiator was visiting the supermarket. He was proceeding down an aisle when he slipped on water on the floor. He hit his head and shoulder when he fell. He did not see the sign. He was taken to the emergency room by an ambulance. There were no broken bones, but he did suffer a slight concussion and torn ligaments in his shoulder. Total medical bills for the emergency room and two follow-up visits were USA$24,500. Rehabilitation therapy for five weeks cost USA$21,000. He lost five days of work totalling USA$3,500. He continues to suffer headaches and 10% permanent disability in his shoulder and is seeking a total of USA$505,000.

RESPONDENT: The insurance company for the supermarket. The manager was aware of the water on the floor and had placed a sign in the aisle warning of the peril. A maintenance person was on the way to clean up the water when the fall occurred. The company argues that the initiator is at fault for ignoring the sign, but is willing to accept some responsibility.

POSSIBLE SOLUTIONS

No possible solutions have been offered. This is to allow the mediation trainers, using appropriate mediation principles, to assist the trainers to develop their skills.

ROLE PLAY SEVEN

PURPOSE OF THE EXERCISE: To give the mediator experience in managing the process by dealing with power imbalance, a highly emotional situation, management of anger and the possibility of using a caucus.

NATURE OF THE DISPUTE: The parties are in dispute regarding the sale and purchase of a new motor car. It is uncertain whether the car is defective or the driver unable to properly operate the car.

THE PARTIES

INITIATOR Mr Hezekiah Brown purchased a new car six months ago, from Auto Sales, for a substantial sum. There were continual problems with the car. The consumer has taken the car back to the dealer four times for the same problem, the car stalls for no apparent reason. When the car stalls, the power steering and brakes shut down. The consumer is handicapped due to a mild stroke and has difficulty walking. He has recently had his driver's licence renewed after re-taking a performance test. Most recently, the car stalled along a highway and the consumer was stranded for over two hours until a truck driver offered assistance. The consumer now demands a new car or to have all his money refunded. He asked his attorneys, Tracy Smith & Co, to file an action in the Civil Jurisdiction of the Supreme Court against Auto Sales and a mediation has been scheduled through the Dispute Resolution Foundation.

RESPONDENT: Auto Sales sold the car to the consumer, Mr Hezekiah Brown. They have tried to fix the car. The company sells many brands, but had only recently introduced this car to the local market and had no experience with its performance, and are receiving only minimal technical support from the manufacturers. At various times they have replaced the starter, the ignition system and the spark plugs. Additionally, they have given the car two complete tune-ups. Although the auto dealer could find nothing wrong with the replaced parts, they still placed new parts in the car in an effort to satisfy the consumer. The dealer can never get the car to stall and contends that the consumer does not operate the car in an appropriate manner. Each time the car was brought in for repairs, Auto Sales has given the consumer a free rental car. However, they refuse to refund the consumer's money or give him a new car. The company's attorney, Leslie Jones, has agreed to attend the mediation along with the company's Marketing and Sales Vice President, Mr Stuart Singh, who has full authority to settle.

POSSIBLE SOLUTIONS

No possible solutions have been offered. This is to allow the mediation trainers, using appropriate mediation principles, to assist the trainers to develop their skills and to find creative solutions to the problem to provide a win/win solution for both parties.

INDEX